The Price Is Wrong

The Price Is Wrong

UNDERSTANDING WHAT MAKES A PRICE SEEM FAIR AND THE TRUE COST OF UNFAIR PRICING

Sarah Maxwell

John Wiley & Sons, Inc.

Published by John Wiley & Sons, Inc., Hoboken, New Jersey.

Published simultaneously in Canada.

Wiley Bicentennial Logo: Richard J. Pacifico

For general information on our other products and services or for technical support, please contact our Customer Care Department within the United States at (800) 762-2974, outside the United States at (317) 572-3993 or fax (317) 572-4002.

Wiley also publishes its books in a variety of electronic formats. Some content that appears in print may not be available in electronic formats. For more information about Wiley products, visit our Web site at www.wiley.com.

Library of Congress Cataloging-in-Publication Data:

Maxwell, Sarah, 1938-
    The price is wrong : understanding what makes a price seem fair and the true cost of unfair pricing / Sarah Maxwell.
        p. cm.
    Includes bibliographical references and index.
    ISBN 978-0-470-13909-7 (cloth)
        1. Prices. 2. Pricing. I. Title.
    HB221.M416   2008
    338.4'3—dc22

                                                                2007032153

Printed in the United States of America
10 9 8 7 6 5 4 3 2 1

*For my children, with love and,
of course, tears.*

Contents

Foreword

I have known Sarah Maxwell for many, many years, starting when she was just "Max" and not "Doctor" Maxwell. She was known back then for her original thinking in marketing and advertising. Now she applies that same creativity to fair pricing, a field that she has been instrumental in pioneering.

A world-class expert in the field, she has written extensively, made countless conference presentations, and conducted numerous industry seminars on the subject of fair pricing. Finally, she has sat down long enough to share her deep insights and profound understanding of what makes a price seem fair.

Sarah has given us a book that is packed with examples of right and wrong pricing, data from her own research in fair pricing, and contributions from all the many different fields that have been concerned with the subject. Although the book is carefully referenced, it is written not for academics but for the general population. It is a quick, provocative read.

Sarah addresses many questions that have not been asked before: Why is it fair for gas stations to charge an extra nine-tenths of a cent per gallon? Why is it fair to pay for blood but not for body parts? Why is it fair to tip a waiter but not your mother-in-law?

She explains why people object when Amazon charges new customers less than old customers, when Coke introduces a soda machine that will increase prices in the summer, when Home Depot gives their outgoing CEO a $210 million bonus.

What Sarah makes clear is that a fair price matters because fairness is the emotional part of economic decision making. Without an emotional base, we cannot make decisions. We have no way to determine what is good, what is bad; what is right, what is wrong. We base these determinations on our personal expectations as well as on the rules of society, rules that we all know intuitively.

In pricing as in a football game, it's unfair to break the rules. We don't like people who don't play fair. And we don't like sellers who don't price fairly. Unfair prices make consumers angry. And they take revenge. Just check out the numerous blogs to see the nasty comments about unfair prices.

Sarah also makes clear that a fair price is much more than just a cheap price. It's giving as much as you get. It's treating consumers with the respect they deserve. It's being above-board and honest in your dealings. It's developing trust and not taking advantage of power.

This is certainly what we try to do at Dunkin' Donuts, Baskin-Robbins, and Togo's. It is what we *must* do to be successful. If we don't price fairly, we'll be at a competitive disadvantage and soon find ourselves out of business.

To treat customers fairly, you have to understand what they want. What can they afford? How can we give them value for their money? At Dunkin' Donuts we have developed affordable lattes and espressos because that is what our customer wants. That is what they think is fair.

We do not invest in easy chairs because that is not what our customer wants, nor what our customer wants to pay extra for. Certainly, our restaurants have a loyal clientele who meet there every day and linger, talking, over their coffee. But most of our customers are short on time and high on need. They want a fast, pleasurable source of energy, and the price should reflect the value of what they get. That is fair.

The subject of price fairness is one that affects us all, whether we are consumers or merchants. Consumers will no doubt benefit from the book's insights and arguments. They will, for example, be better able to negotiate a fair price and avoid the unfair pricing practices of unscrupulous salespeople.

Businesses will also benefit from understanding the emotional aspect of pricing, and students, too, can benefit from appreciating the principles of fair play that underlie our economic system.

As a businessperson, what impressed me most about reading this book was how much we underestimate the emotional part of prices. We worry about the emotional appeal of our stores and advertising. We conduct research to determine the emotional appeal of our products. But we never consider the emotional appeal of our prices. This book makes it clear that we should do so.

As a consumer, I was impressed that we do not consider the social norms of pricing. For instance, we simply accept the fact that the price of a car includes wheels. We accept that we cannot change what is "standard" equipment. But who says that is the way it should be?

Car manufacturers provide many options, but maybe they could get a competitive advantage by providing tire options. Maybe they should provide optional brake systems. Or why not transmissions? These possibilities do not come up in focus groups because standard equipment is accepted as the norm.

We also accept it as the norm that we should not pay our mother-in-law for fixing dinner. We know full well that we should not. I remember seeing a cartoon where departing guests were paying their hosts $50 for a "delightful" dinner. It was funny because we know that such a thing is simply not done.

Sarah gives numerous examples like these that make the reader question why things are the way they are. And she makes clear that they can be changed if we want them changed. We as a society are the ones who determine the social norms of pricing. And we are the ones who can change them.

Maybe we should pay for body parts so that there is an adequate supply. Maybe tips should be included in the bill. Maybe poor people should get discounts to movies. Maybe, like the airline's proposed "bare fares," we should pay for each item we use separately. We should pay for the toilets we use in airplanes. We should pay for the salt and pepper we use in restaurants. We should pay for the elevators in buildings.

As Sarah explains, in most cases, we prefer whatever is now accepted as the social norm. Any change is a violation. But that does not mean that we have to accept the norms blindly and cannot make changes. Social norms of pricing are not telling us what to do, we are telling them. We are the ones who determine what is fair. We are the ones who decide when a price is right—and when a price is wrong.

JON LUTHER
Chairman/CEO
Dunkin' Brands, Inc.

Acknowledgments

I am in great debt to all those who for centuries have struggled to explain fairness in general and price fairness in particular: the philosophers, political scientists, sociologists, anthropologists, psychologists, economists, historians, marketers, and researchers in organizational behavior and social justice. There are so many contributors to the literature that I could not begin to cite them all, which I regret. And I sincerely hope that I have accurately represented the ideas of those whom I did cite.

In the years it has taken to complete this book, many, many people helped with ideas, examples, and encouragement. First are Rosemary Kalapurakal, Peter Dickson, and Joe Urbany whose original fair price model was the impetus for my own work in fair pricing.

Included also are my professors at Florida International University: Frank Carmone, who was an excellent mentor; Barnett Greenberg, who chaired my dissertation committee on price fairness; and Karen Paul, who provided invaluable guidance.

Then there are my marketing colleagues at Fordham University: Richard Colombo, Marcia Flicker, Al Greco, Al Holden, Larry King, Dawn Lerman, as well as our continually supportive former dean, Sharon Smith, and my esteemed partner in pricing research, Hooman Estelami. My graduate assistants at Fordham were also tremendously helpful: Jennifer Suttmeier, who professionally aided in the focus groups; and Juliana Delgado, who expertly handled many tedious details.

I owe a particular debt of gratitude to the insights of my co-authors in fair pricing: Hermann Diller, Ellen Garbarino, Hans Stamer, Marcos Gonçalves Avila, Veronica Feder Mayer, Pete Nye, and my son, Nicholas Maxwell. I also appreciate the constructive advice from other researchers in fairness: Peter Dickson, Stephen Gilliland, and Kent Monroe. And I benefited immeasurably from those patient souls who gave feedback on early chapters: Joe Guiltinan, Arthur

Kover, Sandra Rothenberger, and Richard Schmiesing, as well as my daughter-in-law, Rachel Maxwell, and her mother, Janet Robertson.

In addition, I have been very fortunate to have the creativity and interest of my amazing agent, Jeffery McGraw (I owe a special thanks to Jack Godwin, who recommended me to Jeffery). And I am eternally grateful for the astute insights and recommendations of my editor, Debra Englander. She made me see where I was blind.

Finally, I could not have done it without the help of all my children. They not only advised on drafts but also supplied information and ideas.

Thank you all!

SARAH MAXWELL
May 2007

About the Author

Dr. Sarah Maxwell had nearly 30 years' experience in marketing before getting her PhD from Florida International University in 1997. Prior to that she got her BA from the University of Pennsylvania and her MBA from the Wharton School. She is currently associate professor at Fordham University. She teaches marketing and conducts industry workshops in pricing around the world. In 1996, she cofounded the Fordham Pricing Center, of which she is now codirector. During the past decade, the Pricing Center has hosted the only academic conferences in the world on the behavioral aspects of pricing. Dr. Maxwell is associate editor of the *International Journal of Pricing* and has published extensively on fair pricing and social norms.

PART

BACKGROUND

CHAPTER 1

Introduction

"PLAY FAIR OR I QUIT!"

On a road near me, there are three gas stations, all on the same side of the road. One station consistently undercuts the other two by $.01 to $.03 a gallon. Drivers line up for this station, clogging the road in both directions. Customers wait to save, on average, $.02 a gallon. For a 20-gallon tank, that is $.40. If they wait six minutes each time, that is equivalent to $4 an hour. Hardly a minimum wage. Hardly rational behavior.

Gasoline consumers act irrationally because they are mad. They are mad because the price of gasoline is unfair. They perceive the price to be unfair not only because it is high, having recently gone over $3 a gallon, but also because they think the oil industry is acting unfairly.

OPEC exerts unfair power over oil supply: it now controls some 40 percent of oil production and over 60 percent of crude oil reserves. The oil companies make unfair profits: ExxonMobil has posted the highest profits ever recorded by a company. Oil company executives receive unfair compensation: the ExxonMobil CEO is paid over $144,000 a day. Gasoline wholesalers price unfairly: they use some sort of secret "zone" pricing so that some neighborhoods can be charged as much as $.50 a gallon more than others. And at the pump, customers are charged unfairly: they get less for their money on hot days because the gasoline expands.

3

Consumers react to what they perceive to be unfairness by punishing the oil companies in the only way they can: by demonstrating their anger at the pump. Each one acting individually, consumers wage lonely battles against unfair gasoline prices. But their concerted force is formidable.

Companies can be slow to recognize the force of perceived unfairness. For example, the president of the Western States Petroleum Association, when defending the practices of zone pricing, said "it is a perfectly acceptable form of pricing . . . a way for companies to price fairly in different areas."[1] Consumers disagree. They think it is wrong. And some companies are catching on.

For example, in a recent advertisement for the Sprint™ mobile phone service, there is a photo of some children forlornly reading a sign outside a playground. The sign gives the playground rules. The first two are:

1. "You have to guess how many minutes you're going to use your ball—for the next two years. Don't guess too high or too low, or you'll be sorry."
2. "Whoever is new on the playground is more special. It's just a fact. Therefore, new kids get the new things. Old ones don't."

The Sprint advertisement then points out the unfairness of mobile phone pricing: extra charges for estimating your usage too high or too low, and lower charges for new customers. It could also mention unfair extra charges for "regulatory issues" and unfair confusion caused by multiple plans and indecipherable billing.

The advertisement explains that Sprint is now rewriting the rules "to make things fair." Sprint has been driven to change their policies due to the public's quiet but effective response to the unfair pricing practices of the mobile phone industry. The company evidently gets it that fairness matters.

It also seems that airlines might be getting it. Since the innovation by American Airlines in 1985 of what is called "yield pricing," the airlines have patted themselves on the back for "skimming the consumer surplus," getting each customer to pay the maximum amount that each one is willing to pay.

The problem has been that one passenger could pay only $150 for a flight from New York to Los Angeles while another passenger on the same plane had to pay $1,500. The passengers paying $1,500 were the business-class passengers who did not make their reservations until the last minute and did not stay over Saturday night. To some extent this was accepted; business-class passengers did, after all, receive upgraded service. But was it 10 times better?

The difference in prices paid for the same flight was only part of the problem. The other part was that no one could figure out how prices were determined. The prices did not make sense. They seemed to change by the hour. Customers were left in the dark, and they rebelled. Again, as with gasoline and mobile phones, the revolt was quiet and steady.

Finally, at least one airline responded. Delta reduced its fare choices to just eight and eliminated the requirement of Saturday night stay-overs. The *Star Tribune* reported an airline analyst predicting that the industry was "heading toward a more consistent and fair pricing scheme."[2]

It was, unfortunately for Delta, too little, too late. The public was never made aware of its gesture toward price fairness. The company went into bankruptcy and has only recently emerged.

Printer ink cartridges are still a third example of where a company has responded to the consumers' concern for fairness. Ink cartridges have been priced like razor blades: charge next to nothing for the razor but charge up the wazoo for the blades—or in this case, the ink.[3] Because the company's own ink cartridges are the only ones that work in their printer, the customer had no choice. Customers thought this was unfair.

As a result, court cases were instigated.[4] The media pointed out that printing ink costs more per liter than vintage champagne.[5] Bloggers wrote reams of complaints.

Until recently, however, the printing ink companies have persisted in their pricing strategy. But now the fight for fair prices has been taken up by a competitor: Kodak has produced a printer that may cost more but whose ink costs less than half as much as others.[6] The company is charging customers for what they get. That is fair. And charging a fair price is giving the company a competitive edge.

In addition to gasoline, mobile phones, airlines, and printing ink cartridges, similar battles against unfair prices are being fought in many industries. Sometimes the battle is swift, like the quashing of Amazon's attempt to charge different amounts for the same MP3 player to different customers: some people were charged $233.95, while others were charged $182.95. Due to customer anger, Amazon quickly stopped and offered a refund to anyone who had paid the higher price.

Sometimes the battle is relentless, like the hackers who justify their attack on Microsoft software because they think Microsoft's profits are too high. In the summer of 2003, when they launched an attack of viruses and worms on Windows software, one worm left the message: "Billy Gates, why do you make this possible? Stop making money and fix your software."

Sometimes the combatants are organized, like the elderly who go to Canada to buy drugs because they cost 30 to 50 percent less there than in the United States. Sometimes the results are even lethal. Four people in South Africa died during a riot over the mixed-race community's paying for electricity based on meter readings, while others were paying a small fixed fee.[7]

And sometimes the battle is lost, as in the case of the Victoria's Secret catalog.[8] The company offered males a $25 discount on any $75 purchase, whereas females were offered only $10. The court dismissed the case, but the reason was not that sex discrimination was accepted, but that the case was based on racketeering charges under the RICO statute. The judge found that an irrelevant argument.

A Fair Price

The evidence shows that if sellers do not play fair, consumers will quit. But what is a fair price?

"Fair" has two separate meanings: "acceptable" and "just."[9] Acceptable implies that a fair price is satisfactory. Fair in this sense is a preference as in a "fair maid," "fair weather," or "fair sailing."

A "just" price, on the other hand, is a judgment that the price has been "justified," that it is "free of favoritism or bias; impartial . . . just to all parties; equitable . . . consistent with rules, logic or ethics."

This dual meaning of fair is demonstrated by the two words needed to translate *fair* into many foreign languages. For example, in German one translation of fair is *angemessen* meaning "satisfactory" or "appropriate" and the other is *gerecht* meaning "just."

The difference between an "acceptable" fair price and a "just" fair price is the difference between what is here called *personal* and *social fairness*. It is the difference between a price you prefer because it meets your own personal standards and a price you judge acceptable because it meets society's standards.

A personally fair price is one that is low enough to meet your expectations. In many cases, customers consider a price fair simply because it less than anticipated. As a researcher has commented, "Saying a price is fair may be another way of saying it is lower."[10]

A socially fair price is one that is the same for everyone, does not give the seller unreasonably high profits, does not take advantage of consumers' demand, and so on. Gasoline prices over $3 a gallon are personally unfair; zone pricing of gasoline—where some people have to pay more than others—is socially unfair.

When describing an unfair price, personal and social fairness are often presented in tandem. Pharmaceutical prices are considered unfair both because they are so high *and* because they are more expensive here than in Canada. Textbook prices are unfair both because they are so high *and* because students are forced to make the purchase. Sales taxes are unfair both because they are so high *and* because the poor pay a proportionally higher amount.

The Social Norms

Personal and social fairness is determined by the adherence to *social norms*. These norms are the consensual rules of a society. They apply to every aspect of economic exchange: not only the price itself, but also what is priced, who sets the price, what people get price exceptions, what price information is provided, what is included in the price, and so on.

Social norms are often just tacitly understood. We do not even notice them unless they happen to be violated. They do not dictate behavior but act as commonly accepted guides to what is appropriate.

Some examples of the norms of pricing are given in Table 1.1. The reaction to these examples can be "Of course! That's just how things are." Of course, restaurants are paid to prepare meals and spouses are not. That is obvious. But the social norms are not as obvious as they appear. Just consider the possibilities:

Suppose restaurants charged extra for condiments. Suppose nurses had to be tipped for service. Suppose brunettes and blondes had to pay a surcharge.

You might respond that these things would never happen. But in Slovakia, some restaurants charge tourists extra for mustard and catsup. In India, some nurses demand a tip to bring new babies to

Table 1.1. Examples of Social Norms of Pricing

Scope of Social Norms of Pricing	Examples of Social Norms of Pricing
What is priced	Restaurants should be paid to prepare meals, but spouses should not.
Who sets the price	Sellers should set prices in retail stores, but not in auctions.
What is basis for price	Train prices should vary by age, but not by weight.
What people get price exceptions	Movie prices should be lower for the low-income elderly but not the low-income poor.
Where prices are different	Higher price should be charged for beer in hotels than in grocery stores.
What people get paid more/less	Higher salaries should be paid to physicians than to equally essential school bus drivers.
What is priced higher/lower	Higher prices should be charged for diamond crystals than for salt crystals.
How price is charged	Gasoline charges should include an extra nine-tenths of a cent, but grocery prices should not.
What price information is provided	Prices should be tagged in retail stores but not in flea markets.
What is included in price	Elevator service should be included in the price of offices, but curtains should not.
When price can change	Price increases should be based on increased cost, not increased demand.

their mothers. Foreigners in India are charged more for entry into the Taj Mahal than natives are. To Americans, these charges seem wrong. They are deemed unfair.

There are different social norms of pricing for personal fairness and social fairness. The norms of personal fairness are *descriptive norms*. They stipulate what can be expected based on what has been customary in the past. They indicate what is generally considered to be normal behavior, like driving on the right-hand side of the road.

Descriptive norms of pricing include charging the same amount to mail a letter no matter where it is going, including tires in the price of a car, adding nine-tenths of a cent onto gasoline prices. When these descriptive norms are violated, it is perceived to be personally unfair.

The social norms of social fairness are *prescriptive norms*. They stipulate how people should behave based on society's values. Prescriptive norms are consensually agreed upon rules of society.

Examples of prescriptive norms of pricing include charging all customers the same price, not sneaking in hidden surcharges, not exploiting customers in need. When these prescriptive norms are violated, it is not just personally but socially unfair.

An Emotional Response

When a price is personally or socially unfair, people get an emotional rush. But the intensity of emotion differs depending on the kind of unfairness. The reaction to personal unfairness is mild. The violation of a descriptive norm, such as the expectation of a low price, results in dissatisfaction. An extra charge for bread in a restaurant results in mild annoyance and displeasure.

But in contrast to the relatively mild distress caused by personal unfairness, the reaction to social unfairness is ferocious. When a price is thought to be socially unfair, consumers feel an irrational desire to "get back" at the seller, even if it takes more effort than the money involved. They will argue endlessly with the store manager to get a $5 refund on a defective product. They will drive five minutes longer to avoid a pharmacy that prices unfairly.

Recent studies suggest that the emotional response to fairness is innate. Female brown capuchin monkeys that have been trained to use tokens for money are incensed when the exchange is not fair.[11] This was demonstrated by the actions of the capuchins when separated into adjacent cages where they could observe each other's behavior.

If the first trained monkey received a grape (a treasured reward) without having to pay the usual token, but the second monkey had to pay a token for only a cucumber (a less valuable reward), the second monkey either threw her own token away or refused to accept the cucumber. Just having a grape in the first monkey's empty cage was enough to make the second monkey sulk. "The researchers suggest that capuchin monkeys, like humans, are guided by social emotions."[12]

Fairness, in effect, is the emotional part of economic decision making. Neurological research shows that without this emotional component, consumers cannot make a decision to buy.[13] It is the emotions that generate a fast, convincing belief as to whether a price is acceptable or unacceptable, good or bad, right or wrong. Fairness is an emotional "yes" or "no."

In Sum . . .

A fair price is one that is emotionally okay. It is acceptable and just. It has passed the test of personal and social fairness by adhering to the social norms. But when the norms are violated and the price is judged personally and socially unfair, watch out! Emotions intensify. Tempers flair. Consumers say, "Play fair or I quit!" And companies had better take heed.

To explain fair prices, this book calls on all kinds of evidence: anecdotal, theoretic, and experimental. It incorporates personal experiences, reports from news magazines and web sites, and opinions from bloggers. The underlying belief is that all sources of data are valuable—anything that can help us understand the slippery idea of price fairness.

The organization of the book is in three parts: background, model, and applications of the model in practice. The "background" section comprises this chapter and the following one on the history of a "just" price.

The "model" section explains how personal and social fairness lead to escalating emotions and retributions. Each element in the model is then explained further in subsequent chapters. These chapters show how judgments of price fairness can both increase trust and are supported by trust but can be quickly destroyed by the imposition of seller power. Each chapter includes an inset defining the concepts, which are collected at the end in a Glossary.

In the section on "applications," the model is applied to specific instances of price fairness: tipping, price discrimination, negotiations, taxes, and across cultures. This section addresses why it is the norm not to stiff the waiter, why we care about what other people pay, and why the best tax is an old tax.

Although the first 18 chapters look at price fairness from the consumers' viewpoint, the final chapter considers price fairness from the viewpoint of the seller. Chapter 19 shows how to avoid having customers say, "The price is wrong! And that's not fair!"

Definitions

Personal fairness: Preference for what is considered acceptable outcomes and procedures based on the legitimate expectations of descriptive norms.

Social fairness: Judgment that outcomes and procedures are "just" based on the standards of prescriptive norms.

Social norms: Tacitly understood and consensually agreed-upon rules of a society.

Descriptive norms: Consensual rules of expected actions and outcomes based on custom and tradition.

Prescriptive norms: Consensual rules of appropriate actions and outcomes based on community values.

CHAPTER 2

History

"A 'JUST' PRICE IS NOT GOD-GIVEN!"

A "just" price was the hot topic of the thirteenth century, a century that it is tempting to call "the best of times, the worst of times." Because it was. It was an exciting time when money was just starting to circulate freely. But it was also a terrible time when the market was wild and woolly.

If you were a thirteenth-century urban European housewife, you might have to pay the extortionist price of the fish *forestaller*, the term used for the monopolists who bought up all the supply from the fishermen before they got to market. If you wanted candles, you would have to pay the excessive price fixed by the guild. And the price of wheat could have been exorbitant because another kind of monopolist, an *engrosser*, had bought up all the supply the previous fall.

As a housewife, you would worry that the butcher had painted the dead sheep eyes with blood so they would seem fresh. You would worry that the baker had snuck some moldy batter into the middle of the loaf. And you would wonder if the bread really weighed what it should. You knew, after all, that bakers were often dunked in the river for not selling full weight.

It was the worst of times because so many people—both legitimate entrepreneurs and cunning con artists—took full advantage of the turbulent situation for their own self interest. "Not for nothing," the economic historian Diana Wood writes, "have the Middle Ages been termed 'a paradise for tricksters and the great age of fraud.'"[1]

However, it was also the best of times. Trade was exploding. New international trade routes were opening. Ships laden with spices arrived in Europe from the east. Shiploads of fine cloth were shipped back out. Centers of trade were established in new urban centers, and merchants met to sell goods wholesale at major fairs. "Here counting, measuring, and reckoning had become part of the fabric of daily life, and increasingly such calculations were being made in terms of money."[2] Money became a necessity, and a just price became a major concern.

By the thirteenth century in Europe about a third of transactions used money. For example, "by 1279 the number of rents paid (on English manorial estates) in money had overtaken the number paid in produce or labour services."[3] Even professors were involved in monetary exchange. "Within the universities, every examination taken, every grade passed and degree earned, had a price attached to it."[4]

At the same time, a group of English philosophers at Merton College in Oxford became fascinated with measurement. They were aided by the new technology of the abacus that had been introduced in the tenth century, and their calculations were made easier by the conversion to Arabic numerals that had started in the twelfth century.

"Soon, not only entities that had never been measured before, but also those that have never been measured since, were subjected to a kind of quantitative analysis."[5] Along with the oft-cited number of angels that could dance on the head of a pin, the philosophers enthusiastically measured the depth of Christian charity and Christ's love compared to human love. As an aid to measurement, money took on new importance.

Influence of Aristotle

It was against this background that the medieval church scholars, called the *Scholastics*, debated what constituted a fair or just price. They based their debates on the newly translated philosophy of *Aristotle*. Before the thirteenth century, the philosophy of Aristotle had dwindled to a dim memory in Europe. But when translations of his work did become available, they were instantly popular. The Scholastics liked Aristotle's optimistic view of human reason, his emphasis on understanding nature, and his mathematical approach.

Pope Gregory IX, however, feared that Aristotle's books introduced pagan ideas. This pope was an unusual combination of intolerant churchman and enlightened intellectual. So while he feared the ideas of Aristotle, he still allowed Aristotle's work to be read, with the stipulation that the Dominican friars first purge the work of "anything offensive to the faithful."[6]

Pope Gregory's commission to cleanse the writings of Aristotle was carried out by two remarkable men, *Albert the Great* (1193–1280) and *Thomas Aquinas* (1226–1294). Albert was a distinguished bishop and master of theology known for his "blunt, take-no-prisoner manner of speaking."[7] His celebrated pupil Aquinas was a famed theologian and early economic thinker who had read Aristotle thoroughly while imprisoned for two years by his family. Together, the two theologians did more than just purge pagan ideas from Aristotle: they infused the work with their own commentary, including their own ideas of a just price.

Aristotle directly addressed the subject of justice in Book V of his *Nicomachean Ethics.* Tucked into the middle of a chapter on reciprocity are five paragraphs directly pertaining to money. Aristotle pointed out that money "is a measure of everything,"[8] which is exactly what the Scholastics had realized. And like them, Aristotle was concerned about justice.

Aristotle recognized that a price reflects the value of the labor involved in the goods being exchanged. "The builder must get from the shoemaker the product of his labour, and must hand over his own in return."[9] At the same time, he recognized the influence of demand on prices and wrote that "by social convention, money has come to serve as a representative of demand."[10]

When adding his own comments to Aristotle, Albert defined a just price by fastening on those two aspects of Aristotelian philosophy: the value of the labor involved and the individual demand of the person who wants to purchase the good.[11] Based on the value of labor, Albert held that money was a measure of the inherent worth of the good being sold, including the labor involved in production. Thus, a cost-based price is a just and fair price. But at the same time, recognizing the influence of individual demand, he also held that a just price was whatever a person would pay.

A "Just" Price

Aquinas later added his own ideas to those of Albert. Until very recently, the common belief was that "St. Thomas Aquinas believed value to be divinely determined."[12] It was consequently thought that the "just" price of the Scholastics reflected such a divinely determined value. But Aquinas did not think that a just price is God-given. His thinking was actually driven more by market demand than divine determination. He specifically separated a just price from divine authority.

In support of his position, Aquinas quoted the influential fourth-century theologian, *Augustine*, who separated worth in the eyes of God from worth in the marketplace.[13] In the sight of God, living things are obviously of greater worth than inanimate objects, but in the marketplace, bread still commands more money than a mouse. The difference is between "natural value" and "economic value." Economic value, Aquinas held, was based on demand.

Demand, as cited by both Albert and Aquinas, appears to have meant individual demand, a person's subjective evaluation of a potential purchase. It is the demand of an individual in a negotiation. The just price in negotiations was, according to the legal scholars of the period (the Canonists and the Romanists), whatever two people agreed upon.[14] A fair settlement was based on the Aristotelian idea of the mean: halfway between the two parties' positions. That way, neither party would be harmed more than the other.

In contrast to a just price based on individual demand, the German mathematician and theologian Henry of Hesse (c. 1340–1397), a professor who helped found the university at Vienna, argued that a just price was based not on individual but communal demand. What was just was the current market price, what the populace as a group had decided the good was worth.

In addition to the influence of demand on prices, both Hesse and Aquinas recognized the influence of supply. They pointed out that air is not valued because it is so abundant. Bread is more costly in times of drought. They wrote that this is only to be expected and accepted as just.

Aquinas told a story of a wheat merchant who comes to a town during a drought. He will be able to sell his wheat at a high price because supply is so low. The merchant, however, knows that many other wheat merchants are coming right behind him. Rhetorically,

Aquinas asked whether the merchant could sell his wheat at the currently high market price or whether he should tell the customers that more wheat is on the way. Aquinas answered that it was just for the merchant to sell at the current high price, adding that it would be more virtuous, but not necessary, to tell the customers that more wheat was on its way.[15]

Although the Scholastics accepted a price based on the customer's demand as being just, many Scholastics distrusted the fairness of a price based on the seller's costs. The reason is explained by Marjorie Grice-Hutchinson, a Spanish professor and economic historian: "A cost-of-production theory would have given merchants an excuse for over-charging on the pretext of covering their expenses, and it was thought fairer to rely on the impersonal forces of the market which reflected the judgment of the whole community, or, to use the medieval phrase, 'the common estimation.' "[16]

For example, the Scholastic Luis Saravia de la Calle (c. 1544) wrote that "the just price arises from the abundance or scarcity of goods, merchants and money . . . and not from costs, labor and risk. . . . Prices are not commonly fixed based on costs. Why should a bale of linen brought overland from Brittany at great expense be worth more than one which is transported cheaply by sea?"[17]

San Bernardino of Siena (1380–1444) carried the idea of a market-based price to the extreme. He went so far as to say that the market price is fair even if it is below the producer's costs.[18] The same idea was expressed a hundred years later by Francisco de Vitoria (c. 1480–1546) who argued that prices should be set "without regard to labor costs, expenses, or incurred risks. Inefficient producers or unfortunate speculators should simply bear the consequences of their incompetence, bad luck or wrong forecasting."[19]

Although the Scholastics eventually reached consensus that the market price was the just price, there are several inexplicable contradictions in their thinking. For one, despite their faith in letting the market set the price, they also accepted the right of the ruler to set prices. Hesse, for example, considered it necessary for the public authorities to fix a price "to prevent the rich, the idle, the avaricious, the dishonest, and above all the usurers, from taking advantage of honest workers and the poor."[20]

Another contradiction was that despite their aversion to monopolies, the Scholastics accepted the guild monopolies. Monopolies had been outlawed by Roman law and were still outlawed in medieval times. Albert had specifically admonished the guilds against buying up goods to create artificial scarcity, thus pushing up the price.[21] In the teeth of this admonition, the medieval guilds persisted in protecting both their current prices and the current wages of their members. And the Scholastics tolerated the monopoly.

Since the Scholastics

The Scholastics, backed by Aristotle, dominated academia until the seventeenth century, when philosophers like John Locke (1632–1704) began railing against their dogma. Academics started to prefer empirical research rather than the mathematical abstractions of the Scholastics. In the following century, Adam Smith (1723–1790) moved further away from the Scholastics. He rejected the idea of market-based prices in favor of the idea of cost-based prices.

According to Smith, the exchange value is determined by the cost of labor's "toil and trouble," as well as the "invisible hand." Later, the English economist Alfred Marshall (1842–1924) reinforced the idea of price being determined by supply and demand. The impartial forces of supply and demand were then accepted by economists as the determinants of a fair price. Whether a price was just or unjust was no longer the hot topic in economics.

Recently, however, interest in a just or fair price has been renewed. One reason for this revived interest is that researchers like Sally Blount have demonstrated that the fairness of the market is a social illusion.[22] The forces of supply and demand do not automatically result in a fair price. Another reason is that a concern for fairness has been shown to be a critical factor in consumers' decisions.[23] Marketers and economists alike have realized that the fairness of a price is a factor to be reckoned with.

In Sum . . .

The Scholastics considered a just price the most important concern in economics. They argued fiercely, however, over what constituted a just price. Some held it to be whatever two parties agreed to. Others claimed that it was based on the cost of goods. Still others held it to be whatever the market decreed even if it meant a loss for the seller. They finally agreed that a just price was whatever the market consensually decided.[24] Over time, the impartial, external forces of the market were accepted as the determinants of a just price.

More recently, however, the intrinsic fairness of the market has been questioned. And there has been a resurgence of interest in what is meant by a just or fair price, what are its antecedents and its consequences. It is well to remember, however, that all the issues now being debated were introduced by the medieval Scholastics back in that exciting but terrible thirteenth century.

Definitions

Forestaller: One who discourages or prevents normal sales by buying merchandise before it gets to market or by keeping others from bringing their goods to market.

Engrosser: One who buys up all goods before they get to market in order to gain monopoly power.

Scholastics: Group of philosophical theologians whose school of thought, strongly influenced by Aristotle, dominated the High Middle Ages.

Aristotle: Fourth century B.C. Greek philosopher rediscovered in the High Middle Ages and revered for his work in logic and ethics.

St. Albert the Great: Brilliant thirteenth-century A.D. Scholastic who was the teacher of Thomas Aquinas; with Aquinas, he translated and interpreted Aristotle.

St. Thomas Aquinas: Best known thirteenth-century A.D. Scholastic who is recognized for synthesizing the work of Aristotle with the precepts of the church.

Augustine: Fourth century A.D. theologian, who authored many books on theology and was held as an authority of the church by the Scholastics.

PART II

MODEL

CHAPTER 3

Model

"NOW I'M NOT JUST ANNOYED, I'M FURIOUS!"

A European visitor comes to New York City. She buys a dress for $100, but is charged $108.63. Surprised and not pleased, she demands to know why she is being charged more than what is on the price tag. That, she says, is unfair. She is told that the extra is due to the sales tax. She is still not pleased, but mollified.

Compare this experience with that of a young man who signs up for mobile phone service. The advertised price is $39.95 a month for unlimited local and regional service, but when the bill comes, it is for $56.70. As with our European shopper, he is surprised and not pleased. He thinks the higher-than-expected price is unfair.

Our young man then calls the company to find out why the bill is so much more than expected. He is told that the $39.95 does not include $3.50 for the federal line cost, nor $.25 for local number portability, nor $6.00 for long distance service, nor $2.50 for long distance carrier access, nor $4.00 for service to low-income customers, nor $.50 for 911 emergency service. Unlike our European shopper, he is not only displeased but furious over being tricked. He writes the newspaper, calls the Better Business Bureau, and blasts the mobile phone company to his friends.

In both of the above cases, consumers faced prices higher than what they expected to pay. They both consequently thought the price was initially unfair. Our European, however, accepted the higher price; our mobile phone service buyer did not. The difference between the two shoppers' reactions is due to the justification—the reason why the price was higher than expected. Our European shopper was given what she grudgingly accepted as a legitimate reason for the price. Our mobile phone service buyer was given an explanation that simply compounded his original feeling of unfairness. As a result, he retaliated. The difference in these reactions to a price higher than expected are explained by a *model* of fairness developed by the professor of ethics and decision making, David Messick, working with Cristel Rutte.[1]

In the Rutte and Messick model, the idea is that the fairness of outcomes is first evaluated as a preference. As long as people are satisfied with the outcome—if it was what they expected—it is accepted as fair and no further processing of information is done.

However, if the outcome is a surprise, particularly an unhappy surprise, then people experience distress. They look to reduce their distress by finding a justification for what happened. If a legitimate reason is found, the outcome is accepted as fair. But if the reason is unacceptable, then people become emotional. And they look for ways to retaliate.

The model proposed here extends the Rutte and Messick model to prices, surrounding the fair price decision process with social norms and adding the influence of trust and power. The Fair Price Model (see Figure 3.1) begins with the consumer's perception of the *personal fairness* of the price.

If consumers perceive that the price is personally fair, then they proceed to purchase the good. But if the price is personally *un*fair, the consumer feels *distress* and is motivated to consider the *social fairness* of the price. If that is positive, then the personal fairness is reconsidered. But if the social fairness judgment is negative, the consumer feels *anger* and is motivated to *punish* the person responsible. The intensity of the reaction is influenced by both the *power* of the seller and the consumer's *trust* in the seller.

Personal Fairness

The initial trigger of the consumer's fairness considerations is a cognitive evaluation of the price. According to the social norm perspective, consumers believe that the price *should* be what they expect, how the price is determined and how it is presented *should* be as they expect. When those social norms are followed, the price

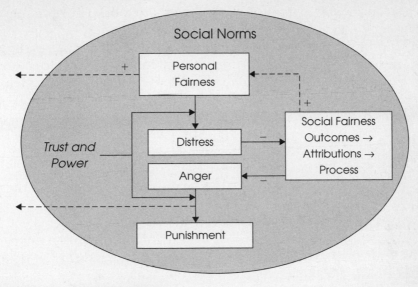

Figure 3.1   Fair Price Model

is perceived to be personally fair and no further judgment of social fairness is required. However, if the outcome is *not* perceived to be personally fair, it causes distress.

Leon Festinger called the distress caused by unexpected outcomes *cognitive dissonance*.[2] It is the uncomfortable feeling that comes when reality does not mesh with prior beliefs, including norms. (See "If Airlines Sold Paint" on page 29.) This discomfort motivates people to find a resolution. The strength of the motivation corresponds to the magnitude of the dissonance.

Imagine, for example, that you are buying a candy bar. The price is $1.50, which is clearly too much. You think, "Grossly unfair!" But then again, it is only a lousy $.25 more than you expected. You can remember having seen similar prices in the past, so it is not really a very big surprise. It causes only minor distress. So the cognitive dissonance produced by the price is not strong, and you think, "Fair or not, why not just buy it?"

In contrast, consider a woman—let us call her Sally—who wants to buy a new sports car. Sally has seen ads touting the price as $35,000. But when she goes to the dealer, she finds to her dismay that the price is actually $45,000. Far more than she expected! The discrepancy causes cognitive dissonance and major distress. The amount of distress is the result of her prior expectations.

Since the amount of stress depends on what is expected, two customers can have totally different responses to the same price. Whereas Sally thought the price of $45,000 was unfair, someone else who expected the price to be $50,000 would think $45,000 was just fine.

In the case of Sally, our frustrated car buyer, she could reduce her stress by changing her underlying beliefs.[3] She could decide "$45,000 is really not that expensive." (This idea, incidentally, is exactly what her sales person has been telling her).

Alternatively, she could change her proposed action: "I don't really need a sports car; a hybrid is much more practical." Or she could consider whether the higher price meets society's standard of social fairness.

Social Fairness

The determination of social fairness is a two-step process: the first step involves the fairness of the outcome and, if that is found wanting, the second step involves the fairness of the process that led to that outcome.[4] These two aspects of social fairness have been termed *distributive*[5] and *procedural*[6] *fairness*, respectively. Both types of fairness are based on social norms.

The primary norm of distributive fairness is the *norm of equity*, which states that economic benefits *should* be proportional to costs (or effort). The idea is expressed in the old adage: "You get what you pay for." But the social norm takes the adage one step further in that you believe you *should* get what you pay for. This belief is what has been called the universal social norm of reciprocity:[7] "quid pro quo," "tit for tat."

Getting back to Sally, she looks first at whether the exchange is reciprocal. At $45,000, would she be receiving an automobile equal in value to the money she paid? If she decides in the affirmative, she will judge the price to be fair and be content with the purchase.

Chances are, however, that she finds the situation ambiguous. As much as she would like the car, she cannot be certain that it is a good deal. As a result, she is likely to search further to understand how the price was determined. She asks to see the manager.

The manager explains that they had to increase the price due to a change in the exchange rate: the dollar is weaker, so imports cost more. This, Sally concludes, is socially fair because it is a legitimate reason: There is a social norm that businesses *should* base prices on their costs. She might, therefore, accept the higher price as fair and make the purchase . . . assuming she can afford it.

But suppose she finds out that the car was imported long before the dollar sank. She might then conclude that the manager is lying. This would mean that the company has broken not only the social norm prescribing fair pricing but the social norm proscribing lies. She will now judge the price not only personally but also socially unfair. She will be angry.

Sally's initial response to the high price had been only mild indignation ("I'm not very happy about the price"), but now that she has found out about the lying, she is in a torrential rage ("Now I'm not just annoyed. I'm furious!").

She is likely to assume that since the manager has broken two social norms, he has most likely broken others. She thinks, "Those bums are only concerned about their own slimy profits. Well, I'll show them!"[8] She is not only furious, she feels morally justified in her fury. She feels that her anger is backed by social norms that are accepted by all good and sensible people. And her anger will have consequences.

In the Fair Price Model, the anger resulting from a judgment of unfairness leads to punishment. The punishment may only be passive: Sally does not buy the car and has a simmering antagonistic attitude toward the seller.[9] But the punishment may also be active: she may complain to the company and to friends, switch companies,[10] perhaps even take legal action.

Trust and Power

The response of consumers to personal and social unfairness depends on whether they have already established a relationship of trust with the seller. Anger and trust can interact in a vicious circle: the anger of social unfairness can diminish future trust, which in turn makes fairness questionable. But the circle can also be virtuous: prior trust can decrease the impact of the anger. If sellers have an established reputation for fair dealing, the consumer will give them the benefit of the doubt.[11] The anger resulting from judged social unfairness will be moderated.

If consumers trust the system as well as the seller, they are more willing to accept a price as legitimate. Even if they find it somewhat unfair both personally and socially, they are likely to feel less anger. However, if the price is deemed grossly unfair, they may well feel that their trust has been betrayed and be even angrier.

Like trust, power also influences the response to both personal and social fairness. It affects social fairness by sensitizing the consumer to fairness concerns. Consumers who feel powerless are primed to watch out for sellers who might take advantage of their weak situation. However, when it comes time to actually do anything about judged unfairness, weak consumers may have to capitulate. Patients without health insurance have to pay however much their medication costs. No matter how unfair they may think a price, they are forced to buy the medicine since they have no alternative. They will, nevertheless, hate the powerful company that acted so unfairly.

In Sum . . .

When consumers evaluate a price as personally unfair, they feel distress. The Fair Price Model indicates that they will then be motivated to investigate the social fairness of the price. If the price is judged inequitable and/or the process by which the price was set is judged unjust, consumers' anger will increase. They will be not just annoyed but furious. And they will exert themselves to retaliate. The following nine chapters will explain each step of the model in greater detail, starting with the surround of social norms.

Definitions

Model: A simplified representation of how ideas are related, often shown graphically.

Distress: A negative emotional state that consists of feelings of disappointment, annoyance, or mild irritation.

Anger: A highly charged negative emotional state that consists of feelings of fury, rage, resentment, and hostility to others.

Power: The ability to make other people do what you want them to do even when they do not want to do so.

Trust: The belief that another person will act in your best interest even when she/he has the power to take advantage of you.

Cognitive dissonance: The discomfort that results from reality clashing with prior expectations.

Distributive fairness: When an outcome adheres to the social norms of how goods (or prices) should be allocated.

Procedural fairness: When a process adheres to the social norms of how people should act in different situations.

Norm of equity: The rule that what you pay should match the value of what you receive.

If Airlines Sold Paint

Customer arrives at United Paint Store.

Customer: Hi. How much is your paint?

Clerk: Well, sir, that all depends.

Customer: Depends on what?

Clerk: Actually, a lot of things.

Customer: How about giving me an average price?

Clerk: Wow, that's too hard a question. The lowest price is $9 a gallon and we have 150 different prices up to $200 a gallon.

Customer: What's the difference in the paint?

Clerk: Oh, there isn't any difference; it's all the same paint.

Customer: Well, then I'd like some of that $9 paint.

Clerk: Well, first I need to ask you a few questions. When do you intend to use it?

Customer: I want to paint tomorrow. It's my day off.

Clerk: Sir, the paint for tomorrow is the $200 paint.

Customer: When would I have to paint to get the $9 version?

Clerk: That would be in three weeks, but you will have to agree to start painting before Friday of that week and continue painting until at least Sunday.

Customer: You've got to be kidding!

Clerk: Sir, we don't kid around here. Of course, I'll have to check to see if we have any of that paint available before I can sell it to you.

(Continued)

Customer: What do you mean check to see if you can sell it to me? You have shelves full of that stuff! I can see it right there!

Clerk: Just because you can see it doesn't mean that we have it. It may be the same paint, but we sell only a certain number of gallons on any given weekend. Oh, and by the way, the price per gallon just went up to $12. We don't have any more $9 paint.

Customer: You mean the price went up while we were talking?

Clerk: Yes, sir. You see, we change prices and rules thousands of times a day, and since you haven't actually walked out of the store with your paint yet, we just decided to change. I suggest you get on with your purchase. How many gallons do you want?

Customer: I don't know exactly. Maybe five gallons. Maybe I should buy six gallons just to make sure I have enough.

Clerk: Oh no, sir, you can't do that. If you buy paint and don't use it, you will be liable for penalties and possible confiscation of the paint you already have.

Customer: WHAT?

Clerk: That's right. We can sell enough paint to do your kitchen, bathroom, hall, and north bedroom, but if you stop painting before you do the bedroom, you will be in violation of our tariffs.

Customer: What does it matter whether I use all the paint? I already paid you for it!

Clerk: Sir, there's no point in getting upset; that's just the way it is. We make plans based upon the idea that you will use all the paint, and when you don't, it just causes us all sorts of problems.

Customer: This is crazy!! I suppose something terrible will happen if I don't keep painting until after Saturday night!

Clerk: Yes, sir, it will.

Customer: Well, that does it. I'm going somewhere else to buy my paint.

Clerk: That won't do you any good, sir. We all have the same rules. Thanks for flying—I mean painting—with our airline.

Reprinted, with permission, from Al Hess.

Norms

"THAT'S WRONG, AND WE ALL KNOW IT!"

My supermarket recently installed a self-service check-out system. You scan your purchases and pay the price all by yourself. Sure, there are cameras watching. But in the end, the store is trusting you to do the right thing.

The first time I used the new system, the machine was stymied by a new kind of melon I had selected. I called for help. While waiting—and waiting—I realized how much easier it would be simply to take the melon without paying. But I did not. And others do not either. And it is not just because of the cameras.

When self-service check-outs were first installed, supermarkets feared that customers would take advantage of the situation by acting in their own self-interest and cheating the system. But in actual practice, "five-finger discounts" did not increase. In fact, they decreased. Customers continued to pay what they owed, and cashiers could no longer follow what was—at least in their minds—a social norm of giving "sweetheart" deals to friends.

Though it may be against our self-interest, most of us pay the price of goods even when not forced to do so. The reason is social norms. Social norms are the generally accepted rules of society. They tell us what should or should not happen, how we should or should not behave.

We tend to believe that everyone else agrees with us on what constitutes a social norm. Norms are therefore not just expectations, but *legitimate* expectations. They are not just what we ourselves expect, but what society in general expects. We learn these norms as children, and they become so much a part of us that we follow these norms even when not coerced.

Social norms apply not just to the actual price for goods but also to all other aspects of prices: what should be priced and what should be provided free, who should set the price and how they should determine the price, what should be included in the price and what should be charged extra, and how the price should be paid. Social norms therefore apply to all aspects of the Fair Price Model.

Descriptive versus Prescriptive Norms

As mentioned in Chapter 1, social norms of pricing are of two kinds: descriptive and prescriptive (see Table 4.1).[1] Descriptive norms describe what is expected as "normal" behavior. We expect a large can of tomatoes to cost about $1. We expect grocery store bags to be provided free of charge. We expect to negotiate prices in a flea market. Violations of descriptive norms are unexpected and judged personally unfair. But the customer's reaction is mild. If a seller in a flea market demands the initially stated price, the customer might be surprised but not particularly angry.

Table 4.1.   Descriptive and Prescriptive Social Norms of Prices

Descriptive Social Norms	Prescriptive Social Norms
Gas prices end with nine-tenths of a cent.	Loyal customers should get a discount.
Elevators are provided free.	The price of water should not go up after a hurricane.
Fine art is sold at auctions.	The price should reflect the quality of the product.
All flavors of yogurt are priced the same.	Complete pricing information should be available before purchase.
Condiments are included in the price of a hot dog.	Prices should be based on costs.
Jumbo-sized products are cheaper per pound than regular-sized.	One should not profit from one's friends.

Prescriptive norms designate not only what is normally done but also what *should* or should *not* be done. Consumers should pay for what they buy. Sellers should give a discount for volume purchases. Loyal customers should receive benefits not available to new customers. Violators of prescriptive norms are punished for being unfair not only to you personally but also to society generally.

Prescriptive norms are backed by a sense of moral rectitude, a belief that what is prescribed is not only normal but right. This is not to imply that such norms are actually right or wrong according to some abstract ethical standard, but only that they are considered right or wrong for a particular situation in a particular culture. (So when I write in this book that something "is" fair, I mean only that it "seems" fair or is "considered" fair.)

Laws are formal and explicit prescriptive norms. "Norms often precede laws but are then supported, maintained, and extended by laws."[2] As an example, the social norm against raising prices after natural disasters is now being formalized into laws forbidding such actions.

Utility of Norms

Over a century ago, social norms were considered to be some kind of ethereal watchdog, some mystic force hovering "out there" that controlled everything that we did.[3] The view today, however, is that norms exist only inside our heads. We create them because we need them. We seem to be natural-born norm makers[4] and norm takers.[5] We create norms that we follow ourselves and expect others to follow likewise. We do this primarily because social norms are useful to us.

Social norms are useful because they help us predict how others will behave and how they will react to how we behave. By predicting how others will act in certain situations, social norms save us time and energy as well as psychic stress. But rules are not functional by themselves. Like driving on the right side of the road, following a norm works only when everybody else also follows the norm. Commonly agreed upon rules keep us from colliding into one another— physically and psychologically.

Social norms are particularly useful in economic exchange because they help us coordinate behavior.[6] For instance, when we pay the stipulated price, we can assume with confidence that the seller will hand over the goods. That is only to be expected. And the seller knows it.

Social norms simplify decision making by providing what is called a *heuristic*—a fast, easy, rule-of-thumb way to make socially acceptable decisions.[7] By following the social norm, we do not have to fret over wearing a business suit or a bathing suit to work; we already know which will meet with approval. We do not have to agonize over whether to use a fork or a spoon to eat our ice cream; the choice is automatic. And we do not have to think about whether we should pay for or steal an item; the socially acceptable answer is obvious.

Norms are also useful because they avoid confusion. When norms are not commonly understood, people do not know how to act. Before women's liberation, men were expected to open doors so women could go through first. With the new gender equality, that norm no longer holds. Both men and women now open doors for each other, not knowing who will go through first. The result is confusion at doorways.

The same applies to pricing. Take tipping. The old norm was to pay 15 percent of the bill, but that norm no longer holds. A new norm, however, has yet to be established. In some cities, the expected tip is 15 percent. In others, it is 17.5 percent or even 20 percent. The result is confusion at restaurants.

Although a norm may be useful at one point in time, it may not continue to be so over time. An example is setting prices to end in a five or a nine, a practice that is today commonplace. The story is that the practice was instituted to force clerks to ring up a sale on the cash register so as to get change for the customer. Since stores then had a record of the sale, the clerks could not pocket the money. Today, with the proliferation of credit and debit card sales, the practice no longer has such a functional benefit, but five- and nine-ending prices endure as social norms of pricing.

Even though social norms can be useful in predicting behavior, simplifying decisions and avoiding confusion, this does not mean that norms are necessarily efficient. Take the problem of setting a price. In the United States, the norm is for the seller to determine the price and post it on a tag. But who says that this method is better than haggling over the price as they do in India? As the Nobel laureate in economics Douglass North concludes, social norms help establish "a stable (but not necessarily efficient) structure to human interaction."[8]

Selfish versus Social

Not only North but many other academics have recently become interested in the role of social norms in the economic system. In addition to economists, there are also psychologists,[9] sociologists,[10] philosophers,[11] lawyers,[12] marketers,[13] and political scientists.[14] A primary concern of these various academics is whether norms act to reinforce or constrain self-interest. In economic exchange, do people use norms just to legitimize their selfish actions, or are they kept from selfish actions by the restrictions of a norm?

On one side are the academics who maintain that particularly in the impersonal context of consumer exchange the only social norm is *opportunism*.[15] These researchers argue that buyer-seller interactions in the consumer market are too short and too impersonal for social norms to develop. Supporting this side are some psychologists who contend that acting in one's own self-interest is a basic social norm.[16]

Certainly, in consumer exchange, self-interest is an overwhelming motivation.[17] Determining the price is a *zero-sum game*: the buyer's loss is the seller's gain. A lower price for the consumer is a lower profit for the seller. And so both parties fight it out to gain the advantage. Although it may be possible for social norms to have an influence in the long-term relations common in business-to-business exchange, some people question the role of norms in consumer exchange.

An answer is provided by the political scientists Gary Goertz and Paul Diehl[18] who claim that norms permeate all relationships, but the norms are of three different kinds. *Cooperative*, social-interest norms evolve in long-term business relationships. *Coercive*, self-interest norms are imposed by powerful companies like Wal-Mart on their weak suppliers. It is the third kind, *decentralized* norms, that apply to consumer exchange. These decentralized norms constrain sellers' profit-seeking through the diffused sanctions of many, many consumers all acting independently. They also constrain buyers' self-interested efforts to pilfer and purloin.

Although it is evident that there are indeed social norms in consumer exchange that constrain both buyers and sellers, there is also evidence of a *self-serving bias*.[19] We tend to view outcomes beneficial to ourselves as being more fair. So consumers tend to think that a cheaper price is a fairer one. But a self-serving bias influences more than just the price evaluation. It also affects what norms we consider when making a fairness judgment.

For example, workers who feel that they have done more than others say that their wages should be based on their contribution. That way, they will receive more than those who have done less. But those who feel they have done less say that wages should be the same for everyone. That way, they will receive more than if wages were based on contribution.

In her insightful book on norms, philosopher Cristina Bicchieri argues that different norms are cued by different situations.[20] Sometimes it is the norm to act in our own self-interest; sometimes it is not. In a situation where we are considering the purchase of one of two identical items, of course we will choose the one that is cheaper because that is in our self-interest. In other situations, however, we will choose what is in the interest of society. For example, we pay for what we buy at the grocery store even though that is against our self-interest.

Which social norm should be followed in which situation is determined by the *scripts* of social interaction that we learn as children. For a given situation, these scripts specify the norms of who does what, when, and how. For instance, it is the norm to leave a tip in a restaurant but not at a dry cleaner. It is the norm to haggle in a flea market but not in a supermarket. It is the norm to pay for the theater beforehand but for the street busker afterward.

We tend to assume that everyone has learned the same scripts, but that may or may not be the case. Some grocery store cashiers apparently think that the script calls for them to charge less to their friends. This is what is called a *personal norm* rather than a social norm; it is an idiosyncratic norm held by an individual but not the group. The actual norm is that one should not profit from one's friends.[21] So it is the norm for an owner of a store, the person who profits from the sale, to give a discount to friends, but not for hourly employees to do so.

Problems arise when people think their personal norms are really social norms consensually backed by the group. Such a misunderstanding, however, can very easily happen. Researchers tell us that it is a human tendency to exaggerate how much others agree with our own idiosyncratic norms.[22]

Back in the 1970s, for example, the radical Abbie Hoffman believed that stealing was not only permissible but commendable. (See "The Personal Norms of Abbie Hoffman" on page 40.) He thought it cool to have a supermarket cashier charge less to friends. And he was convinced that most people agreed with him. However, his personal norm that people should steal whatever they can was not the socially accepted norm.

Emergence of Norms

Nevertheless, even if people have distorted ideas about what constitutes a social norm, general agreement within a society does somehow emerge. For example, in the United States, grocery bags are free; in Germany, they are not. Americans add sales taxes on to a price; Europeans include them in the price. So in every society, a consensus on the social norms of pricing has somehow emerged.

Norms are sometimes instituted on purpose. For example, sellers, in an attempt to establish a competitive advantage by differentiating themselves, can purposely try out new pricing policies. If these policies catch on, they can evolve into norms.

Upscale restaurants, to show that prices are inconsequential, now price menu items simply in dollars with no cents added. Retailers, to satisfy different female shapes, now sell women's suit jackets and skirts separately. Cities like Oslo and London, to improve the quality of life by cutting down on congestion, now charge an entry fee to autos. And shopping centers, to boost profits, are starting to charge for parking. If buyers like a new idea—or at least do not object too strenuously—it can over time become a norm.

In other cases, social norms evolve accidentally. Accidental pricing norms are formed through the trial and error of repeated actions. They are reinforced by repeating "the many seemingly trivial procedures followed in daily life."[23] They evolve over time and are culturally transmitted.

People try out different *behavioral regularities* and settle on those that are somehow beneficial. It is, for instance, beneficial for everyone to drive on the same side of the road, whether it is left or right. Maybe there was once a reason for these norms, but it appears they evolved by chance into descriptive norms of how things are normally done.

Over time, descriptive norms can become so ingrained that they can change into prescriptive norms. As sociologist Christine Horne explains, "Whatever the reason for the initial action, when many people engage in the same behavior, that behavior comes to be associated with a sense of oughtness."[24] What is becomes what should be.

A case in point is the price tag. Posting prices on tags was not done until the 1860s. It then became so common that today it is a prescriptive norm. Indeed, some states like New Jersey now have laws requiring that all supermarket prices be posted.

However, although repetitive behavior can become a descriptive norm, which can over time morph into a prescriptive norm, this does not mean that all behavioral regularities will become norms. Taking off one's hat because it is a hot day is a behavioral regularity, but it is not a descriptive or prescriptive norm. It is not necessarily expected. In fact, some people prefer wearing hats on hot days. In contrast, taking one's hat off in church is indeed a prescriptive social norm.

The difference is that social norms affect not just oneself but also others in the society. Taking one's hat off because it is hot affects only oneself; taking one's hat off in church is a symbolic gesture that affects the entire group.[25] The sideways glances of the entire congregation would signal to offenders that they had violated the social norm.

When men adhere to the social norm and do remove their hats in church, it goes unnoticed. It is only when a norm is violated that it gets attention. For example, imagine buying a car only to find that a battery costs extra. Imagine paying a cab driver $10 for a $6 ride and receiving no change. Imagine registering in a hotel and being told that they did not accept cash.

All these events would be upsetting because they are violations of the social norms of pricing that we all know. Naturally, a battery is included in the price of a car. Obviously, a cabbie will return your change. Of course, a hotel will accept cash. Those are the social norms. Customers believe these are legitimate entitlements; merchants who violate these norms are unfair.

When these social norms are violated, the miscreant is punished. In some cases, it is other people who punish the wrongdoer either actively or passively. They actively fire a cashier who does not charge friends for groceries, or they passively shun a person who does not leave a large enough tip.

Any member of the society of the Pennsylvania Dutch who violates the group's social norms is shunned: no one is allowed to talk to, eat with, buy from, or sell to him or her. Likewise, companies are shunned when they violate the social norms: customers boycott companies that do not follow the rules.

For instance, in New York City, movie theaters were boycotted because they increased prices from $8.50 to $9.50.[26] GlaxoSmithKline was boycotted for cutting off sales to Canadian pharmacies that were then selling pharmaceuticals at low prices to Americans.[27]

In other cases, we punish ourselves. We leave a tip because we would feel bad if we did not. We pay at self-service checkout registers because we would feel guilty not to. In these cases, the punishment for norm violations is internal.

In Sum . . .

Social norms are unwritten rules of behavior for specified situations. They are tacitly understood and believed to be consensually held. In consumer exchange, the social norms of pricing are useful in that they establish and reinforce mutually held expectations. They predict behavior, simplify decisions, and reduce confusion.

Sellers know they have to follow the social norms or face the consequences. Consumers know they have to pay for what they buy. We all know we will be punished if we do not follow the norms. And even if no one catches us taking the T-bone steak without paying, we will feel bad because we have violated a social norm. That's wrong, and we all know it!

Definitions

Heuristic: A "rule-of-thumb" method of solving problems; for example, always ordering the second cheapest bottle of wine on the menu.

Opportunism: Taking advantage of a situation for one's own self interest.

Zero-sum game: Where one person's gain is another person's loss; for instance, negotiating the price of a used car.

Cooperative norms: Rules that develop within an ongoing relationship to the benefit of both parties involved.

Coercive norms: Rules imposed by a more powerful person to further his or her own self-interest.

Decentralized norms: Ubiquitous rules that evolve over time to facilitate exchange, whether economic or social.

Self serving bias: The inclination to think that what benefits oneself is more fair.

Script: A set of rules prescribing a sequence of appropriate actions; for instance, how a negotiation is to be conducted.

Personal norm: An idiosyncratic expectation of how others will behave.

Behavioral regularity: A habitual action repeated over time, but not backed by a social norm.

The Personal Norms of Abbie Hoffman

SUPERMARKETS . . . Women should never go shopping without a large handbag. In those crowded aisles, especially the ones with piles of cases, all sorts of goodies can be transferred from shopping cart to handbag. A drop bag can be sewn inside a trench coat for more efficient thievery. Don't worry about the mirrors: attendants never look at them. Become a discriminating shopper and don't stuff any of the cheap shit in your pockets. . . . Large scale thievery can best be carried out with the help of an employee . . . A woman can get a job as a cashier and ring up a small bill as her brothers and sisters bring home tons of stuff . . . We know one woman working as a cashier who swiped over $500 worth of food a week.

Excerpt from Abbie Hoffman, *Steal This Book.*[28]

Emotions

"YOU'RE NOT BEING FAIR
AND I HATE YOU!"

"I would kill a . . . company that raised their prices 20 percent!"

This statement erupted from a young woman in a research study I conducted. She had just been told that a company had increased prices by 20 percent without any legitimate reason. The company's violation of a social norm precipitated her fierce emotional response.

But note that the emotional response was to *un*fairness, not fairness. Fairness evokes little emotion. It is simply accepted as the norm. It is *un*fairness that causes an emotional outburst.

The emotional response to unfairness has been examined by Norman Finkel, a specialist in psychology and law and author of a notable book on fairness. He argues that the "unfair" end of the fair/unfair continuum "has concreteness, passion, insistence, and primacy, in ways that the 'fair' end does not."[1]

The intensity of emotion to unfairness varies depending on whether the norms of either personal fairness or social fairness have been violated. The different intensities of emotional response to the different kinds of unfairness has been explained by the philosopher Craig Carr. He separates fairness into two kinds.[2] Carr's first kind of fairness is similar to personal fairness: "a person's opinion about something that has affected him or her either positively or negatively."[3]

Personal fairness is thus a measure of positive feelings, a personal preference. And personal *un*fairness is "little more than a person's unhappiness or dissatisfaction with a certain course of events."[4] As explained in Chapter 1, personal fairness is based on descriptive norms that provide a standard for expected prices and pricing policies. Prices are supposed to be predictable and sellers are supposed to act normally. Violations of these norms cause distress.

Carr's second kind of fairness is similar to social fairness in that it is based on prescriptive norms. "Certain transgressions, violations, or disruptions"[5] of these norms make an action socially unfair. The prescriptive norms of social fairness designate not only what is normally done but also what *should* or should *not* be done. Violations of these norms cause fury.

Sequence of Emotional Responses

The sequence of escalating emotional responses to unfair prices was demonstrated in the four *focus groups* I held in the United States. Participants were told that the price of a service had increased 20 percent. Their immediate response echoed the young woman who was ready to kill the company. The others agreed, indicating surprise and annoyance at a price higher than expected, which is personally unfair: *"Twenty percent is a ridiculous increase." "The 20 percent is upsetting me." "Twenty percent is a lot for an increase. It's a big percentage."*

Because of the 20 percent increase, the focus group participants exhibited distress. Their most frequent comment was *"I would be annoyed." "You just get annoyed because you feel less rich. You feel like you're not making enough money to sustain a normal living." "I'm probably frustrated." "I'm not happy about it." "I wouldn't like it either."*

They then wanted some sort of justification for the increase: *"My first reaction would be 'Why?'" "Why are they increasing their prices by 20 percent?" "I'd want to know a reason." "I think [a reason] helps to justify the price increase."*

What the focus groups considered the most legitimate justification for a price increase was equity, the social norm of reciprocity: *"When I hear of price increases, I'm curious to know if they're going to offer me anything a little bit extra." "If you saw that they gave more value for your money, gave you more services, it would be justifiable." "If there isn't anything that offsets the price increase, then I don't think it's worth it."*

It was socially unfair for the company to raise the price without improving the service. That violates the norm of equity.

That made participants furious. *"It makes me mad." "I'm upset. I feel totally manipulated at this point." "I'd feel betrayed by the company." "Price gouging." "I'd be especially pissed." "Me too!"*

And they were ready to retaliate: *"I wouldn't stick with it. I'd quit." "I feel like if I could drop this product, I would drop it."*

Separating Emotional Responses

Most prior research has considered only the response to the social unfairness of a price. For example, in the landmark study by psychologist and Nobel laureate in economics Daniel Kahneman and his associates, they asked respondents the following:[6]

> A hardware store has been selling snow shovels for $15. The morning after a large snowstorm, the store raises the price to $20. Please rate this action as: completely fair, acceptable, unfair, very unfair.

The results were that "82% of the [107] respondents . . . considered it unfair for the hardware store to take advantage of the short-run increase in demand associated with a blizzard."[7]

Replications of the study by Kahneman and his associates have confirmed their results in various groups. A study in Switzerland and Germany found that 83 percent of the respondents found the price increase after the blizzard unfair.[8] Even executives, who are generally keen to make a profit, agree: in another study, 71 percent of them also thought the increase unfair.[9] These studies, however, did not isolate the personal unfairness of a price increase all by itself.

I conducted a follow-up study to separate personal fairness from the social fairness studied by Kahneman and his associates. To separate the two kinds of fairness, I asked one group the same question Kahneman had asked. Replicating the results of their study, 86 percent rated it unfair to increase a snow shovel price after a snow-storm. This indicates social fairness. To isolate the personal fairness of the price alone, I asked another group how they would respond if a seller increased the price of shovels when there was no storm.

> A hardware store has been selling snow shovels for $15. The store now raises the price to $20. Please rate this action as completely fair, acceptable, unfair, very unfair.

Table 5.1.   Percentage of Respondents Judging Price Unfair

Price Increase	Without Storm (Personally Unfair)	With Storm (Socially Unfair)
Remain at $15	8%	12%
Increase from $15 to $17	45%	61%
Increase from $15 to $20	69%	86%

Without a storm, 69 percent rated the price increase unfair, indicating that respondents considered raising a price itself to be personally unfair. An additional 17 percent of the respondents, however, considered the increase unfair when done within the context of a snowstorm. Raising the price after a snowstorm is taking advantage of a consumer in need, which is socially unfair.

To further test the effect of price by itself, I gave other groups the same vignette but in one case with no price increase and in the other case with only a $2 increase.[10] Again, most of the perceived unfairness was due to the price alone. But the social unfairness of raising the price after a storm significantly increased that perceived unfairness (see Table 5.1).

Function of Emotional Responses

The emotional responses to personal and social unfairness are essential to economic decision making. This is made clear by the work of neurologist Antonio Damasio. He tells of a patient who was intellectually intact, showing no sign of psychological impairment. The patient was able to assemble facts and was aware of the social norms, but he had a problem in that he could not come to a decision. His impairment became evident when the patient was given a choice of two dates in the coming month for his next appointment. The patient was incapable of reaching a decision. Instead, he considered endless alternatives:

> For the better part of a half-hour, the patient enumerated reasons for and against each of the two dates: previous engagements, proximity to other engagements, possible meteorological conditions, virtually anything that one could reasonably think about concerning a simple date.[11]

Another of Damasio's patients was given a test in which he was presented with different social problems. He was asked to give possible ways to respond to each problem as well as the consequences of those responses. This patient was able to suggest many legitimate responses and could recognize the possible outcomes of each, but added, "After all this, I still wouldn't know what to do!"[12]

As Damasio explains, the reason the patients could not reach a decision was their lack of emotions due to brain injuries. Both could think rationally, but they had no emotional base on which to make a decision.

Logical thinking alone is not enough to reach decisions. Emotions are needed to determine good or bad, right or wrong. Logic and emotions, Damasio argues, have to work together. Only then can people make plans for the future that will be most beneficial to their survival. Those without access to emotions cannot plan.

The role of emotions has not been a concern in traditional economic decision making. When it comes to the evaluation of a price, people are assumed to be logical and to make decisions based solely on self-interest. That is rational, and rationality is itself a social norm of economic exchange. We are told to "keep a cool head" and "not let your emotions get in the way." But Damasio shows that even though being emotional can sometimes be detrimental to decision making, having no emotions can be devastating.

Emotions are necessary for both learning social norms and following them. Patients who lose access to their emotions at a young age never learn the social norms at all. Since they have no emotional response when punished or praised for either violating or following a social norm, they store no memory of what constitutes a norm. Patients who lose emotional access later in life know the social norms but feel no compunction to follow them. Not surprisingly, such patients are known to shoplift and steal from others.[13]

Emotions also affect whether people enforce the social norms because each norm gets what can be thought of as an *emotional tag*. These tags indicate that following the social norm is important. Due to the tags, we feel it matters whether Amazon is charging different people different amounts. We think it is critical that mobile phone companies use large enough type in their advertisements. We believe that we should care whether airline prices are understandable.

Emotional tags also indicate the acceptability of different actions: stealing is bad, charging all people the same amount is good, taking advantage of the poor is bad, and so on. Based on these emotional tags, customers get a gut feeling about a price. They need no time to work out logically whether a price or pricing policy is right or wrong, fair or unfair. They know it on the spot.

In Sum . . .

Fairness represents the emotional part of economic decision making. If a price is perceived to be personally unfair, consumers will be distressed. They will be motivated to find the reason. They will check whether the personal unfairness is justified by social fairness. If they figure that the reason is socially fair, they will decide to make the purchase. But if the reason is socially *un*fair, they will be more than distressed: they will be irrationally irate. Like an emotional small child, they will blurt, "You're not being fair and I hate you!"

Definitions

Emotion: A strong feeling that arises subjectively rather than cognitively, from the gut rather than from the brain.

Focus group: A market research technique in which 6 to 10 consumers are gathered together to share their ideas with a moderator.

Norm of rationality: The rule that economic decisions should be based on reasoning rather than emotions, with self-interest often considered the primary motivation.

Emotional tag: The association of feelings like "good" or "bad" to beliefs like social norms.

CHAPTER 6

Expectations

"THAT PRICE IS A RIP-OFF!"

I am in shock. My water heater gave up this morning and I was told it will cost over $750 to install a new one. This is unfair! I expect water heaters to cost about $250. Maybe slightly more due to inflation. But not *triple*!

Still, it could have been worse. The plumber could have demanded cash—in advance. He could have told me that he only had one water heater and was going to auction it off to the three customers who wanted it. After the installation, he could have demanded an extra $100 for connecting the heater to the water.

He did none of those things. So he at least followed the descriptive norms of how plumbers are expected to behave. That is fair. But he charged me more than I expected to pay. That is a rip-off! He violated what I considered the descriptive norm of water heater prices. That is wrong!

Descriptive norms of prices and pricing practices are expectations based on prior experience. These price expectations are not just a rational estimate, they are emotional wants. We prefer to get what we expect to get.

The preference for the expected is what William Samuelson and Richard Zeckhauser call the *status quo bias*.[1] They explain the bias as being the result of a status quo norm, which "reinforces the individual's inclination to conform to social norms."[2] Humans prefer the stability of the status quo.

We human beings seem to have some innate drive for consistency, a desire to maintain *social homeostasis*. Stable prices and pricing practices allow us to make plans. We can feel in control. This is good. Changing prices or pricing practices is "a deviation from some norm or steady state."[3] This is bad.

This does not mean that our expectations are exact. Descriptive norms are not precise specifications, but general ideas that can be ambiguous. The norm is to tip in restaurants. That is what is done. But the percentage is left up in the air. And whether to tip other service providers and how much to tip them is not specified.

In some cases, descriptive norms are more than ambiguous, they are downright wrong. The price expectations of contestants on *The Price Is Right* have an error from 19 percent to over 50 percent.[4] Their price expectations are influenced by how much actual experience a consumer has with products in the category. (They have more accurate ideas of the price of frequently purchased goods.[5]) Expectations are, however, skewed by biases.

One bias is the result of optimism. Psychologists explain that we tend to think things that are important to us will really happen.[6] We expect a positive outcome more than a negative one. We consequently have optimistic expectations of price. These optimistic expectations are related to what social psychologists David Messick and Keith Sentis[7] have called the self-serving bias of fairness, as mentioned in Chapter 4.

The self-serving bias leads to price expectations that are in our own self-interest. It is the human tendency "to conflate what is fair with what benefits oneself."[8] Consequently, when we pay less than others (what researchers call *advantageous inequity*[9]), we readily accept it as personally fair. We accept changes as fair if they are in our favor.

Take the pricing of mobile phones. The norm is that customers buy the phone and pay monthly for the service. Often the cost of the phone is included in the service. That is the norm. But when Virgin entered the U.S. phone market, they totally violated the norm. Instead of selling the phone as part of the service, they sold the service along with the phone. This was not the norm. However, it benefited the customer and was immediately accepted.

Due to the self-serving bias to fairness, what we think are descriptive norms, shared by society in general, may actually be only idiosyncratic norms, our own particular ideas of what we would like a price to be. Nevertheless, whether descriptive or only idiosyncratic, norms express strong expectations. When those expectations are thwarted, it is personally unfair.

Expectations of Pricing Practices

Many of the norms cited in earlier chapters are descriptive norms of pricing practices. These norms guide what sellers charge for and what they provide free; what they include in the price and what they add as an extra. These norms indicate how prices are determined: whether by negotiations, by auctions, by the seller, or by the government. And they tell us who is expected to pay the price.

An example is who is expected to pay the bill at a restaurant. When I first started working, male clients were uncomfortable at my paying. And waitresses invariably brought the change back to the male (which one unforgettable client actually pocketed!). The descriptive norm at that time was obviously for men to pay at restaurants, although that has changed over time.

In general, every industry has its own descriptive norms as to how prices should be set. Dry cleaning is charged by type of item. Buffet restaurants charge a flat rate no matter how much you eat. Banks charge a percentage interest charge. Gas stations tack on nine-tenths of a cent to their per-gallon price. Law firms and consultants charge by the hour. In their respective industries, these are the descriptive norms of pricing. Because they are customary and expected, they are fair.

In most cases, companies follow these norms intuitively. They know the rules of the game, and they play along. One continuing difficulty, however, is the descriptive norm of what is included in the price, what is called the *price bundle*. In many instances, what were traditional bundles are now being unbundled, which raises questions about fairness.

It is the norm that parking is bundled into the cost of groceries, but some urban stores are beginning to charge extra for parking, at least for noncustomers. It is the norm that airlines provide food service on flights over four hours, but more and more airlines are beginning to charge extra for food—and it has even been suggested that they start charging for restrooms.

Some hotels now charge extra for housekeeping. Some stores charge a "restocking fee" for returned items. Some newspapers now charge for obituary notices. Delivery services and airlines add surcharges for fuel. Banks charge for overdrafts and the use of automated teller machines. Phone companies now charge for directory assistance. Planes charge for overweight baggage and for tickets bought at their airline counters. Theater ticket sellers charge a processing fee.

These extra fees violate what has been established as the descriptive norms of pricing practices. They are unexpected and consequently personally unfair.

To avoid accusations of unfairness, merchants try to create realistic expectations. Retailers put price tags on their garments. Restaurateurs state prices on their menus. Doctors and lawyers explain their fees in advance. Grocery stores post the price on the shelf. Tours list exactly what is included in the price. And plumbers— even the one who charged me $750 for a new water heater—give prior estimates for their services.

It is the norm that the estimates and posted prices set by sellers will be honored. Consumers are aggravated when a garment on a "sale" rack turns out not to actually be on sale. Homeowners complain when workmen demand more money than they estimated. And customers take retailers to court when scanner prices do not match posted prices. The grocery chain Albertson's, for example, was hit with a $1.85 million fine due to overcharges by their scanners.[10]

Conversely, even a higher price can be accepted as fair when the price has been posted. This was shown in a study of grocery store prices.[11] In this case, the scanner showed a lower price than had been posted on the shelf. Even though the higher posted price was personally unfair, 75 percent of the respondents accepted the higher price since it had been posted.

Expectations of Prices

The expected price has been widely accepted as the "fair price."[12] As one group of researchers concluded, "Under most circumstances, the price we define as the expected price should coincide with the 'fair price.'"[13] Any sharp increase in price is therefore unfair.

The 67 percent hike in the entry fee to the reopened Museum of Modern Art in New York was headlined as a "shock."[14] An increase in gasoline prices, ABC News reported, resulted in 94 percent of consumers being dissatisfied.[15] There was an uproar and eventual Federal Trade Commission complaint when Mylan Laboratories raised the price of its antidepressant drug from $11.36 to some $377 for a bottle of 500 tablets.[16]

Just changing the price too frequently is itself unfair because it is unexpected. Demonstrating a concern for prices that fluctuate, a consultant complained that "when we recently priced an Enterprise rental for a spring trip to Los Angeles, the cost vacillated dramatically: Two hours after we first checked the company's web site, the per-day rate for a full-size car dropped almost $8. Over the next week it continued to yo-yo, ranging from a low of $32 to a high of $73."[17]

A *Los Angeles Times* staff writer had a similar experience of fluctuating prices when buying from Amazon over the Internet.[18] He decided to buy a new cookbook, went to the Amazon site, and placed the book in his electronic shopping cart, but then got distracted. It was not until the next day that he went back to complete the transaction. A pop-up message told him that the price had increased $0.51, from $11.02 to $11.53. Curious, he filled his shopping basket with book orders and let them sit there for several days. When he checked back, nine U.S. books had higher prices and three had lower prices. Later, he found one book that had gone from $225 to $300 overnight. That is not fair!

In recognition of buyers' preference for the status quo, sellers do not change their prices as fast as their costs change.[19] Executives say that changing prices too often would only antagonize customers.[20] An alternate strategy is to keep the price steady but cut the product. This is called *candy-bar pricing* in honor of the candy companies who kept the price of a bar at $0.05 but reduced the amount of chocolate. When consumers catch on to such product reductions, they are angry at being snookered.

In addition to unexpected price fluctuations, any unexpected extra charge is also considered unfair: unforeseen charges for the delivery of furniture, unanticipated extras tacked onto phone bills, unexpected taxes. In the state of Delaware, where they have no sales tax, consumers have to pay an unexpected "rental" tax when they take out a DVD. That is not fair!

Even small extra charges are annoying when not anticipated. I was annoyed when a recent motel bill included a $2 fee for the electronic safe that I did not even use, and when I returned a rental car and was charged $6 a gallon to fill up the tank, and when I signed up for a class that cost $280 and was charged $25 extra in various fees.

Conversely, however, a high fee will be accepted as fair if it is expected. A study by Pacific Gas and Electric Company found that customers' current choice was the best predictor of which service schedule they would chose. Even when customers could get cheaper rates, they preferred the electricity schedule they already had.[21] Even if it is high, people prefer the price they expect.

Reference Prices

Academics investigating price fairness call on the idea of a *reference price*. As one researcher concluded, "the most important factor in determining p* (reference price) is fairness."[22]

A reference price is a standard against which a price is judged to be cheap or expensive. It is the same as the descriptive norm of a price, except that a descriptive norm has emotional content, whereas a reference price is a cold, cognitive calculation. Despite the difference, the research into reference prices is directly relevant to descriptive norms of prices.

Academics explain the formation of reference prices by referring to the nineteenth-century Weber-Fechner law. This law applies to how stimuli like noise or smell affect the senses. The idea is that an average of all previously experienced stimuli act as a reference point against which the intensity of a new stimulus is compared.

For example, if a person has lived in the silence of a desert, the birds and crickets of a farm will seem noisy. But if one has lived in the hubbub of Manhattan, the same farm sounds will seem blissfully quiet. However, after living on the farm for a while, the previous city dweller will then find Manhattan noisy. The reason is that new stimuli are incorporated into prior information so that the reference point is shifted.

Based on the Weber-Fechner law, researchers in the last decades of the 1900s explored how reference prices are formed. They suggested that people calculate some sort of average of all previously experienced prices. When a consumer encounters a new price, it is averaged into the past prices to form a new reference price. This then acts as a standard for judging future prices.

Different researchers came up with different ways of averaging a reference price. Some suggested it is some sort of *rolling average* of past prices.[23] Others said it is the weighted average of previous prices for just that particular brand.[24] Still others have suggested more sophisticated calculations such as taking the exponentially decaying weighted average of all past prices so that more current prices will be given more weight.[25] All these methods of determining a reference price work to some degree. But they all face a common problem. The problem is that people have only a vague notion of actual prices.

Just like the error-prone participants on *The Price Is Right*, repeated studies of grocery store prices in both the United States and elsewhere indicate that barely 50 percent of the people know the actual price of an item they are purchasing, even when they have just taken the item off the shelf.[26] This suggests that a reference price, just like a descriptive norm, is a rough estimate. It is a range rather than a precise point.[27] Consumers have a comparative idea of whether the price is cheap or expensive but not an exact idea of what the price actually is.[28]

In some cases, however, retailers establish specific reference prices through their advertising. In these cases, the reference price becomes a specific expectation which consumers feel entitled to receive. It is the norm.

Customers consequently react ferociously when retailers *bait and switch*. This is when retailers advertise a low-priced item to get the customer into the store, but when they arrive, the retailer says that the product is no longer available. The customer's only choice is a more expensive version of a similar product. This is unfair and illegal. It is more fair for stores to provide a "rain check," where if a sale item is out of stock, customers are given a voucher for the product at the sale price at a later date.

Some unscrupulous retailers try to take advantage of consumers by creating a falsely high reference price. They advertise that a product "Was $79, now only $59." Such a comparison makes the $59 price seem less expensive than posting a $59 price by itself. Researchers have shown that the effect holds even when the comparison is unrealistic: "Was $200, now only $59" still makes the price seem cheaper even though it is unbelievable.[29]

There are, of course, laws against advertising unrealistic reference prices. An item has to have been sold at the regular higher price for a "reasonably substantial period of time" before a store can cite it as the "before" price.[30] However, just because there is a law does not mean that all stores necessarily obey it.

For instance, in Florida, the sale of one store's luggage and mattresses was investigated because "the regular price has absolutely no meaning. . . . The store never sold the item at that price."[31] In another store, investigators found that 97 percent of household goods were sold at "sale" prices; only 3 percent of sales were at the "before" price.[32]

In Sum . . .

A personally fair price or pricing practice is one that meets the expectations of the descriptive norms. These expectations are not precise. Nonetheless, a price that is clearly higher than expected, or a pricing practice that is clearly different from normal, causes an unpleasant surprise. It is personally unfair.

In the case of my water heater, I still feel the price was a rip-off. However, I was stuck because I wanted hot showers and did not want water in my basement. So I paid the price. But I am unhappy because I feel wronged. I am convinced the price was unfair. I suspect that the plumber was taking advantage of my situation, which is socially unfair, the subject of the next chapter.

Definitions

Status quo bias: The inclination to prefer the existing state of affairs.

Social homeostasis: A state of social equilibrium; the status quo.

Advantageous inequity: Getting more than we give in an exchange; getting more than the other party to the exchange gets or more than other people get.

Price bundle: When more than one item or service is included in the price; for example, including the tires in the price of a car.

Candy-bar pricing: Increasing profits by decreasing the size of the product rather than increasing the price.

Reference price: The standard against which a price is judged cheap or expensive, fair or unfair; based on prior experience and information in the environment.

Rolling average: An average based on a set number of past events over time; for example, averaging the past three months at the end of each month.

Bait and switch: The illegal practice of advertising a low price to bring customers into the store but then saying that the item is sold out and showing them a higher-priced alternative.

CHAPTER

Outcomes

"YOU SHOULD GET WHAT YOU PAY FOR!"

When Hillary Rodham Clinton called $1.7 million a "fair price" for their new home, she was referring to the fairness of getting what you pay for.[1] In return for their $1.7 million, they got a 5,200-square-foot, 7-bedroom, 100-year-old Dutch Colonial house conveniently located some 35 miles outside New York City. The $1.7 million price was fair because the exchange was equitable: what they got was equivalent to what they gave.

When the reporter in the *Monterey Herald* wrote that "once upon a time, concertgoers enjoyed first come, first served access to tickets . . . everyone had a fair shot at tickets with fixed prices,"[2] he was considering the fairness of everyone's paying the same amount. This was fair because of equality: everyone had equal access to tickets at the same price.

When the English parliamentarians were concerned about the cost of legal aid being "fair to the vulnerable,"[3] they were thinking about offering special price concessions to the poor. It is fair to adjust a price for the needy. The disadvantaged have a right to the goods required for survival even if they cannot afford them.

What Hillary, the journalist, and the parliamentarians were each saying is that a price outcome is socially fair if the exchange is equitable, the outcome is equal to all, but the price is adjusted for the needy. Equity, equality, and need are the three primary prescriptive norms of distributive fairness,[4] which is the basis for judging the social fairness of outcomes. Although these *norms of outcome* have been identified in theory by social scientists, they have also been shown in practice to be the same standards that everyday people use when evaluating fairness.[5]

The social fairness of outcomes is based on the price society in general finds "just," which is socially fair, as opposed to the price or pricing practice individuals expect, which is personally fair. (See Table 7.1 comparing personal and social fairness of prices.)

Assuming that consumers actually want the product under consideration, a concern for social fairness is triggered by a price that they find personally unfair. It is then that people ask themselves whether the price is justified.

When a price is personally unfair, giving the customer a good reason can be beneficial.[6] If the company can provide an explanation, people will accept a personally unfair price as being socially fair. Researchers have therefore advised companies that they should always give a reason, particularly for adverse actions like a price increase.[7] But the reason has to be a good one. "An inadequate explanation may be deemed more unfair than failure to provide one at all."[8]

A good explanation can be either an excuse or a justification. What constitutes a good excuse is one that demonstrates that no other outcome was feasible.[9] "We had to do it. Our hands were tied."

What constitutes a legitimate justification is demonstrating social acceptability. In a study of requests to cut in front of a line, the conclusion was that "compliance with a request increases when the request is accompanied by a socially acceptable justification."[10] To be legitimate, the action taken has to conform to the social norms.[11] In the case of price outcomes, as with outcomes in general, the norms are equity, equality, and need.

Table 7.1. Personally versus Socially Fair Prices

Personally Fair Prices	Socially Fair Prices
How people perceive that a price is fair to them personally	How people judge that a price is fair to society in general
Adheres to descriptive norms of prices and pricing practices: - Equal to or less than expected price - Follows expected pricing practices	Adheres to the prescriptive norms of prices and pricing practices: - Equity: price reflects product worth - Equality: same price for all - Need: price adjusted for disadvantaged

Norm of Equity

According to the social norm of equity, the price should correspond to the *value* of the product. Clearly, you would not make a purchase if you did not think that what you were getting was worth what you were paying. However, with the social norm, there is an emotional element: you *should* get what you pay for. That is only fair.

But how do we decide what a thing is worth?

Determining worth is difficult since people's value judgments are unstable and easily biased. The instability of value judgments has been demonstrated in a series of exceedingly interesting studies by three researchers who bridge the fields of economics, psychology, and sociology: Dan Ariely, George Loewenstein, and Drazen Prelec.[12]

These researchers showed subjects a variety of products and first asked if the subjects would buy the products for a price that had been established totally arbitrarily: they simply used whatever happened to be the last two digits of each subjects' Social Security number. The researchers then asked the subjects the maximum price they would pay for each product.

When initially presented with a high asking price, subjects said they would pay nearly twice as much as would subjects who had initially been presented with a low asking price. The subjects' evaluation of the product's value was clearly biased by the first price mentioned to them, even though that first price was random.

In a follow-up study, the researchers showed it is possible to shift people's thinking 180 degrees—all the way from thinking they should pay for an item to thinking they should charge for it. They asked one group of subjects if they would each pay $10 to be read Whitman's *Leaves of Grass* for 10 minutes. The researchers asked another group if they would listen to a poetry reading for 10 minutes if they were each paid $10. The researchers then asked each of the two groups to set a price for a shorter, 3-minute reading.

Both groups' responses were biased by whether they had first been asked how much they would pay or how much they would charge. The group that had initially been asked to pay suggested only lower amounts they would pay since the reading was for only 3 rather than 10 minutes. But the group that initially had been asked what they would charge cited only the lower amounts they would charge for less reading time. So even the positive or negative value of a good depends on how the question has been framed. What is paid for in some instances can be charged for in others.

As the researchers point out, this is exactly what Tom Sawyer did when he got people to pay to paint a fence. Another example is that members of American university advisory boards typically donate money to their alma mater, but in other countries, universities have to pay graduates to be on a board. And in a New Zealand seaside town I visited, the mailman was paid for a rural postal delivery, but he then charged tourists to ride along the route.

Not only are judgments of value unstable, but they are also variable. Just as "beauty is in the eye of the beholder," so too is value in the mind of the consumer. This does not make it easy to determine fairness based on the equivalence of the exchange. Those who value the product highly will find the price fair; those who value it less will think the same price unfair.

I am reminded of when I was living in the mountains of Colorado and had to buy a car. Snowstorms up there can be horrendous. When I went to the car dealer and saw a four-wheel-drive pickup truck with monster tires, I fell in love. I knew those tires would make it through any storm. I was ready to pay anything to get that truck. It was worth far more to me than it would be to someone living in Miami. So was it fair for me to pay more? Absolutely.

Evaluations of value are also affected by the social norms of the culture. In the old Union of Soviet Socialist Republics, doctors were paid less than plumbers. The reason, I was told, was that doctors were doing what they wanted to do and plumbers were not. In that culture the social norm was to pay plumbers more.

Services in Germany are generally valued more highly than in the United States. When I was living there I was surprised at the high cost of haircuts, dry cleaning, and photo processing. But workers are valued highly in the German culture.

Estimations of value are also affected by the different factors used as a basis. Hotels are an interesting example. Motel 6 evidently figures that it is fair to charge more for two people in a room than one since the motel guests are reaping twice the benefit. A hotel where I stayed at the seashore figures that it is fair for customers to pay more for an ocean view. In Germany, one creative hotel owner thinks it fair to charge big people more since they take up more space. He bases his room rates on the weight of the customer: $0.64 per kilogram (2.2 pounds).[13]

Another example of different bases of value is how doctors today determine prices compared to how an ancestor of mine did it. He was a physician in Old Salem. Patients in the early nineteenth century paid the doctor only if they were cured. The value was based on the patient's survival. If the patient died—as some of my forefather's patients did from his kite and key treatments—the patient's estate did not have to pay for the treatment.

Today, at my own doctor's, patients have to pay if they miss an appointment or call too late to cancel. The value is based on my doctor's time.

In addition to viewing equity as an equivalence of value and price, it can also be viewed as a comparison of the inputs and outcomes of the buyer versus those of the seller. In order for buyers to even consider such a comparison, they have to have some concern for the welfare of the seller. Not surprisingly, research indicates that this is not the case in consumer exchange.[14]

In today's market, buyers are king. They demand *better* results than what the seller gets.[15] Buyers think that "seller outcomes are unrelated to fairness."[16] It appears that equity with the seller is not a concern as long as the buyer is getting more. It is only when the buyer is getting less—as with the oil companies—that parity with the seller becomes an issue. In most instances, however, buyers show a self-serving bias and think it is fair is for them to get as much—or preferably more— than what the seller gets. That is considered equitable.

An example of an organization that has exerted itself to be equitable is the University of Colorado at Boulder. They charge different rates for parking permits depending on how far a faculty or staff member has to walk from the parking lot to their office. The parking lot has a higher value to these commuters who have a shorter walk. It is equitable to charge them more.

In another example of equity, Jet Blue varies not the price but the product. They give passengers in the back of the plane more legroom than those in the front. Their logic is that the legroom compensates for the front passengers being served faster and deplaning sooner. So the exchange is kept equitable.

Norm of Equality

If the exchange is found to be equitable, it is deemed fair as long as it also satisfies the *norm of equality*.[17] This social norm is based on the American belief that "all men [and women] are created equal" and should therefore be treated equally. They should all be charged the same price.

Equality is the basis of philosopher John Rawls's idea of fairness being when allocations are made behind a "veil of ignorance."[18] His idea is that if we did not know what position we would have in a future society, we would allocate all goods equally. Equality is also the basis of economist Hal Varian's idea of *envy-free allocations,* where a fair allocation is one where no one prefers another's bundle of goods more than one's own.[19]

In consumer prices, both the equity and the equality norms appear to be highly influenced by the self-interest bias to fairness, mentioned earlier. We are all inclined to accept unequal treatment if it is in our favor. But when we have to pay *more* than others, we are angry.

Recent research shows, for example, that consumers are much more likely to object to an increase in price when they know that other people are paying less.[20] Researchers conclude that "the consequences of finding out that another customer received a better bargain seemed to have a much larger impact on satisfaction than the direct effects of the bargain participants received for themselves."[21]

Comparative fairness has been studied extensively in management as it applies to salaries. The amount of a salary is important not only for the monetary return but also for the social significance. Being paid more than another person indicates superiority. In contrast, however, the symbolic importance of getting a better price than another shopper is not so vital to one's ego. Nonetheless, shoppers still do sometimes compare the fairness of what they pay with what others pay.

We think it unfair if we have to pay more than others. We think it unfair that we have to pay double what Canadians pay for prescription drugs and twice what Europeans pay for the same textbooks.[22] Paying more violates our self-interest and the norm of equality.

Even though the norm of equality is heavily influenced by self-interest, the norm actually affects behavior more than self-interest does. The strength of the equality norm has been demonstrated by researchers using a variant of the *dictator games.* In these games there is a *dictator* and a *responder.* They are kept separate and cannot talk to one another. They both know, however, that the dictator has been given a certain sum of money—for instance, $10—to divide between the two of them. In the typical game, the responder can either accept the allotment or refuse it. If the amount is refused, no one gets anything.

In this variant of the game, responders have no choice but to accept whatever dictators allocate to them.[23] There is no threat of punishment and consequently no reason that dictators cannot keep all the money for themselves. But they do not. Dictators still give some amount to the responder. They respect the norm of equality.

In reviewing the results of these games, some researchers have voiced a concern that dictators follow the norm only because they are being observed and not because they are actually concerned about fairness. To test this possibility, researchers conducted a game in which individual actions were unknown to the experimenter.[24] Again, dictators shared some with the responders. People adhere to the social norm of equality even when no one is watching.

Although equality of outcomes is a guiding American social norm, we place still greater emphasis on equality of opportunity, even if it results in unequal outcomes. As sociologist Edward Sampson has written, "The essence of our modern, Western, meritocratic principle [is] that all persons are deserving of an equal opportunity to utilize their energies and talents to achieve whatever inequality of outcomes of wealth and social status is possible."[25]

As applied to prices, the implication is that all consumers are entitled to equal access to goods at the lowest possible price. If I drive across town for a 20 percent discount, it is fair for me to get a lower price than those people who shop at the nearby store. They too have the opportunity to go to the sale. If I made the trip and they did not, I deserve to pay less.

The norm of equal opportunity is violated, however, when inner city stores have higher prices than elsewhere. Many of the local residents patronizing these stores do not have easy access to other stores.[26] They cannot carry huge quantities of discount items from Sam's Club home on public transportation. In these cases, the retailers are taking advantage of people in need.

Special Norms for Need

Social psychologist Morton Deutsch has advocated specialized norms to govern people in need.[27] According to Deutsch, society recognizes that disadvantaged people deserve special treatment not considered by the norms of equity and equality. According to the *norm of need*, outcomes should be distributed so that all people can at least meet their requirements for survival.

In the United States, we respond to the human need for essentials with free food stamps, homeless shelters, and Medicare for the elderly. Airlines provide bereavement fares. Pharmaceutical companies provide drugs free or at a reduced price to the poor. As a country, we are incensed when the government is slow to supply survival basics to the victims of disasters like Hurricane Katrina.

We object when patients without insurance have to subsidize patients with insurance. A study by Premera Blue Cross found that "hospitals in Washington State charged an additional $738 million— or 14.3 percent of their revenue—to private payers to make up for Medicare and Medicaid underpayments."[28] The Wisconsin attorney general has filed a complaint against two hospitals for their unfair practice of overcharging uninsured patients.[29]

We object when insurers charge higher rates to families with lower credit ratings. And we consider imposing regulations to cap the high cost of payday loans taken out by low-income workers. According to the Center for Responsible Lending, annual fees on these loans can be anywhere from 300 percent to 1,000 percent.[30] That is really unfair to the needy.

It is difficult, however, to determine who is needy. The determination itself is based on social norms. According to the U. S. government, the poverty threshold for a family of four is $20,444. But Harvard considers any family earning less than $60,000 as being in need and therefore qualifying for free tuition.

On the other hand, the elderly are treated as needy even though the percentage living below the poverty line has dropped from nearly 35 percent in 1959 to 10 percent in 2004.[31] Nevertheless, senior citizens still get discounts for entertainment and transportation. That is the social norm.

Colliding Norms

On top of the difficulty of determining equity, equality, and need, there is a major dilemma when these norms collide. For example, how can you charge a lower price to a person in need and still treat everyone equally? How can you treat all people the same but give some people discounts? People like low prices for all but also want special bargains just for themselves. Consumers want both "everyday low prices" and special deals.[32]

The drug company Genentech has had to confront these colliding norms. It defends the potential cost of $100,000 a year for its cancer drug Avastin by saying the price is equitable: it reflects the value of the drug's ability to sustain life.[33] But doctors are concerned that the price means some patients will not be able to afford it. Even with insurance, patients' out-of-pocket costs would be between $10,000 and $20,000. Reporters call it "price gouging."[34]

Genetech counters by citing their programs that help needy patients afford the drug, including their donation of some $21 million to charities that aid patients in copayments. The company claims that its price is fair since it saves lives and help is given to the needy. But the public does not accept it. They feel that the company may be adhering to the norms of equity in that Avastin saves lives, but is still violating the norms of need. The norms are in conflict. This is a problem.

Flat fees versus variable fees is another example of conflicting norms. A flat fee is fair because it is equal to all; a variable fee is fair because it is equitable, reflecting the actual usage. This conflict can lead to major clashes. As mentioned in Chapter 1, there were riots in South Africa because members of the mixed-race community were paying for electricity based on usage while others were paying a flat fee.[35] The mixed-race group felt that the others were being given unfairly preferential treatment. They consequently rioted, and four people were killed.

Sociologists tell us that the choice of which norm to follow depends on the social goals of the situation.[36] If the goal is social welfare, need will be the dominant norm so as to help the disadvantaged. That is why college tuitions are often adjusted based on students' financial need. If the goal is to maintain cooperative relations, equality will be dominant so that everyone will be treated equally. That is why Saturn provides a "no-dicker sticker." And if the goal is to promote economic productivity, equity will be dominant so that people will be rewarded based on their contribution. That is why the price of most cars other than Saturn is determined by each buyer's skill in negotiation.

In Sum . . .

If consumers conclude that the norms of distributive fairness have been satisfied, they will accept a price as socially fair. They may not like the price. They may still be dissatisfied and dismayed. They may think it personally unfair. But they will accept it as socially fair if they think it is equitable and equal to all as well as adjusted for the needy.

However, determining whether a price outcome is socially fair is not a simple matter. It is difficult to figure out what is equitable or equal and when concessions should be made for need—and to whom. Although the concepts are clear, the implementation is not. There is no one factor that assures a perception of fairness. As a result, consumers are often unsure as to whether the prescriptive norms of distributive fairness have been met. Hence, the situation is often ambiguous.

In situations where customers think that distributive fairness norms have been violated—whether the violation is clear-cut or ambiguous they will be motivated to investigate the cause. How customers determine the causes of events, particularly adverse events, is the focus of "attribution theory," the subject of the next chapter.

Definitions

Norms of outcome: Consensually agreed upon rules of who should be charged how much in different circumstances.

Value: Subjectively perceived material worth of item or service, which is measured quantitatively by the price.

Norm of equality: The rule that all people should be charged the same amount; all people should have equal opportunity to get the lowest possible price.

Envy-free allocations: A distribution of benefits so no one is jealous of the bundle of benefits received by another.

Comparative fairness: A judgment based on how the individual is treated compared to how others are treated.

Dictator games: A research method in which one person is given a sum of money that is to be shared with another person; if the other person refuses his or her allotted share, neither receives anything.

Dictator: The person in dictator games who is given the money and decides the allotment.

Responder: The person in dictator games who decides on acceptance or rejection of the dictator's allotment.

Norm of need: The rule that special considerations should be given to those who are less fortunate.

CHAPTER 8

Attributions

"THE SELLER IS TO BLAME!"

Consider this typical conversation between two supermarket shoppers:

Woman: "Will you look at the price of that coffee! Why is it suddenly so high?"

Man: "It's the coffee roasters. They're all profit-mongers."

Woman: "Not this company. They have a good reputation."

Man: "Then it's that new manager."

Woman: "Not him. He's a decent sort."

Man: "Then it must be crop failure in Brazil."

Woman: "Yeah, that must be it."

We humans spend an inordinate amount of time ruminating on why something has happened, who is responsible, what was their motivation. When shopping, we ask ourselves: Why is the price higher than what I expected? Who is responsible? Did they do it deliberately or did they have no choice in the matter?

I know because I do this myself. I should explain that I am not one of those "variety-seeking" shoppers. I have bought the same brand

and style of sneakers for the past 15 years. During that time, the price has varied between $19.95 and $29.95. When I recently went back to buy a new pair, however, I found that the price had jumped to $34.95. I was annoyed. That was inequitable and unfair. After all, I was getting the same quality in return for more money. What was the reason, I wanted to know. Just like the woman in the supermarket, I wanted to know why. Why was the price suddenly so high?

We are particularly interested in understanding the cause of an outcome we do not like. We accept good things as being our due, but we want to know why bad things happen. So if a price or pricing practice violates the norms of personal or distributive fairness, we want to know why we have been wronged.

How normal folk in everyday situations figure out what causes events is the subject of a broad stream of research called *attribution theory*.[1] Psychologist Bernard Weiner, who has dedicated his research to this area, points out, "Most consumers are not rocket scientists. They simply ask why an outcome was unsatisfying, whether it will happen again, and who, if anyone, is to blame."[2]

How people answer these questions is not necessarily accurate or even rational because their explanations are based on beliefs, not reality. They are simply conjectures, subjective interpretations, inferences based on people's past experience, snap judgments based on common sense. They are explanations of causality based on what consumers infer from what meager information they have at hand.

If I had gone to the sneaker store time and time again and found their prices consistently fair, then I would figure that $34.95 was a temporary glitch in the system or something that had been forced upon them. But I would not blame them. Not yet. Not until I had repeatedly had bad experiences. Then I would figure—perhaps erroneously—that the increase was permanent, instituted perhaps by a greedy new manager. I would vow never to go back.

According to attribution theory, when consumers like me or the people in the supermarket try to figure out the cause of an unfair price, they have three basic concerns.[3] The first is to determine *responsibility*: whether the cause is internal (my own dumb fault) or external (the benign fault of some thing or the malevolent fault of some person). The second is *permanence*: whether the action is lasting or temporary (a glitch in the system or a long-term plan), and, finally, *controllability*: whether the action is under the control of the person responsible.

Responsibility and Permanence

With my sneakers, maybe the unexpectedly high price was my fault for shopping in that store. But I hate to have to blame myself, because that makes me feel bad. So I try to find something or someone else to blame. Maybe it is the price of oil? Or a new malfunctioning computer system?

If we think the reason for an unfair price is natural or inanimate—an act of God or a mechanical failure—we will be upset, but not as much as if the cause were another human being. Like our customers in the supermarket who accepted crop failure in Brazil as a legitimate reason for coffee prices to go up, we accept a reason as fair if it was not the intentional act of another human being. This is recognized by companies that explain their prices as due to natural causes like crop failures or computer errors or transportation problems, but not the intentional actions of managers trying to make a profit.

If I cannot blame the market or the computer or some other inanimate mechanism for the high price of my sneakers, then I will blame it on another human being. And I will be really mad. The harmful actions of other humans trigger emotions. I know human beings can have nasty motives. I know some retailers will take advantage of me if they can. That really gets my dander up.

The different response to a human versus a mechanical cause of a bad outcome was shown in research using a variation of the "dictator game." In these games, as explained in Chapter 7, "dictators" are given a sum of money, which they are told to divide with "responders." If responders do not accept the amount given to them, neither party gets anything.

In the particular game used in the study, the researchers varied the source of the initial offer: either another person or a computer.[4] They found responders were more likely to accept an unfair offer from a computer than from a person. Evidently, responders interpreted the action of the computer as a chance or random event. But they inferred that the action of a person was intentional. Responders refused an offer from what they thought was a human being in order to punish that person for suspected malicious motives.

Motivations are an important part of attributions. As one researcher writes, "When people perceive a person is motivated by selfishness, they react negatively."[5] If consumers think sellers are increasing a price just to make more money, they judge it to be unfair.

Conversely, if they think sellers are making the increase only to cover unavoidable cost increases, they judge it to be fair.

The importance of motives was demonstrated in a study of bottled water prices after a major earthquake in Southern California.[6] When the respondents were given no reason for a sharp increase in price, 67 percent judged it to be unfair. They seemed to figure that the company was motivated by greed. But when it was explained to them that the price increase had been planned long before the earthquake, implying a normal business motive, then the number of those who thought it unfair dropped to only 35 percent. The difference in perceived unfairness was due to the different assumptions of motive.

To get back to the high price of my sneakers, once I have determined that a person rather than some external factor should be blamed, I still have to decide which person. Should I blame the manager of the store or should I blame the manufacturer? And what about all those people who are in between? They, too, could be the culprits.

For example, students are generally angered at the high prices of textbooks. When I asked them who was responsible, they blamed the publisher, not the retailer.[7] The students estimated that the store makes about a 25 percent profit, which is remarkably close to reality. But they estimated that the publisher makes 50 percent profit, which is unreal. The students evidently did not want to blame the store because they liked the people who worked there, many of whom were students like themselves. But the publishers were seen as uncaring profit-mongering capitalists. Publishers do not have a good reputation among college students.

Just as with the customers in the supermarket, sellers who violate a social norm of pricing will be given the benefit of the doubt if they have a reputation for fair dealing. Research shows that a good reputation makes people infer good motives. When told that a company had a reputation for fair dealings, participants in one study were much more likely to think it fair when the company raised prices.[8]

When I blame other people, my next concern is whether their behavior is typical or not. Is this something that will continue to happen or an aberrant, one-time event? Maybe it's just a mistake. If it is just a one-time problem, then I can ignore it. But if the pricing action appears to be permanent, and if the reputation of the seller is not good, then my concern is whether the person responsible had control over the situation.

Control

Was the unfair action something the person responsible could control? If coffee prices went up because the crop failed, that is understandable: the roaster or the retailer could not help it. If the seller of my sneakers had no choice but to raise the price, that too is understandable. It could not be helped.

In a study of attributions, researchers found that when subjects were told that the seller had some control over the costs, they judged a cost-based price increase to be unfair.[9] When the subjects were told that competitors' prices had not increased—an indication that costs in the market had not gone up across the board—they also judged a price increase to be unfair.

A change, however, seems to have occurred in how much control over costs consumers believe sellers have. In the past, it was assumed that sellers had no control over cost increases. Higher costs from suppliers were therefore accepted as a legitimate reason to increase prices. Over 20 years ago, economist Arthur Okun wrote, "Price increases that are based on cost increases are 'fair,' while those based on demand increases often are viewed as unfair."[10]

But in the current economic environment, the increased cost of supplies is no longer considered uncontrollable. The thinking now seems to be that sellers can control costs. It is their responsibility to do so. The focus groups we held in New York City agreed that it was producers' responsibility to keep the cost of their suppliers under control: *"I would think they should be a better negotiator with their suppliers."* *"Why are they necessarily passing the cost on to me? Have they taken steps to gain efficiencies on their end?"*

Not surprisingly, all three factors of attributions—responsibility, permanence, and control—reinforce each other.[11] People are most upset when they get an unpleasant outcome and they figure the cause is another person who could and should have controlled the outcome and who, moreover, *always* acts in such an irresponsible way. When consumers infer such behavior, they are distressed. Research shows that when behavior is interpreted as being permanent and under the control of the person responsible, consumers are much more likely to intend never to purchase from that seller again.[12]

Attributional Biases

How consumers attribute blame for unfair price is not easy to predict because attributions are swayed by personal and cultural biases. An *attributional bias* influences whether an event is blamed on oneself or another person or fate. For example, females like the woman in the supermarket are more prone than men to attribute good outcomes to external factors and bad outcomes to themselves.[13] In my own research I found that women tend to infer more positive motivations for sellers than men do.[14]

Like most cultures, Americans tend to think that an external factor is responsible for an unfair price. But unlike some cultures, we are more likely to blame another person rather than our stars.[15] We in the Western world tend to take credit for successes and blame others for failures.[16]

In other cultures, people are just as likely to blame an external factor for a failure, but they are not as likely to blame another person.[17] They tend instead to put the blame on some outside factor—stars or luck or fate. Particularly in collectivist cultures, blaming another person is discouraged because it can cause social disruption and disharmony in the group. But blaming fate causes no problem.

In Sum . . .

Attribution theory explains how people, including consumers, infer the cause of everyday events, particularly events with an unhappy outcome. An outcome that violates the norms of personal or distributive fairness leads to an attribution of blame. And attributions of blame lead to questions of who was responsible and why they did it and whether they will do it again.

If blame for a bad outcome like an unexpected price increase is placed on some inanimate object or an act of God, then it is accepted as fair. Just as the supermarket shoppers accepted the high price of coffee when they thought it was due to a crop failure, an unfair outcome may be judged unfortunate but not unfair. As people say, "That's life."

But in the case of my sneakers, I blamed the retailer. I decided the store was getting greedy. They were in a position to control the price, which they obviously had not done. However, my dealings with them in the past had always been satisfactory. After all, they had kept within the price range for nearly 15 years. So I went ahead and bought the sneakers, even at the higher price. But I wondered then how they had determined that price. Was the process fair? The process by which prices are determined is the concern of procedural fairness, the subject of the next chapter.

Definitions

Attribution theory: How everyday people explain the cause of everyday events.

Attribution of responsibility: Person, inanimate object, or force that is named and blamed for an adverse action.

Permanence: Belief that an action will be repeated in the future.

Control: Belief that an event can be influenced by the person responsible.

Attributional bias: Tendency to blame events on either another person, or oneself, or fate.

CHAPTER

Process

"YA GOTTA PLAY BY THE RULES!"

Remember Sally from Chapter 3? The woman who was contemplating the purchase of a sports car for $45,000? Well, she bought it. She took the plunge after getting the sales rep down to $37,500 with 10 percent down and a $7,000 trade-in allowance for her old Jeep.

The sales manager inputted all her information into the computer, which determined her monthly charge. The manager explained that the charge included an "environmental protection package" as well as credit insurance at no extra charge.

What Sally did not know is that the computer automatically slipped an extra $30 a month into her payments. This gave the dealer "room" to provide other products—ones that incidentally had colossal gross margins—while making it sound as if these extras were actually free. (See "'Back End' Sales," on page 81.)

Since Sally had already decided that the price of her cherished sports car was equitable, she did not even consider the fairness of the monthly payments. Poor Sally. She did not even know how unfairly she had been treated. She did not suspect the dealer of using an unfair pricing process.

Instead, if Sally had decided that $37,500 was *not* a fair and equitable price, she would have wanted to know how that price was determined. As ethicist Jerald Greenberg explains, "In attempting to interpret distributive injustices, people seek additional information from their environments about how these particular outcomes came about—that is, procedural justice."[1]

Procedural fairness is based on the *norms of process* that apply to how a price has been determined, the fairness of the seller's pricing strategy. It differs from distributive fairness, which is the fairness of the outcome, the price charged to the customer (see Table 9.1).

But before we address procedural fairness, let us step back and take stock of where we are. We have seen that a personally fair price leads to a purchase, assuming the customer actually wants the product. But a personally *un*fair price leads to considerations of social fairness. Social fairness comprises distributive fairness—the fairness of the price outcome—and procedural fairness—the fairness of the pricing process.

The two components of social fairness (price outcome and pricing process) parallel the two parts of personal fairness (see Table 9.2).

Table 9.1.   Elements of Social Fairness

Fairness of Price Outcomes "Distributive Fairness"	Fairness of Pricing Process "Procedural Fairness"
How people judge the price fair to society in general	How people judge the company fair to society in general
Adheres to the prescriptive norms of price outcomes: - Equity: price should reflect worth of the product - Equality: price should be the same for everyone - Need: price should be adjusted for disadvantaged	Adheres to the prescriptive norms of pricing process: - Voice and choice: process should be controllable - Transparency: process should be understandable - Impartiality: process should be impersonal and unbiased

Table 9.2.   Examples of Social Norms of Price Outcomes and Pricing Process

	Descriptive Norms of Personal Fairness	Prescriptive Norms of Social Fairness
Price Outcome	Ferraris are expected to cost more than Fords.	Students and minorities should not be charged more for a car.
Pricing Process	Back seats are expected to be included in price of car.	The total price of the car should be publicly displayed.

The difference between the social norms of social and personal fairness is that social fairness is based on prescriptive norms, and personal fairness is based on descriptive norms. Descriptive norms are consensually held beliefs of what is normal and expected. Prescriptive norms have a "should" component; they specify how people "should" behave. People believe that society as a whole agrees that prescriptive norms should be followed because they specify what is right and what is wrong.

Now to get back to the concern in this chapter: the social fairness of the pricing process, which is determined by the adherence to the prescriptive norms of pricing. According to the Fair Price Model, the fairness of the pricing process becomes a consideration when the unfairness of a price is blamed on the seller. When a price outcome is judged to be unfair, the customer wants to know how the price was determined.

If the process by which the price was determined is judged to be fair, the fairness of the price itself will be reconsidered. For example, research has shown that plaintiffs receiving an adverse court judgment still think it fair if they believe the process used to determine the judgment was fair.[2] The same applies to pricing: students accept a higher tuition than others if they believe that the university awards financial aid based strictly on income and not on personal connections. That is a fair process, so the price itself is judged fair.

Usually, once the price itself is judged to be fair, there is no motivation to consider the pricing process. In some cases, however, the process later becomes apparent. If the process is found to be unfair, the initial judgment of a fair price will be changed. This was demonstrated in a study conducted in the Chicago traffic courts. The custom there is to dismiss cases without a hearing if the defendant actually shows up at court. The court's thinking is that missing a day of work is sufficient punishment. Nonetheless, even though the results are positive, defendants often feel that the process is unfair because they do not get the opportunity to state their case.[3]

As applied to pricing, a price originally thought fair can become unfair if the pricing process was unfair. For instance, after accepting an offer of a free magazine for a month, consumers can then learn that the small type of the offer committed them to a two-year subscription. Or after buying a house at a price that at first seemed quite equitable and fair, the new owner may find out that higher offers by other potential buyers were not considered due to racial or religious discrimination. In both of these cases, the process is not fair so the price is not fair.

The question, then, is what makes for a fair pricing process? What are the relevant social norms? Researchers in management have identified three social norms of wages that apply equally well to the pricing process: (1) voice and choice, (2) transparency, and (3) impartiality.

Norm of Voice or Choice

The *norms of voice* or *choice* in pricing give customers some control so they are not taken advantage of. The need for voice was expressed by the revolutionary cry of "no taxation without representation." When consumers have some voice in the price-setting process, they are more likely to accept the price outcome as fair.

The effect of voice was demonstrated in a study of a fare increase on the Hong Kong subway. When people were allowed to make an input into the pricing system, they rated the price as more fair.[4] The reason given was that "consumers who participate in price determination through bidding and/or negotiating are more likely to perceive prices as fair."[5]

In some rare cases, buyers are given total voice over the price. Street performers let people pay what they think the performance is worth. Cabbies accept whatever tip riders give them. And in Melbourne, Australia, there is even a small chain of restaurants called "Lentil as Anything," where you pay whatever you think is an appropriate amount.[6] The owners report that most customers do indeed pay a fair price.

Having a choice gives the consumers voice by allowing them to express their opinion. They are not being forced to buy at one preset price or do without. Students, for example, object to the price of textbooks not only because the cost has increased to over $100 a book, but also because students have no choice. They are forced to buy the assigned texts. As a result, a student newspaper proclaims, "Textbook market unfair; few alternatives available."[7]

Strangely, although having too few choices is unfair, having too many choices is also unfair. In a study of mobile phone pricing plans, it was clear that 3 choices were better than 1, and 7 were better than 3. But there are limits to how many choices our brains can handle. When faced with 10 or more "chunks" of data, consumers suffer from information overload.[8] In the study, customers became muddled when given 11 choices and cried "uncle!" when given 22 choices.[9] Too much information was confusing. Being confused makes a consumer vulnerable. And that is unfair.

Norm of Transparency

The process *norm of transparency* holds that how the price was determined should be rational and understandable. The total amount of the price should be clearly explained prior to the sale.

In public utilities, where fairness has long been a concern,[10] commissioners strive to be "impeccably fair." To do so, they focus on process, particularly transparency with "an emphasis on openness and thoroughness."[11] It is when the pricing process is opaque that customers feel at a disadvantage.

A prime example of an inscrutable pricing process is airfares. The airlines' system of "yield pricing" is entirely too complex for a consumer to understand. The outcome, furthermore, violates the norm of equality: as mentioned in Chapter 1, some passengers can pay $1,500 for a flight for which the person sitting next to them has paid only $150. Although the airfare itself is unequal and unfair, consumers also object to the manner in which the price has been determined. As one frequent business flyer complained, the airlines do not appreciate the travelers' outrage over not only the sky-high fares but also the "ridiculous way the carriers set those fares."[12]

Hospitals also have inscrutable pricing (see "The Lack of Transparency in Hospital Pricing" on page 80). They have a detailed list of charges for every procedure and supply. This list can contain as many as 20,000 items. The hospital then specifies the exact amount of every charge in the patient's bill. The problem is that the total amounts are huge and bear no relation to what third-party payers actually pay. Consumers have no way of knowing actual charges, no way of comparing the charges of one hospital against another, no way of taking control of their hospital costs.

An obvious violation of transparency is deceptive price advertising. For example, take the organization that was selling chances on a car. In small print on the back of the sweepstakes form was an authorization for the organization to add a monthly fee to the person's phone bill.[13] When people received the bill, authorized only through trickery, they were outraged.

Another deceptive practice is known as negative option deals: you sign up for free service and unwittingly also agree to a monthly charge unless you notify the company within 30 days. This pricing practice was popularized by the Book of the Month Club nearly a century ago. In the Club's case, the negative option was conspicuous and clear, which made it legal. When a negative option is hidden, however, it is deceptive and illegal. It is blatantly unfair.

Consumers want pricing information to be clear, and there are numerous state and federal laws supporting their right to clarity. Credit card issuers have to explain the annual fees, annual percentage rates, grace periods, and so on. Grocery stores have to post their prices. Mortgage companies have to present the total cost of a mortgage. Making the pricing process transparent levels the playing field for the consumer.

Companies, however, can adhere to the letter of the law and still obfuscate their pricing. TV commercials for automobiles technically alter speech to present price information so fast it is hard to understand. Print advertisements for mobile phones give the contract requirements in type so small it is hard to read. So companies fulfill the legal requirements, but it is still not fair.

Transparency is so important to consumers that, in some cases, they even prefer it to the norm of equity. An example of this is the mobile phone industry, which is considered flat roaming charges. This means that some people will be subsidizing others, which is inequitable. But customer response has been good because the charge is clear and simple. Customers prefer the simplicity of a flat charge to a complex system that laboriously explains the intricacies of differential charges. They do not like being bewildered because that is when they can be exploited.

A price's being transparent, however, does not necessarily mean that it will be judged fair. A fairness judgment depends on whether the information provided indicates that the company is adhering to the social norms. When subjects in a research study were told that the airlines had set the price based on demand, they then thought the price was less fair than when they were given no information at all.[14] It is not the social norm to base prices on demand. That is seen to be taking advantage of the consumers' need, which is not fair. Making it transparent does not make it any more fair.

Norm of Impartiality

The third social norm of process is that pricing procedures should be *impartial.* The process is supposed to be impersonal, not influenced by favoritism.

Having unbiased prices loops back to the equality norm of distributive fairness. Just as all men and women should receive the same outcome, so too should they be treated in the same manner. This is an old idea: the Medieval Scholastics of the thirteenth century preached that tourists should be charged the same price as natives.[15] Today legislators pass bills saying that haircuts for women should be priced the same as those for men. Shirt laundering and bar prices should be the same for both sexes (see Chapter 15 on Discrimination). That is fair.

In Sum . . .

The social fairness of a price is based on the prescriptive norms of outcome and process. If these norms have been followed, the consumer will conclude that the price and the pricing policies are socially fair. Even if consumers have perceived the price to be unexpectedly high and therefore personally unfair, their judgment of social fairness will override their preference for personal fairness. So they will pay the price—assuming they have the money to do so.

But consumers will balk if they conclude that a price and the process by which that price was determined are not only personally but also socially unfair. Sellers are well aware that "ya gotta play by the rules." When they do not, consumers are angry.

Such anger was evident in the focus groups that we held in the United States. When told that the seller had not abided by the prescriptive norms of price outcomes and pricing process, the participants' earlier emotions of dissatisfaction and dismay turned into wrath and rage:

"I'd feel angry." "This smells of greed." "I'm definitely not happy." "Personally, I am really outraged." "I'm upset. I feel totally manipulated at this point. I feel betrayed by the company." "You've lost trust in the company." "As a consumer you feel basically disemboweled as a result of this."

When consumers judge a seller's price and pricing process to be unfair—when they conclude that the seller is not playing by the rules—consumers will be motivated to act. They will then contemplate how to punish the seller for acting unfairly, just as our car buyer Sally does in the next chapter.

Definitions

Norms of process: The rules of how prices should be determined.

Norm of voice and choice: The rule that consumers should have some control over pricing process.

Norm of transparency: The rule that the pricing process should be clear and understandable.

Norm of impartiality: The rule that the pricing process should not be biased or influenced by personal favoritism.

The Lack of Transparency in Hospital Pricing

Until now, the U.S. healthcare "market" has been analogous to an imaginary world in which, say, employers offered to reimburse their employees 80 percent of the "reasonable cost" of attire deemed "necessary" and "appropriate" on the job but, under the contracts negotiated with department stores by the fiscal intermediaries administering this "Clothes Benefit Program," employees had to enter department stores blindfolded.

Only months after a shopping trip would the employee receive for the fiscal intermediary a so-called Explanation of Benefits (EOB) statement, explaining how much the employee had to pay for whatever he or she had stuffed, blindfolded, into the shopping cart on that shopping trip. Framed in bright red on that EOB would be the statement: "Pay X amount." X would represent 20 percent of what the intermediary would have judged, ex post, to be "reasonable prices" for those garments in the shopping cart deemed by that intermediary, ex post, to have been "appropriate" attire for the particular employee's circumstances. It would include 100 percent of the prices charged by the stores for items in the cart that were deemed by the intermediary, ex post, as "not necessary" or "inappropriate" and that were therefore not covered by the Clothes Benefit Program.

Ridiculous though it sounds, such an arrangement closely resembles the current payment system for U.S. health care.

Reprinted, with permission, from Uwe E. Reinhardt,
"The Pricing of U. S. Hospital Services: Chaos behind a Veil of Secrecy."[16]

"Back End" Sales: Rust-Proofing, Financing, Insurance, Service Contracts, Documentary Charges, and Other Add-Ons

The negotiation of a sales price on a vehicle is often called the front-end of a transaction. As much as ninety percent of dealer profits come from the back-end. The consumer typically is led from the salesman who has negotiated the deal to a finance and insurance (F & I) sales manager, sometimes known as the Business Manager, who is responsible for closing the transaction, arranging financing, and selling after-market items and supplemental products and services. Examples include: the "chemicals," such as rustproofing, undercoating, paint sealant, fabric protectant, and vinyl protectant; optional items such as floor mats, bras, and spoilers; financing or leasing; service contracts; credit insurance; and, in some states, gap insurance.

The essence of a dealer add-on is that it is usually discussed after a final price for the car is negotiated, and is a charge to the consumer in addition to the negotiated price for the car, increasing both the consumer's total cost and the dealer's profit. In practical terms, a dealer add-on is usually listed in the sales agreement on a line below the negotiated price for the car, and may even be pre-printed on the form next to taxes to give the impression that it is standard with every purchase.

"Packing" of Back-End Charges

A number of state UDAP (*Unfair and Deceptive Acts and Practices*) regulations find it unfair or deceptive for a dealer to negotiate the terms of the sale of a car and thereafter add the cost of certain items, such as extended warranties, credit life, dealer preparation, or undercoating, to the contract without the consumer's knowledge and consent.*

The dealer can add these costs in one of two principal ways. The more obvious approach is to add these costs onto the negotiated price for the car, and present the consumer with a final contract with these extras included.

One of the more prevalent and surprising techniques dealers use to sell back-end charges does the exact opposite, through the technique of "packing."

---

*Idaho Consumer Protection Regulations, Idaho Admin. Code 04.02.01.234. Other Advertising Practices: Ill. Admin. Code tit. 14, § 475.580, Motor Vehicle Advertising; N.M. Admin. Code tit. 1 §2.2.24 Advertising and Sale of Motor Vehicles; N.J. Admin. Code § 13:45A-26B.2 (add-ons must be individually itemized, showing price for each); Delaney v. Garden State Auto Park, 318 N. J. Super. 15, 722 A.2d 967 (App. Div. 1999) (awarding treble damages for failure to itemize add-ons).

(Continued)

Consumer sales resistance to these extra charges is eliminated because the consumer does not even know these charges are being assessed.

Instead of adding these charges onto a negotiated price, the dealer inflates the monthly payment from that which should be derived mathematically from the negotiated interest rate and negotiated sales price, providing "room" for the dealer to add in other charges to make the numbers come out right.

Third-party providers of credit insurance and other back-end products aggressively compete for dealership accounts, and will provide significant financial incentives, training, and marketing assistance to dealers to get business. One of the principal techniques they teach is the "pack," and, as a result, this practice has become widespread in the automobile dealership industry.

Packing in motor vehicle cases is the intentional misquoting of a monthly payment necessary to retire the debt on a motor vehicle. By adding money to the monthly payment (called "packing" or "loading" the payment) when it is initially quoted to the consumer, the dealer creates "room" into which other products or service can be sold. Because these additional items are "provided" at no increase in monthly payment, consumers are misled into believing there is no charge for the items.

In the normal course of a vehicle purchase, the consumer settles on a particular vehicle and enters into negotiations with a salesperson. The consumer indicates a desired purchase price, cash down amount, trade-in allowance, and occasionally even specifies finance terms. The salesperson takes this information to the sales manager, who inputs the information into the dealership's computer. The computer then calculates a monthly payment, based on either the customer's offer or the dealer's counter offer. This monthly payment is then given to the consumer.

In some cases this payment is a legitimate "stripped" or "bare" payment, in that it will only cover the cost of the car. In many cases, however, the payment will be packed. The desk manager obtains the packed payment by one of three principle methods: (1) adding a flat dollar amount, say $30, to every payment; (2) setting the defaults on the computer program to include a charge for credit insurance or items; or (3) setting the defaults on the computer program to calculate the payment with an unreasonably short term and/or an unreasonably high APR (*Annual Percentage Rate*).

Assuming the consumer agrees to purchase the motor vehicle at the packed payment amount, the salesperson introduces the consumer to the business manager. The business manager prepares the loan papers, which include the charges for the back-end items. The business manager uses an "assumptive" closing technique, indicating that these services "are provided in the monthly payment as part of our optional payment protection plan." Only later (or never) does the consumer discover that the transaction included thousands of dollars of back-end charges.

Originally, the packed payment was used to sell credit insurance or increase financing costs. It can also be used to sell service contracts, vehicle options, or almost anything the dealer can devise. Often whatever service the dealer can make the largest profit on will be the product being "packed."

Reprinted from *Unfair and Deceptive Acts and Practices* (6th ed., 2004), with permission from National Consumer Law Center, www.consumerlaw.org, 617-542-9595.

CHAPTER

10

Punishment

"REVENGE IS SWEET!"

Uh oh! Watch out! Our friend Sally just found out the car dealer snuck an additional $30 a month into her car payments. Sally is understandably furious! What will she do now?

We know how passionately people react to unfairness from the reactions of our American focus groups. Their first thought was revenge: *"They would lose me as a customer." "I would definitely switch." "I'd love to see if there's a better competitor out there." "There's no product that's so unique that you cannot find anything else like it."*

These reactions to judged unfairness are very similar to the reactions of any dissatisfied customer. The difference is in the motivation and the emotional intensity. When confronted with a price that is both personally and socially unfair, consumers are not just dismayed, they are livid. They are motivated not by self-interest but by revenge.

There seems to be a *metanorm* that infractions of norms should be punished.[1] As the social psychologists Richard DeRidder and Rama Tripathi conclude, "Norms imply sanctions."[2] A behavior can only be considered a norm "if any departure of real behavior from the norm is followed by some punishment."[3] Looking at it from the other direction, punishment is defined as "a negative sanction intentionally applied to someone who is perceived to have violated a law, a rule, a norm or an expectation."[4]

Norm of Reciprocity

Theories of why people punish norm violations date back to Aristotle's idea of reciprocity. According to a strict interpretation of the *norm of reciprocity*, a person should repay a kindness with a similar kindness, and a harm with a similar harm. As the Bible says, "Life for life, eye for eye, tooth for tooth." People tell researchers that their motivation for punishment is to "get back at rule breakers."[5] As one researcher concludes, "If somebody is mean to you, fairness allows—and vindictively dictates—that you be mean to him."[6]

Such retaliation appears to be an animal instinct. Frans DeWaal, who is a rare combination of zoologist, ethnologist, and psychologist, tells a story of chimpanzees.[7] This group of chimps had evidently accepted the social norm established by their human keepers that none of the chimps would receive dinner until all of them had returned to their sleeping quarters. Any chimp that came in late would consequently get an angry greeting from the others.

One time, two young chimps stayed out late for many hours. When they finally returned, the other chimps were so angry at the two for having broken the norm that the keepers had to put the wrongdoers in a separate cage for protection. But the other chimps did not forgive and forget. When they had the chance the next morning, the other chimps vented their anger on the two miscreants for having broken the social norm—and delaying dinner for everyone else.

Following the evolutionary approach, researchers claim that a punitive sentiment is "hard-wired" into the human circuitry.[8] People appear to need "strong reciprocity" to punish those within their group who, with malicious intentions, violate a norm.[9] According to sociologist Alvin Gouldner, reciprocity is a *universal norm*,[10] found in all cultures.

But how violations of norms are punished varies depending on the type of norm. Cooperative norms common in business-to-business relationships need no sanctions since they are mutually beneficial to both parties: "You scratch my back and I'll scratch yours." Hegemonic or coercive norms have clear, strong sanctions: suppliers follow Wal-Mart's dictates or suffer the consequences.

The norms of consumer exchange, however, are very different. They are enforced by the expectation that violations will be punished, but the punishment is through many small, independent, uncoordinated actions imposed by individual buyers, each of whom acts on his or her own initiative.[11] This decentralization of punishment fits with the ideas of economist Friedrich Hayek. He argued that a market functions most efficiently through the diffused actions of innumerable buyers and sellers all working independently.[12] And the market is efficiently kept in line by the diffused actions of individuals punishing unfairness.

To ensure that norm breakers are punished in consumer exchange, the norms have to be backed by the force of social obligation.[13] Consumers have to feel a sense of duty in their roles as "norm enforcers."[14] Buyers have to keep an eye on the sellers, judge the fairness of the sellers' actions, and apply *sanctions* when sellers violate a social norm. Buyers have to punish sellers when the price is wrong.

Effort to Punish

Punishment requires effort and possibly some suffering on the part of the buyer. Nonetheless, consumers do exert themselves to punish a seller for unfair pricing. One punishment is simply not to purchase. But going without a product means that customers will have to do without whatever pleasure it might have given them.

Another punishment is to complain. But that requires effort. It means making a phone call and then trying to get someone to answer and forward the call to the right department. Even though the Internet has made the process easier, it is still necessary to find where to send an e-mail and to hope it reaches the right person.

Nonetheless—despite the harm and suffering—consumers do indeed go out of their way to punish misbehavior on the part of sellers. According to one study, about a quarter of a company's customers defected due to what they considered unfair pricing practices.[15] As one group of researchers has concluded, "Angry customers don't come back, they get back."[16]

For example, in just the state of Arizona alone, 2,000 complaints were sent to the Department of Weights and Measures about inaccurate gasoline pumps.[17] In the entire United States, more than 26,000 customers complained to the U.S. Department of Energy about the recent hike in gasoline prices.[18]

Consumers also exert themselves to shun companies they think are unfair. In their pioneering fairness study, researchers Daniel Kahneman, Jack Knetsch, and Richard Thaler asked respondents what they would do if a drugstore raised its prices after another drugstore had been forced to close.[19] They found that 68 percent of respondents would rather travel an additional five minutes than patronize anyone who acted so unfairly. The respondents were willing to go out of their way to punish the druggist who had violated the social norm by taking advantage of customers.

In some cases, consumers organize boycotts as a means of punishment. The evidence is that boycotts are not effective in reducing prices, but they are successfully disruptive. "They serve to punish sellers for 'unfair' price increases."[20]

To organize a boycott, consumers have to devise a system to coordinate their diffuse endeavors, which takes time and effort.[21] In spite of the effort required, an international survey indicates that 50 percent of Americans say they have participated in at least one boycott.[22]

In addition to their own participation, those who join a boycott want to punish those who do not.[23] Ernst Fehr, the economist who has conducted extensive research into fairness, explains that "the kind of person who doesn't punish emerges as a kind of *freeloader*."[24] It looks as if it is not only a norm to punish those who violate a norm but also a norm to punish those who do not join in the punishment of violators.

Another group of researchers showed that consumers respond to unfairness by not only changing to another store or brand, but also choosing a more expensive one just to be vindictive.[25] The researchers concluded that "people appear willing to punish even when it costs them more to do so than the amount of harm they inflict on the target."[26]

Evidence from Dictator Games

Experimental research shows that people are willing to harm themselves in order to punish those who violate social norms. This is clearly demonstrated by the "dictator games" introduced in Chapter 7. In these games there are two players: the "dictator" and the "responder." Dictators are given an amount of money that they can choose to share or not share with the responder. Responders can either accept or reject the dictators' offers. If they reject the offer, neither dictator nor responder gets anything.

From the economic viewpoint that people are strictly self-serving profit maximizers, responders would be expected to accept whatever they are given because it would be better than nothing at all. However, from the social viewpoint that people are influenced by the social norm of equality, responders would be expected to demand equal outcomes. If they do not receive an equal outcome, then the person responsible should be punished.

Actual results are closer to the social viewpoint: responders tend to reject any division that gives them less than 40 percent. It appears that responders accept the dictators' right to keep the lion's share, perhaps in recognition of their position of power. Dictators, in turn, act as if they were aware of how responders would react because they typically give between 40 percent and 50 percent. Only 3.8 percent of dictators give less than 20 percent.[27] It appears that dictators are aware that they will be punished if they do not follow the norm of equality of outcomes.

Using modern methods of brain scanning, economists working with neuropsychologists are now starting to understand how the brain functions when punishing unfair behavior. In one study,[28] researchers had participants conduct a dictator game while their brains were being scanned with functional magnetic resonance imaging (fMRI). The results support the thesis that perceptions and judgments of unfairness have an emotional response. When treated unfairly, responders display significantly higher activity in the brain region associated with negative emotional states such as pain, thirst, anger, and disgust.

Exploring the matter further,[29] researchers investigated how the brain handles the conflict between self-interest and punishment for breaking norms. Again using dictator games, the researchers found that when responders receive an equitable offer, they are quick to accept it. But when given a stingy, inequitable offer, responders take more time coming to a decision. The suggested reason for the time delay is that responders are conflicted between fairness and utility.

Another neuroeconomic study, this time using positron emission tomography (PET), had subjects play a game in which a cooperating player could punish a defecting player.[30] The result was startling: when punishing unfair actions, the *dorsal striatum* of at least men was activated. This is the region of the brain recognized for reward processing properties. It is the part that makes you feel good. So, in effect, punishment provides its own reward. "Revenge is sweet."

A concern with the dictator game research has been that responders were reacting not to the fairness of the offer but simply to the amount of money. People might reject small sums of money under *any* condition just because the amount is small. However, in a study where responders were given information about the size of the pot to be divided, they refused even a big offer if it was proportionally small compared to the total pot. Their response was due not to the absolute amount of money being offered but to the unfair actions of the dictators.[31]

In addition to responders who are directly affected by the dictators' actions, even those not directly involved will go out of their way to punish those who act unfairly. To test the involvement of outsiders, a study was conducted in which a third party could sanction the actions of game players but would incur some cost for doing so. The third party was anonymous and would not interact with the players in the future. Therefore, the third parties had no self-serving reason to impose punishment and had to overcome their own self-interest to do so. Nonetheless, more than two-thirds of the third-party observers punished those who violated the social norms.[32]

The results of dictator game studies are supported both in a meta-analysis of 10 studies[33] and in cross-cultural studies.[34] There are, however, cultural differences in how much sharing is the social norm. In countries where sharing is expected, dictators give more than in countries where it is not expected. When sharing is not the norm, very small offers, as low as 10 percent, are still accepted.[35]

Punishment Is Proportional

In the United States, how intensely price unfairness is punished depends on the degree of consensus to the norm and the strength of norm approval. The greater the number of people thought to support the norm, the more likely is a punitive response to a breach of that norm. And the punishment will be more severe when the degree of social disapproval is greater.[36] So the punishment fits the crime.

In some cases, when a norm is only weakly held, it is not worth the effort to punish the perpetrator. For example, charging different prices in different outlets of a chain store may violate the norm of consistent prices. But if the difference is small, consumers are probably not going to care. It is not worth the effort.

As one participant in our focus groups told us: *"With products you get set in your ways. You expect prices to increase. So if it's a product I like, more than likely I'm going to keep buying it. Whether that upsets me or not, I'm still going to keep buying it."*

However, when customers are riled up enough to do something, the results can be devastating. Take the case of Colman Herman, a consumer living in Dorchester, Massachusetts. He felt strongly that consumers have the right to know the price of goods as was required by state regulation. As a result, he took out class action suits against both Wal-Mart and Home Depot for not displaying prices on their store shelves.[37] Wal-Mart subsequently settled for $7.35 million and Home Depot for $3.8 million, plus the cost of providing shelf prices. Colman has given the money to charity. His motivation was not self-interest; it was punishment for violations of the norm of transparency.

In Sum . . .

People who feel that a price is unfair are highly motivated to punish the seller whom they hold responsible. They will do this even if it causes them personal trouble and expense because revenge is sweet. Which gets us back to our Sally and her sports car. What did she do when she found that the car dealership had unfairly padded her monthly car payments?

First, she called the head of the dealership, who brushed off the incident as only a misunderstanding. She then went to the regional office of the manufacturer, where they said they were "real sorry" and would look into it.

Getting no satisfaction, Sally then fired off letters to the company and the newspapers. She posted her complaint all over the web. And she hired a lawyer. She is now suing the company for $6 million—at a cost to her far greater than the $30 a month extra charge on her car payments. But she is happy. Being able to punish the dealership is reward enough.

Definitions

Metanorm: Norm encompassing many other norms; for example, the norm of fairness.

Norm of reciprocity: The rule that a kindness should be repaid with a kindness, a harm with a harm.

Meta-analysis: Analysis encompassing the results of many other related studies.

(Continued)

Sanctions: Punishment for violating a social norm.

Universal norm: A social rule believed to be held in all cultures.

Freeloader: Someone who takes advantage of the benefits earned by others.

Dorsal striatum: Section of the brain that processes rewards and makes you feel good.

CHAPTER

11

Power

"BEWARE A CUSTOMER WRONGED!"

If you are one of the 58 percent of Americans who commute to work, 88 percent by them by auto,[1] you felt it when gasoline prices after Hurricane Katrina went over $3 a gallon. You were no doubt angry because you thought the oil companies were taking advantage of the situation. And you were not alone. An ABC News poll found that "72 percent of respondents said they believed the rise in gas was a result of oil companies and gas dealers taking unfair advantage after the hurricane."[2]

Newspapers supported the commuters' outcry. Reporters railed against price gouging.[3] Senators weighed in saying there is a "growing suspicion that oil companies are taking unfair advantage."[4] Even the president joined in: President Bush said it was important "to make sure our consumers are treated fairly" by the oil markets.[5]

The public were upset not over the power of the oil companies, but over their violation of a social norm: powerful companies should not take advantage of consumers. That is unfair. This is codified in the Sherman Act, which does not forbid monopolies per se, but only the abuse of power by monopolies.

Powerful companies, like the Mercks and ExxonMobils and Microsofts of the world, often make the news for abusing their power. Editorials refer to "those oil companies, refiners, distributors, or retailers who are 'taking unfair advantage of the circumstances to increase price unreasonably' or imposing 'excessively unconscionable price increases.'"[6] Such price gouging is personally unfair. It is taking advantage of power to bilk the consumer (just as the dealership bilked Sally out of $30 a month). Knowing this is possible makes consumers particularly sensitive to issues of fairness when the seller has power.

Power to the Seller

The time-honored definition of power is that "A has power over B to the extent that he [or she] can get B to do something that B would not otherwise do."[7] A powerful seller can get buyers to pay more money than they expect to pay, more than they *want* to pay.

Economists tell us that certain factors give sellers the power to set pricing. One factor is when demand is strong and rising so that supplies are tight and the industry is pushing its capacity limits. This was the case in the airline industry during the first half of 2006. Air travel was increasing, but airline capacity was down. The combination gave the airlines pricing power. So fares began going up, and passengers began questioning the price fairness.

Sellers get pricing power if the demand for a product is *price inelastic*. In that case people buy almost as much when the price goes up as they do when it remains the same. An example is a life-saving, one-of-a-kind drug. No matter how much a company charges, people at death's door will try to pay the price—but they will not think the price fair.

Pricing power is also high if a company has a monopoly, as did the old Bell Tel. Monopoly power can also be gained by collusion between companies, which is why price fixing is illegal. Archer Daniels was in court for years over a series of price-fixing lawsuits, which economists estimate could cost them some $5 billion to settle.[8] Fixing prices gives companies power over the consumer. This is not fair.

Finally, a company gains pricing power when the customer is clueless. It is similar to American tourists buying a shirt in India. Tourists know they are probably being ripped off, but they have no idea of the normal market price of a shirt in India. Customers of health clubs are also clueless as to their actual future use of the facility, and customers of mobile phones are clueless as to future calls.[9] In all these cases, the buyer is vulnerable. The seller has the power to take unfair advantage.

Conversely, the availability of substitutes decreases power. The desire to find an oil substitute is pushing the development of alternatives to gasoline. If alternatives were made available, we would not be so dependent on the oil companies. It would be a more level playing field, which is more equitable and fair.

Traditionally, sellers have been the ones with greater power in the marketplace. Supplies were limited and consumer information was scarce and biased. The seller was the only one who knew the cost of producing the product. The only information consumers received was what the seller wanted them to know. So consumers were indeed clueless. They were powerless. It was a *sellers' market.*[10] If sellers acted unfairly, consumers had little choice but to pay the price demanded.

That does not mean that consumers had no power all. Consumers have always had economic power. They were the ones putting up the money, which means a lot because "he [or she] who pays the piper calls the tune." But today, the consumer has considerably more power than in the past because supply has surpassed demand. Today, in many industries it is a *buyers' market.*[11]

Of course, some industries continue to have strong pricing power: for example, oil and patented pharmaceuticals. These tend to be the industries where fairness is a pressing issue. But other industries like clothing and automobiles are weak. Consumers have the luxury of picking and choosing what they want to buy. Fairness is of less concern.

Power to the Consumer

Due to the Internet, consumers today have power that they never had before. They have the power of information. And as Francis Bacon observed back in the seventeenth century, "Knowledge itself is power."[12]

Consumers today can check the Internet to find the neighborhood gas station with the cheapest gas. When they go to buy a car, they have the benefit of extensive background information. More than 80 percent of Ford customers come into the showroom having already researched what they want to buy and how much they should pay.[13]

A group of German marketers have analyzed the power of consumers in the new marketing environment.[14] They started from the classic five elements of social power identified by the social psychologists John French and Bertram Raven.[15] They narrowed the five down to three elements that are relevant to consumer prices:

1. *Sanction power*, which comes from the consumer's ability to discipline the seller's prices through rewards and punishments.
2. *Legitimate power*, which comes from the consumer's ability to influence prices in the marketplace.
3. *Expert power*, which comes from the consumer's knowledge about quality and prices in the marketplace.

All three sources of power have been boosted by the Internet. In what the German researchers call "The Old Economy," consumers did not have as much sanction power as they might because of the high cost of punishing recalcitrant sellers: the time and bother of making calls, writing letters, and organizing boycotts. In the new economy, sanctions are much easier since they can all be handled over the Internet. Consumers now have greater sanction power.

In the old economy, consumers could have but little input into prices. They were simply price takers. Today, consumers can set their own price in an eBay auction or on a Priceline web site. They can express their price opinions in blogs and company sites. Consumers have gained legitimate power since they can now have direct influence on the seller's price.

In the old economy, consumers had little access to information about the product, and the information available was primarily the biased advertising of the seller. Today, the Internet provides vast quantities of information not only from sellers but also from happy or not-so-happy consumers of the product. Buyers can check prices and get price comparisons over the web. Consumers now have expert power.

However, even though the Internet provides a mind-boggling wealth of information, it does not empower consumers as much as it could. First, the Internet is not as transparent as it appears. Companies have learned to use the media effectively. They can, for example, feature slightly different models on their web site than in their stores, making price comparisons difficult.

Second, web transparency is clouded by the vast quantity of data available. Even though extensive pricing information may be available, it can be difficult to find. Furthermore, it may be inaccurate. A supposedly trustworthy word-of-mouth report from a dissatisfied customer over the Internet may be due to the person's having had entirely unrealistic expectations.

The third problem is that web coverage is uneven. There is a massive amount of information on automobiles, but much less current information on local services: the reliability of the corner dry cleaner, the prices of the local supermarket, the skill of the nearby dentist.

As a result of these problems—and, no doubt, of natural laziness and lack of interest—consumers do not use the web for price information as much as they might. A sign of this is that the early prediction of price convergence has not panned out. Despite the forecast that the Internet would make all prices converge, online price dispersion is still as wide as in traditional brick-and-mortar markets.[16] So, as the German research team concludes, the Internet provides potential but not actual consumer power.

Nevertheless, even with less-than-optimal use of the Internet, the market generally favors consumers. The *Economist* asserts that "The claim that 'the customer is king' has always rung hollow. But now the digital marketplace has made it come true."[17]

Constraints on Power

There is a debate over whether social norms constrain power or social norms are imposed by the powerful.[18] The debate is resolved by recalling the different kinds of norms (see Chapter 4). Outside the consumer market, coercive norms are imposed by powerful operators, and relational norms are developed by cooperating partners. But in the consumer market, the decentralized norms arose to protect the consumer against more powerful sellers.

It is important to remember that the decentralized norms of prices evolved over hundreds of years, during which time sellers had the power advantage. As recently as in the 1980s, researchers were still commenting on the "power advantage held by retailers vis-à-vis consumers."[19] Social norms evolved to constrain the overweening power of those sellers.

As a result of social norms, sellers with pricing power do not exploit it as much as they might.[20] Powerful sellers like Johnson & Johnson follow the norms to protect their reputation. They do not want to be known for being unfair. And they are wary of a consumer backlash. As economist Robert Frank argues in his book, *Passions within Reason*,[21] it is the potential of consumers' irrational emotions of unfairness that act as a constraint on the seller. Sellers have to beware a customer wronged. They are forced to adhere to the social norms.

Although norms constrain more powerful sellers, a problem today is posed by sellers who lack power. When sellers are weak, they connive to find ways to skirt the norms. According to transaction cost economics, being dependent (which is the diametric opposite of being powerful) leads to opportunistic behavior.[22] Sellers who are dependent on consumers try many devious tactics.

Not being able to command a price, weak sellers try to sneak price increases past the buyer. They dupe the buyer into paying hidden fees, padded monthly payments, and fictitious surcharges. They reduce the quantity of product in packages. They add on "shipping and handling" and "processing" fees. They tack on fuel surcharges.

Some weak sellers institute automatic upcharges on a monthly car payment, a fee for a fictitious tax, or an unnecessarily complex agreement. All these practices are against the social norms of our society. By breaking the social norms of prices, weak sellers are acting blatantly unfair. And today's more powerful buyer will retaliate.

In all fairness, it should be pointed out that although sellers are readily accused of breaking the norms, the accusation is rarely levied against the consumer. Because the social norms of pricing evolved to constrain more powerful sellers, there are few norms constraining consumers. Certainly, it is illegal for a buyer to steal: consumers are expected to pay for what they purchase. It is illegal for consumers to use their receipts to return duplicate items from the store instead of the items actually purchased. But that is about all.

Even though consumers are quick to anger when sellers are not acting fairly, they demonstrate no compunction about acting unfairly themselves. For example, consumers who form into buying groups feel justified in demanding rock-bottom prices from sellers or taking their business elsewhere. When companies do this—for example, Wal-Mart—they are accused of monopsony, the illegal abuse of buyer's power. But consumers evidently feel justified in abusing their own power. They happily use "mob rule" to haggle for cheaper prices.[23] They seem, in fact, to take fiendish pleasure in being powerful.

In Sum . . .

Sellers have traditionally had greater power than consumers. And some sellers, such as the oil companies, still do. When sellers have power, they can use it to their own advantage. They have the potential of acting unfairly. They are, however, constrained to some extent by the social norms.

Now, however, power has shifted to the consumer. They have the power of information. They are living in a buyers' market, where supply exceeds demand. Today, "the customer is king."

Customers seem to take delight in their newfound power. It gives them a feeling of control. Research in organizations shows that a feeling of control increases judged fairness.[24] This suggests that consumers will feel that a market in which they have more power is a fairer market. That being the case, the consumers' sense of greater fairness may lead to greater trust in the seller, which is the subject of the next chapter.

Definitions

Price elasticity: The extent to which the quantity sold responds to the price charged, the assumption being that as the price increases, sales will decrease.

Sellers' market: A situation where sellers have greater power than buyers due to demand being greater than supply.

Buyers' market: A situation where buyers have greater power than the seller due to supply having outstripped demand.

Sanction power: The ability to control another person's actions through rewards and punishments.

Legitimate power: The ability to influence another person's actions such as setting a price.

Expert power: The ability to manipulate prices due to superior knowledge.

CHAPTER

Trust

"FAIR PRICE? I DOUBT IT!"

In rural India, housewives can buy their milk directly from cowherds. These cowherds, however, are not always to be trusted: to increase sales, they have been known to water their milk down before selling it. A recent test of 200 milk samples in India found that almost all of them had 10 to 20 percent added water.[1] The women—like women everywhere—do not appreciate this. They consequently pay a premium to get their milk from a cowherd they can trust to provide whole milk.[2] They pay extra to get not only peace of mind but ease of purchase. With trust, they do not have to think about the milk problem anymore. And—like women everywhere—Indian housewives have many, many more interesting things to think about besides the price of milk.

Trust helps not only Indian women but all consumers by simplifying the buying process. Trust acts as a heuristic: a rule-of-thumb method to make consumer decision making easier.[3] Trust reduces complexity and makes happy outcomes seem certain.[4] Hence, trusting buyers can make price decisions faster. They have less anxiety and less cognitive strain. This is a huge benefit: we all tend to conserve our limited and very precious cognitive resources.[5] Like the Indian housewives, we have more important things to think about than the price of milk.

At the same time that trust helps the consumer, it also helps the seller because trusting customers come back for more. Since trusting consumers are more confident in their decisions and less anxious about making purchases, they can enjoy the buying experience more. And they tend to be less price sensitive: just like the Indian women buying milk, consumers will pay more if they trust they are getting what they are paying for.

Not everyone agrees with this sanguine view. Some economists claim that trust is irrelevant and confusing in commercial exchange,[6] and that the emotional aspect of trust hinders the calculating decision making needed for market transactions. They consider the normal reaction of consumers to be a cynical "Fair price? I doubt it!"

According to this view, both buyer and seller are motivated solely by self-interest. Other economists consider such a view of the market as being "under-socialized."[7] For example, Kenneth Arrow, the Nobel laureate in economics, holds that every commercial exchange contains an element of trust.[8]

Recent marketing researchers support the importance of trust in consumer transactions. In services, researchers have proclaimed, "Trust is perhaps the single most powerful relationship marketing tool."[9] And in e-commerce, trust has taken on particular importance. To the surprise of many, customers do not always select the cheapest source of an item found in a shopping bot; they go to a source they can trust. In e-commerce, consumer trust has consequently become a well-documented marketing concern.

Modern marketers try to transform impersonal exchanges into personal relationships: they want consumers to be committed to the brand, committed to the company, and loyal! Such a transformation requires consumer trust. Without trust, a brand loyalty relationship is not possible.[10] With trust, "businesses can extract themselves from brutal price wars by proving to customers that they deliver true value."[11] Marketers consequently are creating "trust indices," like Edelman's Trust Barometer (see Table 12.1), so companies can measure their customers' trust.[12] "Trust Marketing" is the new mantra.[13]

It is a problem, for example, that only 25 percent of the opinion leaders in Europe trust McDonald's. As a result of this lack of trust, when an activist farmer attached his tractor to the roof of a McDonald's and yanked it off, he became a national hero.[14]

One definition of trust is "making a decision as if the other person or persons will abide by ordinary ethical rules that are involved in the situation."[15] A reputation for trustworthiness arises from following

Table 12.1.   Edelman Trust Barometer 2005[16]

	Percentage of Opinion Leaders Who Trust Corporations*	
Company	United States	Europe
Procter & Gamble	74%	44%
Coca-Cola	69%	45%
McDonald's	58%	25%
Citicorp	56%	25%
Shell	46%	40%
Danone	58%	55%
Siemens	57%	60%

*Based on surveys of 1,500 opinion leaders in eight markets

the "diffuse social norms of obligation and cooperation."[17] Consumers trust sellers who can be counted on for fair pricing.

Being "fair" and being "trustworthy" are very similar ideas. Both imply behavior that meets expectations by following societal rules. The difference is in the time orientation: fairness is an evaluation of whether past behavior has conformed to social norms, trust is a belief that future behavior will conform.

Levels of Trust

There are three levels of consumer trust: *individual trust, cultural trust,* and *context-based trust.* Trust at the individual level is a personal predilection: "an optimistic expectation on the part of an individual about the outcome of an event or the behavior of a person."[18]

Some people are born to be more trusting than others.[19] Differences in trust have been explored in neuroeconomic research using functional magnetic resonance imaging (fMRI) of people's brains. The results indicate that a predisposition to trust may be due to the neurochemical involved in the control of maternal behavior: when this neurochemical (neuropeptide oxytocin) was increased in the brains of the fMRI volunteers, they became more trusting.[20]

In addition, some people live in a more trustworthy society than others. Those who lived through Russia's "Wild West" transition to a market economy would be expected to be less trusting of sellers' prices than those who lived in Norway during the same period.

Social scientist Francis Fukuyama defines cultural-level trust as "the expectation that arises within a community of regular, honest, and cooperative behavior, based on commonly shared norms."[21] It is part of what has been called *social capital*.[22]

Social capital has economic benefits in that it increases communication and reduces *transaction costs*, which are the costs involved in making an economic exchange. They include the costs of policing sellers so they do not take advantage of the situation. A high-trust society needs fewer rules and regulations as well as fewer people to see that those rules and regulations are being followed. As a consequence, everything is cheaper.

Trust at a cultural level can be generalized to the entire population or limited to one's extended family. Japan and Germany are high in generalized trust. Brazil is high in family but not generalized trust. And the United States was once high in generalized trust, but is no longer.[23]

According to a recent survey by the market research company Yankelovich, consumer trust in the United States has sunk to an all-time low.[24] In this survey, 66 percent of the respondents agreed that "if the opportunity arises, most companies will take advantage of the public if they feel they are not likely to be found out." This lack of trust does not encourage brand loyalty.

Although trust in consumer exchange has individual and cultural components, it tends to involve primarily context-based trust. Context-based trust is short term. It is the temporary optimism of a buyer that a seller actually is trustworthy.[25] All of us exhibit context-based trust every time we walk into a new store, every time we order from a new web site. We trust that sellers will follow the social norm that when we pay the price, they will hand over the goods. If we go back to the same store or site and continue to find that the seller continues to act according to the social norms, we develop long-term trust.[26]

In the Fair Price Model of Chapter 3, prior trust—personal, cultural, and context based—is shown to have a reciprocal relationship with both personal and social fairness. Trustworthiness is influenced by fairness,[27] and a perception of fairness is influenced by trust.[28] The one reinforces the other.

Many researchers confirm that fairness leads to trust. One researcher reports that it is the seller's adherence to fair rules that leads to trust.[29] Another says, "Trust is the result of 'right,' 'just,' and 'fair' behavior."[30] And still a third concludes that: "Customers often base their level of trust/distrust in a company on their perceptions of the fairness of their company's pricing of products and services."[31]

At the same time, trust leads to judgments of fairness: if people trust a seller, they will accept a price that might otherwise be dismissed as unfair.[32] For example, at a trusted store, a one-time breach of a pricing rule will be thought temporary and perhaps accidental. The seller will be given the benefit of the doubt.

Motivations

In early research, trust was associated with one person's confidence in another person's motives.[33] If a seller raises prices, suspicious consumers will ask themselves: "Is the seller just trying to make a fair profit or is she or he motivated by greed?" How consumers resolve this question depends on whether they trust the seller. If the consumer has experienced a series of fair dealings with the seller or if the seller has established a solid reputation for fairness in the community, the consumer will accept the price increase as fair and continue to trust.

For example, when a bottled water company had a reputation for fair dealing, the increase in the price of water after a disaster was more readily accepted as a cost of doing business and not an unfair use of power.[34] Conversely, when the company did not have a reputation for fairness, respondents assumed the motive was greed.

However, if a trusting consumer sees that a seller has made an entirely too serious breach of a norm or has done it entirely too often, watch out! Trusting consumers react even more negatively than nontrusting consumers.[35] "Loyalty may act as a buffer against dissatisfaction but it perversely amplifies the effects of any unfairness perceptions, if they occur."[36] Instead of just an infraction of social norms, prior trust makes unfairness seem like a betrayal of beliefs. And people explode emotionally when they feel betrayed.[37]

Research has also provided empirical evidence that old customers feel betrayed when firms give new customers special benefits.[38] It can be a mobile phone company that gives new customers a cheaper rate than existing customers, or Amazon charging a lower price to a first-time consumer. Infractions like these demolish all the previous trust businesses may have so carefully nurtured.[39]

When consumers feel betrayed, they have an intense desire for revenge. In a recent survey on the "State of Consumer Trust," market research company Yankelovich found that 97 percent of consumers who feel betrayed take some sort of negative action against the company that betrayed them.[40]

Some evidence suggests that without trust, consumers will assume that price increases were motivated by greed: the desire to increase profits. To some extent this is accepted. Consumers seem to condone some profit making.

For example, the focus groups we held in New York City were told that a company had increased prices by 20 percent, and was predicted to earn record profits in the coming year. Even though the high profits suggested a motive of greed and possible exploitation of customers, the focus group participants did not think that a company's high profits necessarily made its price unfair—as long as the profits were not *too* high, like the oil companies.

Evidently, at least in the United States, it is a social norm that businesses *should* make a profit. That is reasonable and acceptable behavior from a trustworthy firm. *"Whether they're taking a loss or a profit, it doesn't bother me. I'd expect them to make a profit, that's what they're there for." "(Higher profits are) good for them. They're doing something right." "They're there for a profit, too."*

A popular pricing textbook supports the focus group's observations.[41] It points out that the consumers' perception of fairness has very little to do with the company's profits. Many popular organizations—state lotteries, Godiva chocolates, Häagen-Dazs, and so on—are very profitable. And the public does not mind. It appears that consumers are not concerned about a firm's profits as long as they trust that it is acting fairly.

Trust and Power

Trust and power work together in that greater power on the part of the seller requires greater trust on the part of the buyer. This is demonstrated by seller-administered prices given on price tags. The consumer has given up the right to negotiate prices and let the seller set them. Giving power to sellers raises an issue addressed by what is called *fairness heuristic theory*.

According to fairness heuristic theory, "ceding authority to another person raises the possibility of exploitation . . . people frequently feel uneasy about their relationships with authorities."[42] As a result, consumers look for information to determine whether the price-setting seller is trustworthy. If the more powerful seller is deemed trustworthy, consumers trust that the price is fair.

However, if a more powerful seller gives back some of that power to the consumer, it is possible that the buyer will gain trust. Research indicates that "one trusts those whom one can control."[43]

The marketing research firm Yankelovich recommends that sellers should counter the current lack of consumer trust by "putting consumers in control . . . (because) consumers now expect to be able to dictate the terms of any transactional relationship."[44] The idea is that giving consumers more control will lead them to consider the seller to be fair. By thinking the seller fair, consumers will trust them more.

In Sum . . .

Even though consumer exchange is often impersonal and contains a certain rational component, the element of trust is important. A seller builds trust by reliably following the social norms of prices and pricing. When consumers feel that the seller is trustworthy, they give the seller the benefit of the doubt when the seller commits a seemingly unfair act. Conversely, trust is destroyed when a trusted seller does not behave according to the social norms of fairness.[45] And the greater the trust in the seller, the greater the outrage when the seller acts unfairly.

The women in rural India are a good example. Angry with the untrustworthy cowherds, they have done the unthinkable: they are now running dairy cooperatives on their own. More than 1,000 women are now ensuring the safety of their own milk.[46] They pay a higher price for the raw milk they process, but the price is equitably based on fat content. The untrustworthy cowherds have missed out twice: they missed out before on getting a price premium, and they are missing out today by having lost customers.

Definitions

Individual trust: A predisposition to have optimistic expectations about events or behavior.

Cultural trust: The expectation that people in one's group will act in accordance with the social norms.

(Continued)

Context-based trust: Short-term optimistic expectation that another person will be trustworthy.

Social capital: A network of cooperative relationships based on commonly accepted social norms that facilitate productive activity.

Transaction costs: The costs associated with making an economic exchange.

Fairness heuristic theory: The idea that giving another person authority increases one's sensitivity to issues of fairness and concerns about the other's trustworthiness.

PART

III

APPLICATIONS

Modifications

"SORRY! THE RULES HAVE CHANGED!"

Is it fair to charge a price for human eggs? For missed appointments? For a British peerage? Is it fair for a spouse to charge for cooking dinner? For making the bed? For having sex?

These are but some of the many things in the world that were once free of charge and are now being priced—or could be priced, if people so agreed. This is part of a trend that started in the Middle Ages: going from free or bartered goods to priced goods.

People, however, typically think that charging for previously free goods or services is unfair. Any new charge is unfair. It is a change in the rules. And it is infuriating to be told midway into a game, "Sorry! The rules have changed."

Charging for previously free goods is unexpected and against one's self-interest. It is personally unfair. And it is also socially unfair because the previous exchange of getting the goods for free was considered equitable. So how can a new charge still be a fair exchange? It violates the social norm of equity.

The imposition of a charge for a previously free good or service is considered fair if the customer perceives added value. The ring tone on cell phones is a case in point. It adds value to have a distinctive ring tone—one that signifies what kind of person you are and distinguishes calls to your phone from other phones nearby. The new charge for a ring tone is equitable and fair.

A charge for incoming calls, however, is not fair because no value has been added. The same applies to charging for entry into London or for parking at shopping centers or for restocking in retail stores. These are charges for what had previously been provided at no charge. Customers consequently complain because the new charges are inequitable and unfair.

However, in our society—as in any society—what was thought to be unfair in the past can be accepted as fair in the future. Social norms do change. Children were once expected to do chores for no pay; today, they are more and more likely to be paid. Water was once provided free of charge or at least bundled into community taxes. Now water is a separate and significant charge.

Trend to Market Solutions

A major change in the social norms of prices is being brought about by the trend to market solutions: allowing supply and demand to set the price. The question is whether these solutions are fair. For example, is it fair to tax those who emit greenhouse gases, or should they be able to purchase the rights to global emissions? If it is fair to charge, how do you place a value on those rights? Do you let the market decide?[1] Or do you determine the price based on the cost of environmental damage?[2] These were the debates that raged at the Kyoto summit.

The United States, with its belief in the market and its successful experience in selling *pollution rights*, wanted a system whereby rights to emit greenhouse gases were sold as tradable permits. The holders could then sell them to countries that put a higher value on them. The belief was that through trading, a fair price would be established.

Europe, however, with its distrust of the market, wanted a system of regulation. The resolution was an agreement on a "flexible mechanism" of implementation, following the U.S. market-driven system. The sale of pollution rights may become the norm.

As another *market solution, The Economist,* a champion of the free market, advocates the privatizing of water because governments can no longer afford to handle it.[3] Their contention is that "the way to make water available to everybody, everywhere is rather simple: to price it at a level above the cost of its provision and disposal."

The objection to charging for a previously free good like water is that it limits the sale of a scarce and necessary product to those who can afford it. Such rationing raises questions of fairness because it means that the rich benefit and the poor suffer. It violates the social norm of equality. An *Economist* commentator counters these objections by arguing it is possible to charge for water but at the same time subsidize the poor, as they do in Chile.[4]

Market solutions have even been suggested to handle life-and-death issues. Selling human organs to the highest bidder is clearly against the social norm. But organs for transplant are in short supply. This is a problem. One proposal is to charge for organs and let the market determine the price.[5] The advocates say the market would then provide a quantity of good-quality organs: "Market forces would ensure high quality of human organs, just as they do of hot dogs."[6]

The opponents of a market solution say that that everyone has an equal right to life; society has the "obligation to ensure that every person—whether rich or poor—has equal access to medical benefits."[7] Charging for body parts—just as with charging for water—would mean that human organs would go to the rich and not the poor. A monetary incentive, furthermore, would encourage poor people or poor countries to begin selling organs. In our society, this is not considered fair.

As a consequence, the revised Uniform Anatomical Gift Act of 1987 forbade the sale of human organs. It did, however, allow charges for handling and transporting bodies. Companies can now make some $7,000 from processing a donated body so it can be used in medical research. This price provides some incentive and is still fair because the price is, at least theoretically, based on costs.

Unlike the sale of body parts, a market solution to the sale of blood and sperm and human eggs has become accepted. Their sale has been made possible by medical research that can safely remove and store and ship them. But even if it is now accepted as fair to sell something like human eggs, what is a fair price to charge for them? That question has not been resolved.

Buyers of human eggs pay hugely varying amounts. The Bedford Stem Cell Research Foundation pays donors some $4,000 to cover their costs of travel, time, and child care.[8] But other agencies pay as much as $20,000. And still others pay nothing at all. Society has yet to reach a consensus on a fair price for human eggs.

In the case of the market value of a human life, Americans seem to have agreed on how to determine a fair price. Our method, however, differs from that in other countries. In the United States, compensation for death is usually based on the anticipated earnings of the victim.[9] That appears to have become the social norm.

In contrast, when three young girls died in a traffic accident in China, the father of one was dismayed to find that he was entitled to only $8,500, whereas the other parents received $25,000. The reason was that the first man came from the countryside while the others came from the town.[10] In China, children of peasants are not worth as much as the children of urban dwellers. That would not be considered fair in the United States.

Other market solutions are not as emotionally super-charged as human life or body parts. In some cases, the market is being used simply to discipline consumer behavior. Resources like water or even hospital parking were once abundant and therefore free. But they have now become scarce and therefore costly. The economists have fought for pricing because "if a finite resource is free, human beings tend to use it all up, regardless of the consequences. If it has a cost, they tend to use it more rationally."[11]

To discipline patients, doctors now charge not only for missed appointments but also for late cancellations. The charge is not motivated by profit: one doctor even donated all late fees to a local charity.[12] Ostensibly also to discipline passengers, airlines have instituted fees for changes in flight schedules.

Congestion pricing (charging for peak-time travel in city cores) is a way to discipline traffic in congested urban centers. When originally proposed in London, congestion pricing was vigorously opposed. The main argument against it was "perceptions of fairness. By charging for something that was once 'free' it may be seen as unfair."[13]

Prior to the implementation of congestion pricing in London, it was reported that "politicians have mostly turned a deaf ear, fearing that charging for something that was previously free was a quick route to electoral suicide."[14] But after implementation, it was generally accepted by the public. The mayor who advocated congestion pricing was actually reelected. Plans are now being made to expand the program in London and to implement similar programs in cities around the world. Congestion pricing may become accepted as the norm.

Social Trends

Some shifts in social norms of prices are due to social trends. A major shift is in women working outside the home and grandparents living in another town and often working themselves. These social changes have required changes in pricing norms. Child care was once provided free; now it is usually paid for. Food preparation was usually free; now, more and more, it is paid for in restaurants and take-outs.

Another shift in society is the new value placed on time. People today are willing to pay to save time. For example, you can pay extra to bypass the line waiting to go up to the top of the Empire State Building. Drivers in San Diego pay extra to drive in congestion-free HOT (high-occupancy toll) lanes, which have been converted from previous HOV (high-occupancy vehicle) car-pool lanes. It has also been proposed that airline passengers who are in a hurry can pay extra so they can get more quickly through the security lines without wasting time removing their shoes.

These actions again raise the question as to whether it is fair to give privileges just to those people who can pay. Preferential treatment is, after all, counter to the norm of equality. "The Ethicist" in the *New York Times Magazine*[15] said that in an egalitarian democratic society like ours, it is not fair for someone at the back of a long line to pay $5 to someone up further to buy them a beer. His point was that vexations should not be distributed based on money. That is not fair.

Some researchers have argued that over time any pricing strategy will become the norm and will therefore be accepted as fair. This was the case with driving on the right-hand side of the road. Similarly, they claim, the yield pricing of the airlines is now becoming accepted.[16] But it appears that yield pricing is accepted only when prices vary consistently based on when a consumer makes a reservation.[17] It is questionable whether yield pricing that is not so transparent—that varies capriciously over time—will ever become accepted as a social norm.

Countertrends

At the same time that market solutions are being proposed so that previously nonpriced items are now being priced, some previously priced items are now being provided free of charge. Anything free is accepted as personally fair.

An example of free goods is the week-long Burning Man Festival in Nevada. For nearly two decades, the participants have provided all food and services to each other at no cost (except for the $300 site fee and charges for coffee, tea, and ice). The cofounder and director of the festival, Larry Harvey, says his quest is to spur a "spiritual redefinition of what is value."[18]

The Burning Man Festival is not alone. In software, we have *freeware* like the R statistics software. In music, we had a flurry of free downloads through Napster and still have them available from other sites. Wikipedia now provides us with a free encyclopedia. Creativecommons.org allows artists to make their work available at little or no cost.[19] Ryanair's CEO Michael O'Leary provides free seats on some off-peak flights. He even claims that "there is absolutely no reason why we could not eliminate fares altogether on off peak flights."[20] (This evidently is made possible by the revenue they get from on-flight services.) Such free services are happily accepted as fair.

In Sum . . .

The social norms of a fair price change over time as society and the economy change. One long-term trend is toward a monetized society where people pay for things previously outside the money system. There is also a shift to privatization where services previously paid for with taxes are now being priced in the marketplace.

A problem arises, however, when the established norm is that a good or service should be provided free. It is then judged unfair to charge for it. There are now rumbles that there will be charges instituted for the Internet. That will no doubt cause a cry of "Unfair!"

However, norms can change—and do. Londoners now accept congestion pricing. Parents pay for child care. Homeowners pay for water. But during the period when the social norms are in flux, complaints of unfairness will be voiced. And sometimes those voices will drown out the advocates of change. Despite an ongoing barrage of voices speaking out for marketizing the sale of human organs, it is still not legal.

Definitions

Pollution rights: An assigned allotment of pollution that a country can produce and potentially trade with other countries.

Market solutions: Allowing supply and demand to determine prices without government interference.

Congestion pricing: Charging for traffic into the center part of a city; adjusting charge by time of day to reduce peak-hour traffic.

Freeware: Software provided at no cost over the Internet.

CHAPTER

TIPPING

"JUST DON'T STIFF THE WAITER!"

Thanksgiving dinner was spectacular. Never had your mother-in-law cooked such a succulent turkey. In appreciation, you slipped a 20-dollar bill under your plate. Afterward, your father-in-law took you aside and firmly returned the $20. Ruefully, you accepted it.

Later that weekend, you went to a New York restaurant. The meal and service were sublime. The tab was about $200. In appreciation, you slipped a 20-dollar bill under your plate. Afterward, the maitre d' took you aside and firmly explained that the usual tip is 20 percent. Ruefully, you handed over another $20.

So what gives? Why is it wrong to leave $20 for you mother-in-law and yet wrong *not* to leave an extra $20 for your waiter? The reason is the social norm of tipping.[1] When asked why they leave a tip, most people explain that tipping is the social norm.[2]

A person who follows the social norm of tipping projects an image of trustworthiness.[3] It is all "about appearance and ego, a litmus test for the kind of person we are perceived to be, and the kind of person we perceive others to be. We want to come across as fair though not excessive, prudent yet not cheap."[4] If other patrons notice that a person has not left a tip, they think she or he is a "cheapskate."

For example, a writer tells of a friend who went on a date and picked up the tab. "The woman he was with—it was their third date—offered to pay the tip. She calculated 12 percent to the penny. That was the last time he asked her out."[5] She was not prudent; she was cheap.

The evidence indicates, however, that people tip not just for the approval of others but also for their own feeling of self-worth.[6] If it were only the social influence of what others thought, patrons would tip more at restaurants where they are known. But this is not the case. A 1986 study found there was no significant difference between what people would tip at home or away from home.[7] My own recent replication of that study yielded identical results.[8]

Studies show that although frequent patrons of a restaurant are inclined to tip a bit more,[9] people still leave socially acceptable tips even in one-time restaurants.[10] In addition, lone diners actually leave higher tips than those at tables with two or more.[11] So tipping appears to be a norm sanctioned by internal guilt as much as by social approval. People feel shoddy because they know "you just don't stiff the waiter."

Evolution of Tipping

Although tipping is now established, it was not always a social norm. It consequently provides a nice example of how a norm can evolve. In the case of tipping, it appears to have become a norm due to a combination of risk reduction for the restaurateur and power for the customer even though it conflicts with the social norm of equality.

Folklore has it that the word *tip* originated in England sometime in the sixteenth century. Pub patrons would give the waiter a coin wrapped in paper marked T.I.P., "*T*o *I*nsure *P*romptness."[12] Tipping then became customary in England and soon spread to Europe. But it did not come to the United States until the end of the nineteenth century, when the upper classes who had traveled to Europe brought back the practice.

When first introduced to the United States, tipping caused an uproar. The practice was condemned as elitist. Tipping was considered un-American in that it fostered a *class society*, a master-servant relationship that was counter to the American value of equality. The public thought tips were just a devious ploy of managers to pay servers lower wages. Outraged anti-tipping associations were formed. In 1916 William Scott wrote an entire book on the evils of tipping.[13] As a result of the ferocious outcry, six states banned tipping outright.

Strangely, however, it was not in the United States but in Europe that objections to tipping led to its demise. Today, in Europe it is most common for a standard *service charge* to be added to the bill in lieu of a tip. Europeans think that "tipping is incompatible with the cardinal principle of democracy: the equality of citizens."[14] So tipping evolved into a norm in the United States but not in Europe. (See "American versus European Views on Tipping" on page 124.)

Reasons for Tipping

While tipping became unacceptable in Europe, it became the norm in the United States.[15] One reason this happened appears to be the benefits of tipping to the restaurateur. Not only does tipping potentially lower operating costs and possibly control quality, but it also spreads risk.

Like the early anti-tipping demonstrators, most people today still believe that restaurateurs cut costs by having part of the waiters' compensation come from tips. They think that "many table servers earn less than minimum wage and, whether you think it is fair or not, many depend on tips to make a basic living."[16] This belief is not entirely accurate: it is based on the idea that waiters are paid less than the minimum wage so that tips must then make up the rest. In actuality, this is true in some states like Massachusetts but not in others like California. In California, tips are received over and above the minimum wage. So tipping may or may not cut a restaurateur's cost.

Another potential reason for tipping is that it efficiently controls the quality of a decentralized service. Rather than the proprietor having constantly to watch each and every waiter, the theory is that patrons themselves will monitor service quality. The belief is that "tip payments are a preferable means of rewarding intensity and quality of service work when it is very costly for employers to enforce contracts and the quality of service is important to customers."[17] Again, this may or may not be the case. Although the idea makes intuitive sense, evidence suggests otherwise.

If tips were an efficient means of supervising the quality of decentralized service, it is logical that they would spread from restaurants to all decentralized services. But they have not. Waiters are tipped, but grocery store cashiers are not. Parking lot attendants are tipped, but bank tellers are not. Doormen are tipped, but nurses are not. Evidently, doctors and dentists are tipped in Hungary, but not in the United States.[18]

Evidence from countries that have no tipping also counters the idea that tipping ensures service quality. Since tipping fosters a class society, it has generally not taken hold in *egalitarian societies* like Scandinavia.[19] But according to reports, the absence of tips does not appear to hurt quality: "Countries where there's no tipping—like Australia and Japan—don't have worse service than the United States."[20]

In addition, if tipping is to ensure quality, it would be more common in frequently visited restaurants. But as we saw earlier, people leave tips even when they go to a distant restaurant where they will never return. In addition, the actual difference between tips for very good or very bad service is very small, an average only 1.5 percent more for excellent service,[21] perhaps too small for a waiter to actually notice. Consequently, it does not appear that a tip is actually used as an incentive for good service or punishment for poor service. So tipping may or may not be a means to control service quality.

However, tips certainly do reduce management risk. This is important since the restaurant business is highly risky. A restaurant can be empty one day and so crowded the next that it has to turn patrons away. By tying servers' wages to the volume of customers, the management is able to spread its own risk to its servers. "It shifts a lot of risk onto the server for bad business—if no one comes in, the server gets paid less for working the same hours."[22]

Another risk of the restaurant business is that one table will order a complete meal along with cocktails and fine wines, while another table will order only a snack. But both parties can fill the same number of seats for the same amount of time. By basing the amount of a tip on a percentage of the bill, the manager shares this risk of high/low tabs with the waiter. The result is that very low paid employees share the risk of owners, but they do not share the potentially high return traditionally connected with such risk. Which is unfair.

Although it cannot be proved, it is suspicious that risk reduction was the prime motivation for instituting tipping as a norm. This idea is supported by the fact that while the debate over tipping was being waged in the early twentieth century, restaurants were proliferating and beginning to organize. In 1916, at the same time that Scott was writing his anti-tipping diatribe, restaurants in Kansas were starting what became the National Restaurant Association.[23] So, possibly, that organization promoted the norm of tipping as a service to its members.

Customer Attitude Toward Tipping

The evolution of the tipping norm was facilitated by the fact that customers found they liked it. Contrary to the earlier resistance to the practice, customers today are in favor of tipping and their positive opinion has actually increased over the years. In 1978, a Roper survey found that 55 percent of those polled supported the practice of tipping.[24] In 2002, 73 percent said that "tipping is a fair way to compensate people for various services."

Some researchers argue that there has to be some sort of benefit from a social norm—particularly when a norm is as costly to maintain as tips certainly are. Otherwise, they claim, the norm will erode over time.[25] The fact that approval of tipping has increased over the years suggests that people must receive a good feeling in return. They apparently "derive benefits from tipping, including impressing others and improving their self-image as being generous and kind."[26]

Restaurant patrons also like tipping because it gives them a sense of power. As Kerry Seagrave, a historian of tipping,[27] has written, "It reinforces a sense of superiority in a society that says it does not believe in classes, and it allows Americans to establish feelings of dominance and superiority over others. It's all about control."[28] Customers like having the power to pay for service according to what they feel the server deserves. They believe that "a restaurant tip should be earned, not automatic."

The power to decide on the amount of the tip, however, does not override the social norm of leaving at least some sort of gratuity.[29] As a blogger writes, "Tipping is not really optional. The norm is always to leave something, even if it's a lousy tip."[30] Even for very bad service, the expert in manners, Letitia Baldridge, recommends leaving a smaller than usual amount and then quietly explaining to the server why you have done so.[31]

Despite the acceptance of tipping as a social norm, leaving an overly generous tip can be an insult because it reinforces a class distinction. For example, a doorman in New York City told a reporter that his Christmas tips range from $3 to $800.[32] A blogger complained that such a disparity of tips is just so "the rich bastards can show off how generous they are."[33]

Despite its elitist aspect, the social norm of tipping has become so ingrained in the American psyche that an outcry went up when an elegant restaurant, Per Se in New York City, recently switched from tips to a service charge. The restaurant is now adding a flat 20 percent fee to bills, an amount that is actually less than the average 22 percent tip that patrons had been leaving. So the motive is not to make more money. It is instead, the restaurant explains, to pool tips so that the chefs in the back of the house can earn as much as the waiters in the front. In New York City, servers in exclusive restaurants are reported to make as much as $75,000 a year while the back-of-the-house staff can make as little as $30,000.[34]

In Sum . . .

In the more than a century since the introduction of tips, tipping has become an established social norm in the United States. It appears to have been established by restaurateurs as a means of risk reduction. It has been reinforced by patrons as a means to wield power. Over time, it has become accepted as the social norm even though it goes against the American norm of equality—for there is no denying that tipping is elitist. One tips only those in subservient positions. It is insulting to tip one's equals or one's superiors. That is the social norm. Masters tip their servants. Sons-in-law definitely do not tip their mothers-in-law.

Definitions

Class society: A society that supports obvious levels of social rankings.

Service charge: Percentage automatically added to restaurant bills for service provided.

Egalitarian society: A society that supports all people's being on the same level.

American versus European Views on Tipping

"Being in a foreign city attending a conference, having had a cup of tea and a piece of hot chocolate fudge cake of mediocre quality in a coffeehouse I will never visit again, I still leave an additional one dollar bill on the table before I stand up and leave. I do so not out of habit or because I pity the wait staff. Rather, I feel strangely compelled to act in this way, to quite voluntarily incur an additional cost that I could equally have avoided without any sanctions."

An American[35]

"Europe has the right idea when the cost of food includes the costs of food, food preparation, and a decent living wage for staff. The United States is confusing . . . 10 percent? 15 percent? 18 percent? If the waiter is so damn good do you tip him 50 percent and add him as a dependent on your W-4?"

A European[36]

Discrimination

"IT'S UNFAIR TO CHARGE ME MORE THAN OTHERS!"

One day an Internet user decided to clean out the cookies on his computer. After doing so, he went to the Amazon site to recheck the price for a DVD he wanted. To his surprise, the price had magically dropped from $26.24 to $22.74.[1] His cookies had evidently identified him as an old Amazon customer, and the company was apparently giving new customers a lower price than old customers.

The news of Amazon's discriminatory pricing tactics circulated at breakneck speed through the Internet. On DVDtalk.com, the bloggers ranted, "I find this extremely sneaky and unethical." "Amazon's pricing practices qualify them as the shysters of the Internet."[2] Such *price discrimination*, the bloggers agreed, was unfair.[3]

Charging different prices to regular customers as opposed to new customers is socially unfair because the discriminatory charge violates the social norm of equality. "If customers perceive no differences between offers other than price, they are likely to feel victimized."[4] However, even though it may make customers feel ill treated, charging different prices to different people is usually *not* illegal. This is contrary to what most people think.

According to a study by the Annenberg Center at the University of Pennsylvania, two-thirds of the population do indeed think it is illegal "for an online store to charge different people different prices at the same time of day."[5] An even greater percentage (71 percent) think it is illegal for bricks-and-mortar chains to charge different prices for the same product in different stores. In actuality, discriminatory pricing—the charging of different amounts for the same item to different people or groups of people—becomes illegal only when the discrimination is based on race, religion, or gender. So when equally qualified African-Americans and Latinos are charged more for mortgages, that is clearly a cause for legal action.[6]

In the United States, group discrimination is illegal according to the antidiscrimination laws of the 1960s. Extending these laws to pricing, states like Iowa, Florida, Pennsylvania, and New Jersey have followed California in enacting laws against gender-based prices.[7] In those states it is illegal to charge women more for haircuts or to charge them less at "happy hour." In New Jersey, it has even been judged illegal to charge women less at a happy hour one day a week even when charging men less another day.[8]

Although people think that all discriminatory pricing is unfair and have the mistaken belief that it is illegal, in many cases they still accept price differences as fair. One obvious case is when the preferential treatment is in their favor.

As indicated earlier, we all tend to accept as fair any price that is lower for us than it is for others. But even in cases where we ourselves do not benefit, we sometimes still accept price differences as fair. As political economist Edward Zajac wrote, "The public's attitude to price discrimination is not capable of rational exposition. Broadly speaking, it dislikes discrimination, but special cases are tolerated."[9]

The marketplace is rife with situations where it is acceptable for some people to get preferential treatment over others. Examples include no-cost frequent-flyer fares, quantity discounts, "early-bird dinner specials," and sales for special customers only. These discriminatory prices are all accepted as fair. The question is, then, what makes price discrimination fair?

Price discrimination is considered fair if the difference is due to a socially acceptable reason. These are the same reasons that make any price fair. The price or pricing practice has to adhere to the social norms:

- The descriptive norms of personal fairness: tradition and the status quo.

- The distributive norms of social fairness: equity, equality of opportunity, and need.
- The procedural norms of social fairness: voice, impartiality, and transparency.

Descriptive Norms of Personal Fairness

In some cases, the reason for price discrimination is just tradition. It is fair because that is the way it has always been. It is the descriptive norm. As we saw in Chapter 6, what is customary is reinforced by the status quo bias. This means that once a pricing practice has been established, it is expected to continue.

Take the practice of giving senior citizens discounts at movies. The practice was initially fair because it gave preferential treatment to a needy segment of the population. But today, the highest level of wealth in the United States is with people over 50.[10] So it would now be fair to charge seniors the same as everyone else. The senior citizen discount, however, is still considered fair just because it has been established as the status quo.

Distributive Norms of Social Fairness

Many price differences are accepted as fair because they adhere to the norm of equity: the difference in prices reflects the different costs in providing the product or service. Higher prices west of the Rockies are therefore thought fair because of assumed higher transportation costs. A higher price for unaccompanied minors on airplanes is fair because they require more work.

Different prices in different kinds of stores can also be equitable because of difference in costs. A now famous study shows that people expect to pay more for the same beer when buying it from a resort hotel than when buying it from a neighborhood store.[11] The difference is considered fair due to consumers' implicit understanding that resort hotels have higher operating costs than neighborhood stores.

Paying different prices can also be equitable if buyers receive correspondingly different benefits. Thus, higher prices for lower tiers in a theater are fair because one can see and hear better when closer to the stage. Higher prices for football games against winning teams can be justified by the expectation of a better game. A higher price for music downloads of more popular songs can be defended due to the perceived better quality. Conversely, lower prices for off-peak service—as is common practice for electricity, telephones, and restaurants—are fair because users are receiving a service at a less convenient time.

As mentioned earlier, it is considered equitable and fair for one person to get a better price than another person by shopping at a sale. After all, the sale shoppers have been clever enough and energetic enough to find the sale and get there when it was going on. Since they have greater inputs, it is only fair that they should get better prices.

So, too, is it equitable for some people to get a lower price due to rebates or coupons. Those people who take the extra time and effort to send in the rebate or hold on to the coupon deserve the lower price. That is fair.

Sales, coupons, and other discounts are not always thought to be fair. Until 2001, laws in Germany forbade any discount of more than 3 percent. Coupons were not allowed. Sales to clear stock were permitted only twice a year. Everyone was charged the same price, which was thought to be fair. Now, however, the system in Germany has shifted. Germans, too, are recognizing that it can be fair to get a bargain.

In the United States, it is fair for some shoppers to get lower prices because they belong to large wholesale grocery chains like Sam's Club or smaller supermarket chains like Stop and Shop. In both cases, consumers pay extra to get a lower price. At Sam's Club, consumers pay a fee. At supermarkets, consumers pay with demographic information that the store can then sell. In both cases, it is considered a fair exchange.

Quantity discounts are equitable because there are economies of scale that the seller shares with the buyer. It is therefore expected that a larger-size package will be cheaper than a smaller-size package. A few years ago, consumers were upset to learn that large cans of tuna actually cost more per pound than medium cans. Researchers subsequently found many other products that were priced in a similar manner: on a per-pound basis, large cans of pork and beans cost more than medium cans, large tubes of toothpaste cost more than medium tubes, and large containers of whipped topping cost more than medium containers.[12] Sellers were accused of taking advantage of buyers' legitimate expectations of a quantity discount.

However, the real reason why the per-unit price of many medium-sized grocery store items is less than larger-sized items is that the medium-sized cans are the most popular; they are what stores feature in advertisements. A medium-sized can is the one that customers use to make price comparisons, and it is therefore priced competitively.[13] Competition is an established social norm in our economic system. We accept it as a means for ensuring consumers the lowest price, which is in our self-interest. Competition-based prices are accepted as fair.

A quantity discount is also expected to apply to loyal customers who have, over time, bought more.[14] Unlike the example of Amazon's charging *new* customers less, consumers seem to think the norm is that *old* customers should be charged less. Providing frequent-flyer miles to reward loyal travelers is fair. It is an entitlement that regular flyers think they deserve. Every time an airline even contemplates a change to a frequent-flyer program, they hear from those travelers who feel the rules and conditions are sacred.[15]

Looking at it from the other side, mobile phone customers object that lower prices are given to switchers.[16] Loyal customers feel betrayed when their own company gives new customers a lower price. They are angry when, as the Sprint ad cited in Chapter 1 said, "Whoever is new on the playground is more special." That is unfair.

To provide equal opportunity, the norm is that all people should have equal access to low prices. It is unfair to limit access to only a certain privileged few. This was what bothered Tom Sherlock, a Canadian, who thought it unfair that Air Canada offered Internet users lower fares than other people.[17] He sued the airline. The ruling went against poor Tom, because the judge said that the Internet is now available to everyone. There was equal opportunity for all to get the lower price. The special Internet deal was judged legal and fair in Canada.

In addition to the distributive fairness norms of equity and equality, the other major justification of discriminatory prices is need. Disadvantaged people deserve a lower price (see Chapter 7). Society consequently supports subsidized housing for the victims of hurricanes, food stamps for the poor, and tuition discounts for the less wealthy.

Procedural Norms of Social Fairness

Price discrimination is fair if it adheres to the procedural norms of social fairness: if it gives consumers voice, is impartial and transparent. For example, negotiated prices are fair because consumers have voice. They are in control. Even if you can get a better price on a new car than I can get, that is fair, albeit annoying. The reason is that we each have control over the price. I, after all, did not have to accept the sales rep's price. I cannot attribute the fault to another person. It is my own doing. So I have to accept it as fair.

But it is not fair when the price is not impartial. An example is *price segmentation*: when sellers charge different prices to different segments in the market depending on how sensitive the consumers are to prices. This means that different people are charged different prices for the same item, based on whether they care about the cost. Such a practice is inequitable and unequal. It is taking advantage of the customer. Consumers will fume that "it's unfair to charge me more than others."

Price discrimination is now possible on the Internet in what is called *dynamic pricing*. Sellers on the web can adjust a price when potential customers have already found competitive information on the web. They can pinpoint where customers live and figure their income level, so they charge accordingly. As economist Paul Krugman concludes, "Dynamic pricing is . . . undeniably unfair: some people pay more just because of who they are."[18]

The industry most renowned for the use of dynamic pricing is the airlines. Using a system which the airlines call *yield pricing*, they price according to actual and projected demand. If actual demand is high and future demand is projected to stay high, the cost of seats is increased. Although legal, the airlines' pricing is generally judged unfair.[19]

Discriminatory pricing is now spreading to stores with the new *price optimization software*, which is designed to determine the ideal price for each item in a particular store, given that store's clientele. This software not only sets the original price but also decides when that price should be marked down, all based on the different levels of consumer demand in different stores rather than on supplier costs.

As a case of discriminatory pricing, the local television station reported that Target and Wal-Mart charged different prices in different Denver neighborhoods depending on the residents' ability to pay.[20] The same liquid Tide that was sold at one Wal-Mart for $12.83 was sold at another for only $9.58.

In a survey of nearly 4,000 viewers that followed the Denver television report, 40 percent were surprised at the difference in prices and thought that the discriminatory pricing practice was wrong.

Although Wal-Mart gave no response, Target defended itself by saying that they do not adjust prices between stores "out of fairness" to their customers.[21] But it seems that they do indeed adjust prices between stores. And, as they themselves say, that is not fair.

Although we consider it unfair for chains to charge different prices in different stores, we consider it perfectly fair for one chain to charge different prices from other chains. In fact, we applaud it. If Wal-Mart undercuts Target, that is considered a benefit of competition. Competitive-based prices are fair.

Sellers seem to think fairness is not an issue as long as consumers are unaware of price discrimination; for example, fairness is not a concern if buyers do not know they can bargain with a car salesman or they learn afterward that moving costs can be negotiated. However, when customers do find out that they have missed an opportunity for getting a better price—a price that others received—they are furious.[22] There is evidence that the longer after the event a person learns about a saving that they could have had, the more unfair they judge the loss to be and the more angry they become.[23]

For example, if shoppers have just put some yogurt in their carts when they find that they could get an additional one free, then it is no problem. They simply take another. But if they learn that they missed out on a free yogurt after they get home, they will be really annoyed. The only way in which they can remedy the missed deal is to waste time and energy returning to the store. They will be livid. However, customers really appreciate being informed by the checkout clerk that they are entitled to a free yogurt. That is very fair.

Part of the anger over Amazon.com's dynamic pricing can be explained by the company's lack of transparency: how Internet sellers identify potentially higher-paying customers is a mystery. It is not the same as driving into a car dealership in your Mercedes and being pegged as an affluent buyer. Online, a person "may not realize that her high wages and pricey lifestyle are translating into pricey plane tickets."[24] That is not fair.

In Sum . . .

Discriminatory pricing is a clear case of some people getting a better deal than others. Yet buyers continue to accept it, particularly if they are the ones getting the deal. Buyers delight in getting a bargain that others do not get. That is thought to be fair.

But in some cases, buyers accept it as fair even if they themselves are not benefiting. These are cases where discriminatory pricing has been established as the custom, or where the distributive norms of equality, equity, and need as well as the procedural norms of transparency, voice, and impartiality have been upheld.

There is, however, increasing potential for unfair discriminatory pricing. With the Internet, the possibility for price segmentation is exploding. "In the future," an Internet consultant has said, "what you pay will be determined by where you live and who you are. It's unfair, but that doesn't mean it's not going to happen."[25]

Others, however, point out that sellers had better be prepared for a backlash if their customers find out they have used discriminatory pricing. As one researcher declared, "Get caught, and you're dead."[26] And an industry analyst concluded, "Amazon.com's biggest mistake was getting caught."[27]

Definitions

Price discrimination: Charging different prices to different people for the same product or service (also called "differential" pricing).

Quantity discount: A lower price based on buying a larger quantity.

Price segmentation: Grouping together consumers based on their price sensitivity.

Dynamic pricing: Discriminatory pricing that can change quickly; usually applied to discriminatory prices on the Internet.

Yield pricing: Discriminatory pricing that changes based on predicted demand. Usually applied to discriminatory prices for airfares.

Price optimization software: Computer software that determines discriminatory prices based on local customer demand; usually applied to discriminatory prices in retailing.

CHAPTER 16

Negotiations

"SPLIT THE DIFFERENCE. THAT'S FAIR!"

When in Marrakesh, I wanted to buy a djellaba, one of the long, cowled gowns worn by Moroccans. On the way to the souk, I found a dreary, ill-lit store with just what I wanted. When I asked the price, the bored shopkeeper said 200 dirham (DH), which is about $24. Knowing that they negotiate prices in Morocco, I offered him 150 DH ($18). He said 185 DH ($21), take it or leave it. I took it. Was it fair? Absolutely. We split the difference. That is fair.

My fellow traveler also wanted a djellaba, but in black, which the shopkeeper did not have. So we wandered deep into the souk, and there we found a beautifully lit clothing store with a black djellaba, exactly like mine, in the window. The price, the charming shopkeeper said, was 900 DH ($107). I was aghast. My friend only smiled. She offered him 200 DH ($24). After much flirting and laughing and passionate exchanges, she got him down to 400 DH ($48), which she triumphantly paid. I was quiet. She had just paid more than twice what I paid! Was that fair? Absolutely.

The negotiation was under her full control. She could have left at any time. Both she and the seller were willing partners. Of course, when one party has vital information that the other party does not, then it is still possible for a freely negotiated price to be unfair. But in my friend's case, she knew that the exact same djellaba was available at a lower price. It was her choice to pay the higher price. So it was fair.

The belief that a negotiated price is a fair price is an old idea. According to both Aristotle and Roman law, a price determined through free bargaining—without coercion or deceit—is a fair price.[1] In a negotiated price, both parties to the transaction have control over the outcome. They both have a voice. That is fair.

A concern for fairness is evident in many business-to-business negotiations. Some, of course, are one-sided, in which the stronger negotiator simply demands "my way or the highway." But other business negotiations involve extensive trade-offs. Price is just one consideration among many. The goal is that both parties come out ahead, to conduct what are called *win-win negotiations*.

Such business negotiations are often conducted over and over, year after year, frequently with the same people. Labor unions negotiate and renegotiate contracts. Car manufacturers negotiate prices with suppliers on an ongoing basis. Consultants negotiate contracts with the same clients over time. To maintain good relations in future negotiations, both parties need to uphold their reputations for fairness. As a result, they both have an incentive to follow the social norms of fairness.

Consumer negotiations, however, differ from business-to-business negotiations because they involve only price. One person's gain is another person's loss. People selling their cars want to get as much as they can; the people buying the cars want to pay as little as possible. These are *win-lose negotiations*.

Consumer negotiations also differ from business negotiations in that they are often only one-time deals. Perhaps plumbing services are negotiated on a repeat basis, but most consumer negotiations are not. A person buys a house from another person only one time; a person sells a car to another only one time. There is no incentive to maintain a reputation for fairness. But, remarkably, even in consumer price negotiations, reputations still matter. Fairness is still a concern.

Personal Fairness of Negotiations

Just as with any price, negotiators determine the personal fairness of a price by comparing it to their reference price, as explained in Chapter 6. If they have recent information as to what others paid for the same item, they will use that as a measure (with the exception of my friend in Morocco). They then form an idea of a fair price range.

Both buyers and sellers come to the bargaining table with a range of prices in mind. These prices extend from what they would most like to pay to what they would totally reject, what is most fair to what is totally unfair. It has been accepted as obvious that any settlement will take place between the highest price the buyer would pay and the lowest price the seller would accept, what is called the *zone of agreement*.[2] That is fair to both buyer and seller.

When we are negotiating, our biggest fear is that we will unwittingly pay an unfair price. We worry about being exploited, taken in, hoodwinked, swindled, scammed, bamboozled, fleeced, ripped off, taken for a ride. The multitude of colorful words for paying an unfair price shows how much it is feared.

In addition to the price itself, personal fairness is also based on the descriptive norms of the negotiating process. These norms establish what prices are negotiated and what prices are not. For example, it is the norm to negotiate cars or used furniture or house repairs but not kidneys or shoes or train fares. Other descriptive norms also establish how a negotiation should be conducted.[3]

According to norms of the *negotiation script*, one person makes an offer and the other responds with a counteroffer. Everyone knows that the initial offer is wishful thinking, simply a means to test the water. Everyone expects the seller to lower the price and the buyer to increase the offer until a settlement is reached. When these expectations are not met, it is unfair. Negotiators respond by making stingy counteroffers. They become angry and vindictive. They quit or threaten to quit.

For example, suppose you go to a flea market to buy a pitcher. The dealer says $10. You respond with $5. The dealer then says, "No, now I want $12." You are annoyed and leave because that is not how the script is supposed to go. "Most negotiators honor the code that maintains that an offer, once made, should never be withdrawn."[4] Reneging on a past commitment is unfair.

Or suppose you want to buy a chair and the dealer says $50. You say $30. The dealer says $40. You say $35. But the dealer then says, "No, I'm not selling." That is not the expected response. What is expected is, "Let's split the difference." That is fair. Simply cutting off a stream of reciprocal offers is not part of the script. That is not fair.

Scripts, however, can change. About 10 years ago, I wanted to buy my current house. I knew the script for negotiating house prices: the seller sets the price, the potential buyer offers 15 percent less, and they then negotiate. Because I really wanted the house, I foolishly offered the full asking price and expected a fast, cordial settlement.

I was not aware that the real estate market was shifting from a buyers' to a sellers' market, which had a different script. The owner did not think the old script applied. He did not consider the price as fixed. He had no intention of negotiating. He thought it was an auction. So he dragged his feet and waited for other offers to come in. None came, so I got the house. But I felt the sale was unfair, because the owner had not played the game according to what I thought were the rules.

Social Fairness of Negotiated Outcomes

The personal fairness of negotiations is not difficult to achieve as long as both parties know the same rules and follow them. But the social fairness of negotiated outcomes is hard to achieve because the outcomes are potentially both unequal and inequitable.

The outcome of any price negotiation is potentially unequal because neither partner to the exchange really wants equality. Both want a better return than the other. They compete to get the best deal for themselves. And their ideas of what is fair can be severely biased in their own self-interest.[5]

Both buyers and sellers come to the table with unrealistic ideas of the outcome. They are influenced by what they happen to remember and, due to the self-interest bias, they tend to remember and retrieve from memory only information that supports their own interest.[6] They consequently form biased expectations of what would constitute a fair outcome.[7] They are prepared to battle for what they think is their own fair return.

Negotiated prices are also potentially unequal because the outcome depends on the skills and motivation of the negotiators. Because I am a lousy negotiator, I paid full price for a house you would no doubt have negotiated for less. However, we both would have had equal opportunity to negotiate. So that is still fair.

What is unfair is when one group of consumers is targeted for unequal treatment. In two studies of over 500 negotiations to buy a car, researchers found that white men consistently get a better deal than African-Americans and women.[8] This is blatantly unequal treatment—grossly unfair.

In addition to inequality, negotiations can easily be inequitable. Equity—in the sense of the price's being equivalent to the value received—is difficult to determine in negotiations, since it is often only the seller who knows the true value of what is being sold. When selling a house, the seller may know that the basement floods every spring but may choose not to inform the buyer. This gives the seller an unfair advantage.

Sure, there are laws about sharing information. For example, house sellers have to inform prospective buyers of any structural problems with the house. But the laws are few. And if the basement floods next spring, the prior owner can say that is the first time it ever happened. That is a problem. It is potentially unfair because it can violate the norm of equity.

It is somewhat surprising, therefore, that despite the strong adversarial aspect of consumer price negotiations, price negotiators can still demonstrate some concern for fairness.[9] Fairness evidently has utility to them.[10] Researchers tell us that "doing the right thing is clearly a motive for many people."[11]

Both buyers and sellers often appear to want to reach a settlement that is both fair and self serving. They have both a competitive drive to get the best of the bargain and a cooperative incentive to reach a fair conclusion. This idea, which has been formalized into what is called the *Dual Concern Model*,[12] has extensive research support.[13]

How the Dual Concern Model works is shown in the dictator game discussed in previous chapters. Even though dictators act out of self-interest, they are also aware of the social norm of equality, that people should receive equal outcomes. They have empathy with the other party in the game.

Like dictators, negotiators also act empathetically. When deciding on an offer, they put themselves in the shoes of the other and mentally consider how the other party will assess the fairness of their action. Will it be thought fair? Will it make the other party angry? Will the other party walk away?

Negotiators are motivated to act fairly because they recognize that their opponents can punish them by walking out. They are caught between wanting the best deal and not wanting to anger their opponents so that there is no deal at all.[14] That is their dual concern.

Social Fairness of the Negotiation Process

Just as with personal fairness, the fairness of a negotiated price depends as much on the fairness of the process as on the fairness of the outcome. The importance of a fair process in negotiations can be affected by *priming*. Priming is a way of encouraging specific thoughts, of bringing to mind certain concerns. It is accomplished through the power of suggestion.

When negotiators are primed to like their opponent and to consider their viewpoint, the self-serving bias is reduced.[15] When they are primed to think of fairness, the range of prices negotiators consider a fair settlement price shifts toward the seller, indicating a concern for how much the seller makes in the bargain.[16]

Fairness-primed negotiators bargain more cooperatively: they make bigger concessions, settle more quickly, and are more satisfied with the results.[17] They generally act more fairly. When people themselves act more fairly, they rate the outcome and their opponent as being more fair.[18] They seem to generalize from their own fairness to the fairness of the other.

The negotiating strategy that is generally seen to be most fair is a *cooperative strategy*, one in which the negotiator gives big concessions to the other party.[19] A cooperative strategy leads to a swift conclusion, but a cooperating negotiator runs the risk of being "walked all over."[20] In contrast, a *competitive* strategy, one in which the negotiator hangs tough, is seen as unfair and often results in the negotiators' reaching an impasse.

Some negotiations are doomed before they even begin because one or both negotiators start with a presumption of competitive behavior on the part of the other.[21] They perceive the other party as an adversary, not as a human being.[22] And they play "hard ball." They stand firm and force the other to yield.[23] If such aggressive behavior is reciprocated, as it often is, both parties become more and more competitive.[24] The negotiation then falls apart.

The most effective strategy is a *reciprocal strategy*: tit-for-tat— respond generously when opponents give a big concession; respond stingily when they give a small one.[25] Researchers have found that "the person following a tit-for-tat strategy was seen to be as fair and honest as one following a cooperative strategy and more intelligent and stronger than individuals following a unilaterally cooperative strategy."[26]

Most negotiators follow a reciprocal strategy.[27] It works best not only in reaching a satisfactory settlement but also in being perceived as fair. But it has to be reciprocated in kind. If negotiators' reciprocity is not returned, they retaliate vindictively.[28]

Whatever strategy is used depends on some deception. In negotiations, it is not the norm to be frank and open. The need for deception has been pointed out repeatedly: "To conceal one's true position, to mislead an opponent about one's true settling point, is the essence of negotiations."[29] "Minimal truthfulness is necessary for a valid agreement, but absolute candor is not."[30]

Negotiations are like poker games where you keep your cards close to your vest. You never smile when you have a straight flush. Deceit is expected. But deceit has its limits. Just like players in a poker game, negotiators cannot cheat. They cannot keep a card up their sleeves or use mirrors to see opponents' cards. They have to play fair. In negotiations, the norm is that major problems have to be explained, as with the law saying structural problems of a house have to be reported.

The norm-limiting deceit was recognized by Thomas Aquinas in the thirteenth century. He held that "there is no need to publish beforehand by the public crier the defects of the goods one is offering for sale."[31] But he stated that it was necessary to point out any defect that might be dangerous or cause a considerable loss. He defined a considerable loss to the seller as being a price less than half the "just" price. So he actually allowed considerable leeway in what information had to be made available. Some deceit in negotiations is therefore to be expected, and the possibility of deceit makes trust of great importance.

Trust and Power in Negotiations

Since a negotiation involves a repetition of offers and counteroffers, there is sufficient time for trust to evolve even between strangers. When a negotiator acts fairly—in a predictable manner, particularly a concessionary one—trust is built. Once built, trust leads to risk taking, to making larger concessions.[32] Trusting negotiators therefore reach settlement faster and are assumed to be more fair.[33]

Trust is particularly vital when a price is negotiated before the delivery of a product or service, for example, when negotiating roof repairs. The buyer is then dependent on the roofer to deliver as promised.

Suppose a house owner had negotiated really aggressively and had driven the roof repairer down to a rock-bottom price. The distrust developed in such a rancorous negotiation could come back to haunt the owner. The roofer could repay the owner with a shoddy job. The house owner would then be angry.

To protect themselves against unscrupulous roofers and other such sellers, buyers rely on reputation. The building contractor has to have a reputation for making good on promises; the realtor has to have a reputation for presenting houses honestly. That is why buyers often ask around to see if sellers have behaved fairly in the past. They check with the Better Business Bureau to see if there are complaints and whether the company has responded. So reputation is important, even in a one-time negotiation.

In addition to trust, power also has an obvious influence on price negotiations. It affects how people negotiate. Negotiators who have more power make smaller concessions and force their lower-power opponents to make larger concessions.[34] More powerful negotiators consequently get a better deal than their opponents, and they judge the deal as being more fair.[35]

In some cases, it is sellers who have greater power because they are more experienced negotiators and have better information.[36] In other cases it is buyers who have the power because they have access to alternatives.

When power is equal, buyers get the better outcome. And buyers perceive themselves to have more power than sellers no matter what the actual situation.[37] So settlements tend to favor the buyer.

As researchers have concluded, "A curious, consistent, and robust finding is that buyers tend to outperform sellers in symmetric negotiation experiments."[38] It appears that the norm of equality, at least in negotiations, is slanted so negotiations typically favor the buyer (again, with the exception of my friend in Morocco).

In Sum . . .

A negotiated price is fair because both parties have a voice in determining it. They have control over the process and the outcome. They can walk away from what they perceive to be an unfair price or unfair negotiating tactic on the part of the other.

At the same time, a negotiated price is unfair if it involves something like a heart transplant or if the negotiators do not follow the proper script. It is unfair when the outcomes are unequal and one party gets the best of the deal. It is unfair when the exchange is inequitable because the seller has concealed information. And it is unfair when the more powerful negotiator forces concessions.

Social norms limit how unequal outcomes can be, how much deceit is acceptable, and how much power can be imposed. By adhering to the social norms, negotiators lessen the danger of their opponents walking out. The settlement will be quicker and more durable. It will be fair.

Definitions

Win-win negotiation: Bargaining over price, product, and services so that both negotiators come out ahead.

Win-lose negotiation: Bargaining where one person's gain is another person's loss as in price negotiations.

Zone of agreement: The range of prices between the highest price the buyer will pay and the lowest price the seller will accept; settlement is expected to take place within this zone.

Negotiation script: Expected sequence of buyer-seller behavior when bargaining.

Dual concern model; A negotiation model in which both parties have a concern for not only their own self-interest but also the interest of the other.

Priming: Planting an idea so that it becomes important when decisions are made.

Cooperative negotiation strategy: The use of conciliatory negotiating techniques: making large concessions and not bluffing with threats to leave.

Competitive negotiation strategy: The use of aggressive negotiating techniques: making small concessions and bluffing with threats to leave.

Reciprocal negotiation strategy: Copying whatever the other party does when bargaining: making large concessions when they do and being stingy when they are, counter-bluffing when they bluff.

What Is a "Fair" Price?

As long as there is no coercion, a fair price is whatever a willing buyer and a willing seller agree upon. Let me illustrate.

Say I went into the bottled water business. Knowing that people like to buy bottled water when it's hot and they're hot, I approach Tour 18 Golf Course in Flower Mount, Texas. I negotiate a deal with them where I can walk the course and sell my water, giving them a cut. It's been a good, hot day and I have only two bottles left. I decide to head for home.

I cut through the woods and notice the Irish plumber lifting up logs trying to find his golf ball. The sweat is pouring from his brow. Aha, I think, I can sell another bottle.

"Wanna buy some water?" I ask.

"How much?" asks the Irish plumber. "It better not be too much. I'm Irish, after all, and I work for a consolidator. Every dime counts."

Just then, Randy Hilton drops from a tree he had climbed in an effort to better survey the landscape looking for his ball. I smell the sweat before I see it. Great! I can sell out.

"I'll give you two bucks," says Hilton. "It's all I got on me."

"Sold," I say, tossing him a bottle.

Hilton hands me two sweaty dollar bills and takes a swig. "Heck of a deal," he says.

Irish looks at me slyly. "I've only got a dollar," he says.

I think about it. What the heck, it's my last bottle.

"Wait a minute," says Hilton, "you charged me two dollars. If you sell it to the Irish plumber for a buck, I want a dollar off."

"You just said two dollars was a heck of a deal," I say.

"That was before," he says indignantly.

"What if I told you I normally sell water for three dollars and already gave you a dollar off?"

While Hilton is scratching his head and Irish is salivating, Frank Blau bulls through the brush. "Are you guys going to play golf or what? Let's get with it."

"We're buying water," says Irish.

"Hey, that sounds good. How much?" asks Frank.

"What's it worth to you?" I ask.

"Five dollars."

"Hey, wait," says Irish. "I just found a fiver. I'll give you six for the last bottle."

"No Irish plumber's going to outbid me," says Frank. "Ten."

"Eleven," says Irish.

"Twenty," says Frank. "I'll just put it in overhead and make a profit on it. What do I care?"

"Twenty-one," says Irish.

Suddenly, Randy Hilton pipes in, "I'll sell you the rest of my water for ten."

"I'll give you five," says Frank to me.

"What happened to twenty?" I ask.

"Do you want five or not?" says Frank.

"I'll give you ten," says Hilton.

"Sold," I say quickly before the price drops again.

Hilton takes a swig, then hands the rest to Frank. "It's ten bucks, Frank. Same as Irish paid. It's my flat rate price."

Pretty silly, huh? Silly or not, when was the price unfair? At no time. Where there is a willing buyer and a willing seller, it is impossible to sell at an unfair price. It's IMPOSSIBLE!

By Matt Michel;[39] reprinted with permission from *PM Magazine*.

CHAPTER

Taxes

"PAYING TAXES IS AS AMERICAN AS DISLIKING TAXES"

Buy a suit in New York state, and you will be hit with an average of 8 percent extra in sales tax. Buy a quart of liquor and you will be charged $1.61 in excise taxes. Stay in a hotel, and the room rate will be increased by 13.375% for city and state taxes, plus another $2 occupancy tax and a $1.50 unit tax. Purchase a gallon of gas, and 23.9 percent of the price will be excise taxes. With gasoline currently at $3 a gallon, that is $.72 per gallon for business taxes, federal excise tax plus a "spill" tax.[1] In sum, nearly 13 percent of New Yorkers' income goes to local and state taxes. Add to that an average of 22.2 percent in federal taxes, and New Yorkers pay over 35 percent of their incomes in taxes.

Other Americans may pay less in taxes than New Yorkers, but they still pay a lot. According to the Tax Foundation, a nonpartisan tax research organization, Americans' taxes now average 31.6 percent of their incomes.[2] In 2007, American taxpayers had to work from January 1 to April 30 just to pay their taxes. They worked more days to pay taxes than for all their food, clothing, and medical care combined.

The focus in this chapter is on individuals' income taxes. What is amazing is that most Americans pay them: over 90 percent of Americans comply voluntarily.[3] A study of the United States and 15 European countries shows that Americans are the most

145

intrinsically motivated to pay taxes.[4] We have what is called a high *tax morale*. We take pride in paying our taxes.

Political philosopher Benjamin Barber proclaimed that taxes are "emblematic of what it means for Americans to be constituted as a people."[5] Supreme Court Justice Oliver Wendell Holmes said that "taxes are what we pay for civilized society," a quote now engraved on the Internal Revenue Service (IRS) building in Washington, D.C.[6]

The IRS Oversight Board conducted an independent poll in 2005 that found 96 percent of the respondents agreed "it is every American's civic duty to pay their fair share of taxes."[7] The Pew Research Center in a similar study in 2006 found 79 percent of the respondents said that "cheating Uncle Sam was morally objectionable."[8]

Certainly, Americans pay their taxes because they have to: ever since 1943, taxes have been automatically withdrawn from paychecks. But people also comply because they think it is fair. Polls show that most Americans think only "a few" people cheat on their taxes.[9] Paying taxes, just like leaving a tip, is a social norm.[10] It is what Americans believe most people do. This belief is important because "taxpayers' judgments about the compliance of others have a strong impact on their intrinsic motivation to pay taxes."[11]

To research the influence of other people on tax compliance, a study in Minnesota tested the effect of two different letters sent to taxpayers.[12] One letter gave a rational argument for paying taxes: "Your income tax dollars are spent on services that we Minnesotans depend on." The other letter was based on compliance by other people: "Audits by the Internal Revenue service show that people who file tax returns report correctly and pay voluntarily 93 percent of the income taxes they owe." Only the letter based on the compliance of other people significantly increased compliance.

Personal Fairness of Taxes

In the United States, even though the social norm is to pay taxes, following the norm is not the same thing as liking the norm. Research shows that 59 percent of Americans think federal income taxes are too high.[13] Although they are willing taxpayers, Americans think the tax burden is more than what it should be, which is personally unfair.

Part of the problem is that, even though paying income taxes is a norm, how much should be paid has yet to be established. The reason is that the tax rate keeps changing. It has varied from a top rate of a mere 5 percent during the Civil War to a monstrous 94 percent during World War II.[14] Recently, the top rate has fluctuated from 50 percent in 1985 to 39.6 percent in 1995 to 35 percent in 2005. Since the rate keeps changing, what constitutes a "normal" tax rate has yet to settle down and become a descriptive norm.

So taxes are personally unfair both because they are higher than people would like and because the amount cannot be anticipated. When taxes are expected, they are onerous but not surprising. People learn to cope with them. As the adage goes, "the best tax is an old tax." It is an unexpected tax that is an unpleasant surprise. And surprises are unfair.

One unexpected tax is the *use tax* that more and more states are demanding. A use tax is a tax on goods or services purchased from another state, for example, books purchased over the Internet. Due to a Supreme Court ruling of 1992, a sales tax can be imposed only if the seller has a physical presence, or "nexus," in the state. This means that Wal-Mart, which has stores in every state, has to collect sales taxes for all products sold over its web site, while Amazon, which has distribution centers in only a few states, is mostly free of sales taxes.

The states, however, have ruled that they can impose a tax on the *use* of a product in that state even if it has been purchased elsewhere. Instead of paying for the sale, the purchaser is paying for the use of the goods. But the amount of money is the same. However, since it is new and unexpected, the use tax is seen as personally unfair.

Another example of an unexpected tax is the alternative minimum tax (AMT), which parallels the federal income tax. The AMT has only two tax rates (26 percent and 28 percent) and no deductions for dependents or for state and local taxes. It was created in the late 1960s to catch tax evaders like the 155 high-income people who paid no taxes in 1967.

Since the threshold for paying AMT was not indexed to increase with inflation, even middle-income families can now earn enough to be pushed into the AMT. Those who qualify have to figure two taxes, the regular income tax and the AMT. They then have to pay whichever tax is higher. Again, since it was unexpected, the AMT is seen as personally unfair.

Distributive Fairness of Taxes

According to the Fair Price Model described in Chapter 3, when an unexpected price is seen as personally unfair, we are motivated to consider the social norms of distributive fairness: the norms of equity, equality, and need.

The concern with equity is whether taxpayers are getting a fair return for their tax dollars. How the government spends tax money is a major concern of taxpayers, even more important than how much they pay in taxes. In a recent poll, people were asked, "When it comes to paying taxes, which bothers you more—how much you pay in taxes or how the government spends your taxes?" Seventy-one percent of those polled answered that how taxes were spent was more important.[15]

But it is difficult to find out how tax dollars are spent. "The hard thing about taxes," says Patricia McGinnis, president and CEO of the Council for Excellence in Government, "is it's a lot of money, a chunk of a person's paycheck, and it's not always clear where the money's going or what the benefits are."[16]

People suspect that tax money is being squandered. Their suspicion is fueled by politicians who decry the waste of "the workers' hard-earned tax dollars" being spent on $1,000 toilets and by news reports that lament the billions of dollars being spent on the war in Iraq. As a consequence, 65 percent of Americans do not feel that they get an adequate return from the taxes they pay.[17]

Americans have not always felt the return on taxes was inadequate. During World War II, people overwhelmingly supported taxation because the taxes were going to support the war effort. In 1944, even with the high tax rate, 90 percent thought their taxes were fair; today, the percentage is down to 61 percent.[18]

In addition to equity, there are constant questions about the equality of the tax burden. People ask, "Does the tax system treat similarly situated individuals similarly? Does the tax system account for individuals' different capacities to bear the burden of the tax?"[19]

The concern for equality clashes with the concern for equity in the debates over regressive or progressive taxes. A *regressive tax* decreases proportionally as income increases: the less you earn, the higher proportion of income paid in taxes. A *progressive tax* increases proportionally as income increases: the more you earn, the higher the tax rate.

A regressive tax, like a sales tax, is fair because it is equal treatment: everyone pays the same percentage. But 20 percent of $200,000 means less to a rich taxpayer than 20 percent of $20,000 means to a poor one. A progressive tax is fair because it is equitable: everyone pays in proportion to their income. But the rich then have to pay a greater amount than the poor. So both kinds of taxes are, in a sense, fair. But both kinds result in some people's suffering more than others, which is unfair.

The federal income tax in United States is progressive: wealthier people pay more taxes not only in absolute terms but also as a percentage of their income: the top 0.1 percent pay over 30 percent of their income, and the bottom 20 percent pay less than 5 percent.[20] Most Americans find that acceptable. In an NBC News poll, 61 percent of the respondents agreed that they were paying a fair share of taxes.[21] At the same time, however, 77 percent thought the tax system should be overhauled.

To overhaul the system, two major changes have been proposed. Proponents claim that both changes would be fairer because they impose an equal burden on all taxpayers. They are also touted as being simpler and more transparent than the current progressive tax structure.

One proposal is a *flat tax*, which was advocated most prominently by Steven Forbes in his campaign for president. In a flat tax, everyone pays between 20 and 30 percent of all earned income.

A flat tax is considered regressive because it harms the poor more. However, a flat tax is considered fair because "nobody could be construed as receiving a favorable or 'unfair' tax advantage . . . Fairness literally is when everybody is the same."[22] As described in Chapter 7, charging the same rate to everyone is considered fair because it is equal.

The benefit of a flat tax, in addition to charging everyone the same amount, is its simplicity. An entire tax return could be sent in on a postcard. The cost of preparing and auditing taxes would be much reduced. And the possibility of some people's exploiting tax loopholes would be decreased.

Such a flat tax is already used in five states that have rates ranging from 3 percent in Illinois to 5.3 percent in Massachusetts. A flat tax has also been introduced in several of the former communist countries as well as in Russia itself. These countries have experienced high growth rates, which some have attributed to the flat tax. At the same time, however, there is evidence that a flat tax leads to greater income disparities. In Estonia, for example, where they have a flat tax, "calls for a progressive system of taxation are getting louder"[23] so as to equalize incomes.

In the United States, an alternative to the flat tax has been proposed, sponsored primarily by Republicans. They propose to replace the income tax with a national retail sales tax or consumption tax—what they call a *Fair Tax*. A Fair Tax Act has been introduced in Congress every year since 1999. The Act calls for a 23 percent sales tax on the sale of all goods and services to replace the income, payroll, estate, and gift taxes. Such a tax would be similar to a federal *consumption tax*. "A consumption tax is a tax on spending rather than on income; income is taxed when spent (consumed) not when it is saved."[24]

Both consumption taxes and sales taxes are regressive. Since the poor have to spend all their income, they would be taxed on 100 percent of it. Since the rich spend only part of their income, they would be taxed on only that part. Whereas the current progressive system tends to favors the poor, a flat or sales/consumption tax would tend to favor the rich. Thus, there is a conflict of interests.

In a recent poll, Americans demonstrated their conflicted opinions about different tax structures: 33 percent preferred a flat tax; 20 percent, a national sales tax; and 21 percent, the current tax.[25] The preference correlated directly with income: the higher the income, the greater the preference for a flat or sales tax and the lower the preference for the current tax structure.

These differing preferences demonstrate what we have seen before: when confronted with the conflicting norms of equity and equality, people's choice is influenced by the self-serving bias to fairness. They seem to think, "What is most fair is what is fair to me."

Although the fairness of a progressive versus a regressive federal income tax is debated, most Americans accept it as fair when taxes are adjusted based on need. There appears to be a consensus that necessities should not be taxed and that the very poor should get special tax consideration. Essential products like food and medicine are usually not taxed. Essential services like child care and education are given special consideration. There are now, for example, 16 different tax breaks for education.[26]

To offset the costs of Social Security and Medicare, the poor can get earned income tax credit. If the credit is greater than the taxes owed, poor people are paid the difference. Society condones these income tax adjustments since they are based on need, which is a distributive norm. That makes it fair.

Besides income taxes, other taxes can also be either equitable or equal as well as adjusted for need. For example, *sin taxes* are levied equally on all. They are designed not only to raise money but also to discourage consumption. Cigarettes are an obvious example. The amount of taxes varies depending on the perceived "sin" of smoking: from $.07 a pack in South Carolina[27] to $3 a pack in New Jersey.[28]

An example of an equitable tax is the *luxury tax*, which is levied only on the rich. The rich, however, are vocal in saying that such taxes are unfair, that luxury taxes penalize the rich just for being rich. In 1990, for example, Congress voted in a luxury tax on jewelry, furs, yachts, and cars over $30,000. That tax, however, was quickly repealed when the rich complained,[29] although some states still tax luxury clothing.

Whether a tax is fair depends on how you look at it. How viewpoints can vary is demonstrated by the gasoline tax. In Europe, gasoline is seen as a limited resource, which should not be wasted. It is therefore taxed heavily as both a luxury and a sin. As a result, gasoline in Europe costs four times what it costs in the United States.

The reason for the low tax on gas in the United States is that gasoline is considered a necessity. Workers need their automobiles to get to work. In response to need, the percentage of tax in the price of gasoline has actually dropped over the years. "Taxes used to represent as much as 40 to 50 percent of the price you paid at the pump," says Tom Kloza, a gasoline analyst. "Nowadays, it's a much lower figure than that because they haven't changed in 12 years."[30]

Politicians are loath to increase gasoline taxes because of voter outrage. They are now selling toll roads to private firms rather than raising gasoline taxes to pay for road maintenance.[31] Americans feel a higher tax would be unfair.

Procedural Fairness of Taxes

In addition to whether taxes are fair based on the norms of equity, equality, or need, whether taxes have been set using fair procedures is also a factor in determining fairness. To be fair, a tax system has to be transparent and taxpayers have to be treated with respect.

Income taxes are considered unfair because they are not transparent: 80 percent of Americans think the current tax system is somewhat or very complex.[32] The current tax code, along with the many, many regulations and IRS rulings, now fill more than 60,000 pages, compared to 40,500 in 1995.

There are currently 582 tax forms, up from 475 tax forms in 2000.[33] As an indication of the complexity, 60 percent of taxpayers have to have professionals compile their returns.[34] And even professionals differ when determining how much tax is owed.

Complexity is not only unfair but also leads to tax evasion and tax errors. "Complexity obscures how, when and on whom a tax is imposed, which increases confusion, frustration, and the perception that the tax is unfairly imposed and thereby decreases compliance."[35] Complexity provides a would-be evader with a convenient cover. If audited, a person can claim, "It was so confusing, I just didn't understand."

With the goal of making "the tax code simpler, fairer, and more conducive to economic growth,"[36] President Bush created an Advisory Panel on Federal Tax Reform in January 2005. The panel recommended fewer tax brackets, lower tax rates, and fewer tax breaks. A guiding principle was that "a good tax system . . . needs to be understandable to those who are expected to pay the tax." That would be fair because it would be transparent.

The other way to make taxes more acceptable is to treat taxpayers with respect. Showing respect to the taxpayers has been shown to lead to greater compliance.[37] The two countries with the highest "tax morale"—the United States and Switzerland—are two countries where taxpayers are treated with respect. As evidence of this respect, a poll of American taxpayers who had some experience dealing with the IRS showed that over 90 percent of them thought that they had been treated fairly.[38]

Power, Trust, and Taxes

The traditional view has been that tax compliance is due to enforcement. Economists hold that rational people pay taxes because they fear the penalties of non-compliance, and people weigh the probability of being caught against the fine if they do get caught. The conclusion is that governments should use their power to enforce tax payment.

Although the idea of enforcement certainly has merit, it has been shown to consistently overestimate how many people will evade paying taxes.[39] And it does not explain why many countries have relatively high tax compliance even though they have relatively low enforcement.[40] Not only that, but enforcement has been shown to actually have a negative effect on compliance.

Studies have shown that the intrinsic willingness to comply with taxes can be *crowded out* by coercive actions.[41] This finding is based on the work of social psychologist Edward Deci, who argues that external motivation crowds out internal motivation.[42] According to his theory, paying children for good grades will reduce their intrinsic motivation to get good grades. Similarly, enforcing tax compliance will reduce—or crowd out—the intrinsic motivation to comply.

The crowding out theory has been upheld in several studies. The government of Guatemala, which has reduced penalties for nonpayment of taxes, is the Latin American country with the highest willingness to pay taxes, the highest tax morale.[43] In Costa Rica, research shows that imposition of penalties reduces tax morale, and the possibility of audits damages morale even more.[44] And in Germany, researchers conclude that it is factors other than deterrence that drive tax morale.[45] The conclusion is that tax morale is hurt—not helped—when the government uses its power to force compliance.

What helps tax morale is trust. The more taxpayers trust the government, the greater their rate of tax compliance. For example, in Russia, after the transition to a market economy, it was found that "trust seems to be a key determinant of tax morale."[46] (In the case of Russia, where only 24 percent of the taxes are actually collected, it is perhaps more accurate to say "*distrust* is a key determinant of the *lack* of tax morale.")

As we saw in Chapter 12, trust is built on perceived fairness. Taxpayers' trust in the government and the legal system is built on honesty and is destroyed by corruption. The greater the belief that government officials are corrupt, the lower the level of tax compliance.[47] This is demonstrated in Latin America, where the belief that government officials and tax collectors are corrupt has been found to significantly lower tax morale.[48]

In contrast, in Sweden, where taxes are nearly double what they are in the United States, people trust the government. As a result, 98.7 percent of billed taxes are collected,[49] and "Swedes don't complain."[50] They trust their government to act fairly, so they believe their taxes are fair.

In Sum . . .

Most Americans pay taxes because they think it fair to pay them. Paying taxes is fair because it is the social norm. It is the social norm because most Americans do pay them. Most Americans pay them because they think they are fair, and so on. This virtuous circle has led to the acceptance of federal income taxes in the United States.

The debate, however, will continue to rage as to which tax structure is most fair: whether it is one based on the norms of either equity or equality and how it should be adjusted for need. Any solution will favor one group over another, satisfying that group's own biased view of fairness but being unfair to the others.

In addition, Americans object to the complexity of the current tax code, which they cannot understand and think unfair. And they do not trust the government to spend tax dollars fairly. They question whether they are getting a fair return for their tax dollars.

Nonetheless, most Americans still do pay their fair share of taxes because that is the social norm. It is the fair thing to do. As the San Antonio *Business Journal* concludes: "Paying taxes is as American as disliking taxes."[51]

Definitions

Tax morale: Having an intrinsic motivation to pay taxes.

Use tax: Taxing the use of a product instead of the sale of it.

Regressive tax: A tax that has less impact as income increases, for example, a sales tax that is the same percentage for everyone, no matter how much income a person earns.

Progressive tax: A tax that has more impact as income increases, for example, the current income tax system where the percentage of tax increases when the income a person earns increases.

Flat tax: A tax where everyone pays the same percentage of income.

Fair tax: A tax based on a percentage of all sales; a tax on amount spent rather than the amount earned.

Consumption tax: Same as a "fair" tax.

Sin tax: Tax on items which are generally considered harmful to society or individuals.

Luxury tax: Tax on big-ticket nonessentials.

Crowding out: The replacement of internal, intrinsic motivation with external motivation.

CHAPTER

Culture

"BUT I NEVER ORDERED ANY BREAD!"

Two Americans, Bob and Carol, are visiting Spain for the first time. They have dinner in a charming little restaurant with wooden tables and checkered tablecloths. The bread is particularly delicious: hot, fresh, and crusty. When the bill comes, it is three euros more than they expect. They learn that they have been charged extra for the bread. "But," Bob complains, "I never ordered any bread!" "But," the waiter replies, "you ate it."

Americans are typically surprised when they are charged extra for bread in Spain—or for appetizers in Brazil or for condiments in Slovakia. We are equally surprised by the opposite: for example, ordering more beers than we actually drink in China but being charged for only what we consume. In all these cases, we are surprised because the social norm in the United States is to pay for what you order and *only* what you order. Anything served unordered is assumed to be free. That is fair in American culture. In Spain, fair is being charged for what you eat.

Although a concern for a fair price is universal,[1] the social norms of what counts as fair vary from society to society. The social norms are influenced by culture but not completely determined by it. As we saw in Chapter 4, norms tend to reflect cultural values, but they can also evolve by chance or be instituted by sellers. Consequently, even though two societies may have a similar culture, their norms can still be quite different. Because the fairness of a price is based

155

on following the social norms, what is considered fair also varies in different societies.

To understand how consumers' views of fair prices vary in different societies, my colleagues and I conducted focus groups in Brazil, Germany, India, and the United States.[2] Those countries were selected to represent differences in what cultural psychologist Harry Triandis called *cultural syndromes*. Triandis defines syndromes as patterns "characterized by shared beliefs, attitudes, norms, roles and values that are organized around a theme."[3] The two themes that have the greatest impact on the norms of pricing are what Dutch cross-cultural researcher Geert Hofstede[4] called individualism/collectivism and power distance.

Power distance refers to the acceptance of differences in power within a culture. It can be divided into large power distance in a *hierarchical culture* and small power distance in a *flat culture*. In hierarchical cultures like India and Brazil, inequalities between groups are accepted as the norm. In flatter cultures like the former West Germany and, to a lesser extent, the United States, inequalities are less acceptable.

Individualism or collectivism refers to whether people usually think of themselves as separate entities or as members of a group. Individualists define themselves in terms of the self, and collectivists define themselves in terms of the group to which they belong. The United States is considered the most individualist country in the world. Germany, at least the former West Germany, is also individualist, but not as fiercely individualist as the United States. In contrast, India is a collectivist country and Brazil is even more so.

Cultures that are collectivist tend also to be hierarchical, and cultures that are individualist tend also to be flat. (See Figure 18.1 comparing countries' cultural themes.) Whether a culture is individualist or collectivist and whether it is hierarchical or flat affects many aspects of what is considered a fair price.

Personal Fairness across Cultures

Not surprisingly, people in all cultures respond emotionally to a higher-than-expected price or a different-than-expected pricing practice. They are surprised and not pleased. But each culture has its own social norms describing what is expected, what is normal in that particular society. As explained earlier, the norms that describe what is considered "usual" are called the descriptive norms of pricing.

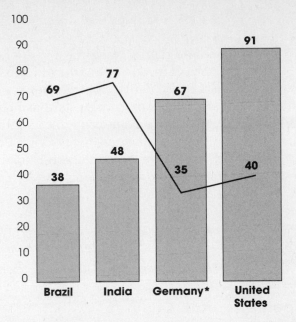

Hofstede's indexed ratings of four countries[5] on the cultural themes of

Individualism/Collectivism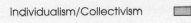

Power Distance (Hierarchy) ▬

*Note: Since Hofstede rated countries prior to the unification of Germany, the ratings are only for the former West Germany.

Figure 18.1   Comparison of Countries' Cultural Themes

Anyone who has traveled to a foreign country has experienced different descriptive norms of pricing:

- The high price of services in Germany.
- The low price of services in India.
- The free bicycles on the streets of Oslo.
- The refusal of tips in Chinese restaurants.
- The inclusion of taxes in European prices.
- The absence of coupons in Indian newspapers.
- The charge for grocery bags in German supermarkets.
- The haggling of prices in Morocco.
- The demand for "baksheesh" or tips in Egypt.

- The inclusion of breakfast at English hotels.
- The extra charge for bread in some European restaurants.

When consumers think that the descriptive norms have been violated—as when charged for bread you did not order—the Fair Price Model presented in Chapter 3 suggests that people feel distress and subsequent anger. This response appears to be universal. Around the world, perceived unfairness results in anger because it is unjust. An analysis of studies of Americans and Europeans found that after "relationships," unfairness in the sense of "injustice" was cited as the most common cause of anger.[6]

In all our focus groups, the participants expressed their anger when they thought that the social norms of pricing were being violated. They then wanted some justification for the violation of the norms.

Fair Outcomes across Cultures

In our focus groups, one universally accepted justification for an unexpected price or pricing action was equity. According to the norm of equity, a price should reflect the value of the product/service being purchased. If a price were increased by 20 percent, the focus groups all agreed that the value should be increased correspondingly in order for the price to remain fair.

Although the norm of equity appears to be universal, the norm of equality varies depending on whether the culture is hierarchical or flat. Hierarchical cultures prefer inequality where some people are treated differently because of their power, class, or status. For example, in the hierarchical country of India, it is considered fair to charge a higher price to the rich. As the Indian focus group participants explained, *"The shopkeeper will charge me higher prices because he knows that I can pay." "[The price] depends on the kind of clothes you are wearing, the purse you are holding, the kind of vehicle you have arrived in."*

In cultures that are collectivist, different norms apply to different groups of people. Collectivists form their identity based on their social group, what is called their *in-group*. This group is composed of extended family and close friends—people who are "just like me." In collectivist cultures, the norm is to be generous to members of one's in-group. They lend each other money and whatever is needed no matter what the other can give in return.[7]

In collectivist cultures, it is the norm to give better prices to those in the in-group. *"If you know a shopkeeper, then you go straight to him, knowing that you can get a heavy discount. A lot depends on a personalized discount." "The shopkeeper may give a discount not only to a permanent customer but to someone he is otherwise obliged to. He may be a relative or have some work with you."*

Unequal treatment of customers violates the social norm of equality found in flat, individualist cultures like the former West Germany. In cultures like those, the norm is to treat all customers the same. Although some preferential pricing may be given to family and friends, it is not as common as in collectivist and hierarchical cultures.

Because individualists believe in equal treatment of everyone, people in the United States and Germany respond more to the need of workers than do people in Brazil and India, which are collectivist. In the focus groups, the Germans condoned a price increase that was due to an increase of wages: *"A wage settlement would be perfectly understandable." "Wage settlements are a very good thing in Germany."*

Brazilians, however, were skeptical of price increases due to wage increases. *"Fair reason?" "I'd question justifications like that. It doesn't hold water. Too fuzzy."* (Their hesitance to give workers a wage increase is probably only partly due to their acceptance of inequality. No doubt it also stems from the Brazilians' great fear of inflation.)

As we have seen in Chapter 8, violations of social norms lead to blaming the person responsible. But different cultures cast blame in different directions. Collectivists tend to blame fate for both good and bad outcomes. Individualists, however, tend to take credit for anything good that happens and to blame others like the seller for anything bad that happens such as a price increase.

Fair Process across Cultures

The Fair Price Model of Chapter 3 indicates that if blame for a price is cast on the seller, the price setting procedures of the seller will then become a concern. These procedures are constrained by social norms. These norms give buyers some control, which is considered fair. When buyers anywhere feel they lack control, they cry "unfair."

For example, a Brazilian complained, *"That's totally unfair. You don't have a choice."* Another added, *"I get madder when I don't have any choice."*

Echoing this sentiment, an American participant exclaimed, *"You have no control and you're mad about it."*

However, although all people want some control, people in individualist cultures demand more control than those in collectivist cultures.[8] In addition, people in hierarchical cultures accept control from those in power, but people in flat cultures resent others having more power.

An example is Germany, an individualist and flat culture, where they reject any government control over price: *"The government in general is not allowed to set prices. It would not be a free market economy."*

By way of contrast, in Brazil, a collectivist and hierarchical culture, people are more accepting of government intervention (even though, as we will see, they distrust the government). Our Brazilian focus groups said that price increases are fair if *"the government decided on a surcharge." "Increases based on such contracts are fair. They may not seem fair to the consumer, but they are foreseen in the contract made with the government."*

And in India, our focus groups held the government primarily responsible for setting prices. *"The government should fix the prices of basic commodities." "We can't do anything about this [huge profit] until and unless the government works out these problems." "If because of the public demand some particular item is costly, they can create pressure on the government. The government can provide subsidies to lower the price of that item."*

As seen in Chapter 9, it is considered fair when sellers make their price setting procedures transparent. But consumers' demand for pricing transparency varies. The difference in their demands depends not on the culture but on the economy: whether it is a buyers' or a sellers' market. In the seller's market typical of developing countries, lack of transparency may be disliked but is still accepted as the norm. In Brazil, a focus group participant lamented, *"There's very little transparency in relation to investors or consumers. In more developed economies there are rules about the information passed on to people who are used to having these kinds of information."*

Reaction to Unfair Pricing across Cultures

Culture affects whether and how consumers punish infractions of social norms. The desire to punish norm violations is highest in the United States and lowest in Hong Kong, with Germany in between.[9] Westerners evidently find asserting one's rights to be an acceptable problem-solving behavior, whereas Asians do not. Complaining publicly can disrupt social harmony, which is counter to Asian collectivist ideals.

If a price is unfair, individualists tend to complain both privately to their friends and publicly to the company or over the web. Collectivists complain only privately by telling their in-group. But their word is so well respected within their in-group that they are very effective at convincing their friends to avoid an unfair company. A study showed that most Korean consumers (86 percent) told friends and most (56 percent) convinced them not to deal with an unfair company.[10] Even though most Americans (78 percent) also told friends not to deal with the company, only 35 percent were successful in convincing their friends not to do so.

Some researchers have suggested that public complaint behavior is associated with affluence rather than individualism/collectivism. For example, one group wrote that "positive attitudes towards complaining were found to be positively associated with the level of a country's economic development."[11]

Increased affluence may be the reason that the Brazilians, although collectivists, are becoming more vocal in their complaints: *"We have gotten less tolerant, more demanding about the quality of services." "If you don't act, don't switch, don't complain, the service company will always think that you are not price sensitive." "For sure I'd complain."*

However, why some cultures complain and others do not has yet to be understood. Both theories—that public complaining increases with either increased income or with greater individualism—suggest that consumers in both Germany and the United States would complain. But although complaining is the norm in the United States, it is not in Germany.[12]

In the four focus groups we held in Germany, all the participants agreed that they would not complain to the company, at least not in person. The participants said, *"I don't see that you could provoke any reaction." "I feel you only get on their nerves." "I know from others that some customers did complain and that the company was annoyed if there are always people calling and complaining."* Maybe, the Germans said, they would send a polite letter. But that was all.

Americans, however, are quick to complain publicly. They lodge complaints on IhateStarbucks.com and Fordsucks.com as well as with companies' well-staffed customer complaint departments. Although it is the social norm that unhappy customers should not complain publicly in Germany, complaining is the social norm in the United States and is becoming one in Brazil.

Other Effects of Culture

Culture affects trust, as explained in Chapter 12. And trust can lessen anger due to an unfair price or an unfair pricing practice. In collectivist countries, people tend to trust members of their in-group and distrust outsiders. They have what the prominent writer on trust, Francis Fukuyama, calls "low generalized social trust."[13] In individualist countries, people tend to trust all other people equally; they have "high generalized social trust."

For example, individualistic Germany is considered high in generalized trust.[14] This trust was apparent in focus groups where the participants exhibited great trust in the government. For example, one German said, *"I think we can be quite relaxed in Europe . . . because our laws and regulations are quite strict. If something like [a cartel] happens, the national and EU public authorities would be there right away and would check it . . . I personally would rely upon their evaluation."*

Collectivist Brazilians, however, appear to distrust both the government and business in general. As the focus group members told us, *"The problem is that when the government gets involved it seems that you are being duped." "You tend to think that the company is taking advantage of you right off the bat." "It's a conspiracy . . . everybody is against you." "They're lying!"*

Culture also affects what is considered a fair negotiation settlement. When buyers in the United States have power, a settlement favoring the buyer is considered fair. But in Japan, a more hierarchical society, the norm is that powerful buyers should take care of their less powerful opponents. Hence, a fair settlement is considered one favoring the seller.[15]

As for taxes, individualists like Americans believe in self-sufficiency and special treatment for those who have earned it. They therefore prefer the equity of a progressive tax such as the current federal income tax in the United States. Collectivists like eastern Europeans stress relationships within the group and prefer equality of treatment to foster harmony. They therefore want everyone to be charged an equal proportion of taxes, which may explain the success of a flat tax in many former communist countries.

Finally, the norms of tipping vary by culture. Tipping is generally more common in countries with a hierarchical culture; for example, in

Greece, Portugal, Turkey, and Brazil.[16] In those countries over 20 different professions are tipped. Compare this to a very flat culture like New Zealand, where only three professions are tipped. However, even though United States is not a hierarchical country, it has the highest number of professions that are tipped. This demonstrates that culture may influence but does not totally determine the social norms.

In Sum . . .

The Fair Price Model of Chapter 3 applies in general across cultures, but there are differences in what social norms of pricing have evolved and how people punish violations of those norms. Some of the differences can be explained by differences in the cultural themes of individualism/collectivism and hierarchical/flat.

But no culture is a pure example of these themes: all cultures represent paradoxical combinations. Even though people in the United States are highly individualist, they are also good team players.

In addition, although some norms may reflect the culture of the society, other norms have evolved by chance or decree. Consequently, there is no neat and tidy way to explain all the different norms of pricing in different societies. They simply have to be recognized and accepted.

So you may not have ordered that bread in the European restaurant, but if you take just one little bite, you will be charged extra. That is the norm. And that is fair.

Definitions

Culture: The values, beliefs, and attitudes of a society; what has been called "the software of the mind."[17]

Cultural syndrome: The shared beliefs and values of a society that constitute a theme that differentiates that society from others.

Power distance: The extent to which a culture accepts preferential treatment of some groups based on their power.

Hierarchical culture: Culture in which differences in power and status are accepted; where the norm is that individuals with more power should be granted special privileges.

(Continued)

Flat culture: Culture in which differences in power and status are less accepted; where the norm is that all people should be treated equally.

Individualist culture: Culture in which people take their identity from their own individual accomplishments.

Collectivist culture: Culture in which people take their identity from the group in which they belong.

In-group: The group of similar individuals—extended family and close friends—in a collectivist society.

A Fair Price Utopia Gone Wrong

Once upon a time there was a fair price utopia. In it, prices were set according to a theory of fair pricing. The price was based on the average product cost of all firms plus a standard percentage markup. Even if the costs of production for an identical good varied, the price was kept uniform for the customer. Although prices responded dynamically to changing average costs of production, this dynamism was tempered to maintain price stability. There were no unpleasant surprises. Buyers were supposed to enjoy complete transparency and control: by law, they could review the producer's accounting and participate in determining the price. And the prices of basic staples like bread were subsidized to help the needy.[18]

Beginning to sound familiar? That is because this utopia was the pricing system of the former United Soviet Socialist Republic. It was a pricing system designed to be fair. So what went wrong?

It might have been fair in theory, but not in actuality. Prices did not reflect the value as perceived by the consumer. The determination of value was done by overblown governmental departments based on complex calculations of cost and profit plus distribution costs, as well as consumption value and utility. Consumers had no idea how prices were actually determined. Supply did not respond to demand. Consumer goods were always in short supply no matter how strong the demand.

The system was imposed from above so that consumers had no voice. They consequently felt no compunction about flouting it. The black market flourished. Although in theory all consumers paid the same price, in actuality they did not.

The pricing system was inequitable, unequal, uncontrollable and opaque. The prices were wrong—and that's not fair.

Practices

"SO HOW IS A COMPANY SUPPOSED TO PRICE FAIRLY?"

I f you are a manager, you want your customers to think your price is fair so they will buy your product. That is obvious. But how you price fairly is not so obvious. It is particularly difficult because there can be fair and unfair aspects to many of the basic pricing strategies.

According to pricing textbooks, there are three basic strategies: the "three C's" of pricing. These are *competitive-based*, *cost-based*, and *customer-based* pricing. To these, add a fourth "C" for *custom-based* pricing, the traditional method used in an industry. (See Table 19.1 for examples of fair/unfair pricing strategies.) These strategies are fair when they follow the norms of personal and social fairness.

Custom-Based Pricing

Let us start with custom-based pricing, because this is easiest. Custom-based pricing is the traditional pricing system used in an industry. It is the pricing system that most sellers follow. It may have one of the other three C's as a basis, but will have aspects unique to that industry.

Custom-based pricing is personally fair to buyers because it adheres to the descriptive norms of what is normal. It is what buyers expect. Buyers expect rebates with electronics, price tags in department stores, and the weird nine-tenths of a cent added onto gasoline prices. They expect quantity discounts on bigger boxes of soap flakes.

Table 19.1. Examples of Fair/Unfair Pricing Strategies

Industry	Pricing Method	Fairness Belief	Perceived Adherence to Social Norms
	Custom-Based		
Clothing store	Posting price on tag	Personally fair	Adheres to descriptive norms
Flea market	Haggling to set price	Personally fair	Adheres to descriptive norms
Law office	Bundling cost of elevator into price of office visit	Personally fair	Adheres to descriptive norms
Street entertainment	Passing hat after performance	Personally fair	Adheres to descriptive norms
	Competitive-Based		
Office supplies	Offering to match any competitor's lower price	Personally fair	Follows norm of competitive pricing
Electronics	Lowering price over time	Personally fair	Follows norm of lowering price due to demand
Shoes	Maintaining price over time by finding cheaper suppliers	Personally fair	Conforms to social norm of status quo
	Cost-Based		
Auto repair	Charging for parts plus standard hourly rate for labor	Socially fair	Adheres to social norm of equity: "get" equals "give"
Convenience store	Adding markups to cost of item	Socially fair	Adheres to social norm of equity: "get" equals "give"
Gasoline	Basing price on affluence of community	Socially unfair	Violates social norms of equality
Pharmaceuticals	Basing price on costs plus share of all research and development	Socially unfair	Violates social norms of equity and need

Industry	Pricing Method	Fairness Belief	Perceived Adherence to Social Norms
		Customer-Based	
Airlines	Basing price on fluctuations in consumer demand	Socially unfair	Violates social norms of status quo, transparency, equality, and need
Laundries	Charging less for washing men's shirts than women's	Socially unfair	Violates social norm of equality: same price for all
Fine art	Auctioning off paintings	Socially fair	Conforms to social norm of giving customer voice
Industrial parts	Basing price on customers' perceived value	Socially fair	Adheres to norm of equity: "get" equals "give"

They expect all flavors of yogurt to be the same price. They expect to negotiate the price of a car and to have fixed prices for cosmetics.

Consumers do not think about the fairness of custom-based pricing until a descriptive norm is violated, when a price is unexpected. That is when people judge it unfair: unfair to charge for riding an elevator, unfair to haggle over department store prices, and unfair to auction off a much sought after doll since dolls are usually sold at a fixed price.[1]

Competitive-Based Pricing

Like custom-based pricing, competitive-based pricing (or market-based pricing) is also considered fair. It is fair because competition is basic to our free market economic system. Competition forces sellers to charge as low a price as they can to beat the opposition. Consumers consider this personally fair.

In contrast, it is unfair when competitors collude to keep prices high. Competitors may do this quite legally, without actually talking to each other. They may simply not undercut each other's prices. For example, grocery store prices in Finland used to be higher than elsewhere in Europe because all the companies kept prices high. Then, after Finland joined the European Union, the German discounter chain Lidl entered the country and prices plummeted. Now Finland has grocery store prices that are highly competitive and very fair.[2]

The opposite of competitive pricing is monopoly pricing, which is considered basically wrong. Monopolies reduce choice, which is unfair to the consumer. Monopolists can exploit their market power and take advantage of the consumer, which makes the price even more unfair.

Consumers also object to the near monopoly powers of cartels like OPEC, which can influence gasoline prices. And they resent the power created by the consolidation of credit card companies, for example, the acquisition of the credit card company MBNA by Bank of America. As a result of mergers, some credit card companies are now in a position to change the terms on contracts with only 15 days' notice.[3] They can impose fees for foreign currency conversions. And they can condemn consumers as poor credit risks if the consumer happens to be late paying any other creditor. These pricing actions are clearly unfair.

Cost-Based Pricing

Cost-based pricing (or "cost-plus") is sometimes considered fair and sometimes not. It is commonly considered fair[4] because it conforms to social norms: it is thought to be equitable, equal to all, and easy to understand. But it can also be unfair when the costs are not legitimate or transparent.

Cost-plus pricing is based on the cost of labor and supplies plus some extra to compensate sellers for their time, effort, and risk. It is what economist Adam Smith considered the just price based on the "toil and trouble" required in the production of the good.[5] Cost-plus is thought to be equitable because it reflects the seller's own costs, which is taken as an indicator of the good's true value.

Sellers have recognized that consumers accept cost-based pricing and commonly use it to justify their prices. The bookseller Barnes and Noble, for example, published a folder explaining why textbooks cost so much. The reason given was that "like every college bookstore across the country—and indeed like every retailer—our cost determines our price."[6]

When companies want to increase prices, they frequently cite increased supply costs as the justification. They blame the increase on uncontrollable external factors. They defend their actions by saying, "I didn't want to raise my prices, but I had no alternative!"

Companies sometimes take advantage of the public's belief in the fairness of cost-based pricing. They do this by raising prices when costs go up but not lowering prices when costs go down. The coffee industry provides an example. Retail coffee prices have historically been increased when the cost of green coffee increased. But when green coffee prices go down, the retail price does not necessarily follow.

Take what happened to coffee prices after the International Coffee Agreement ended. Until 1989, a cartel of coffee-growing countries had worked together to keep the price of coffee high. But when their agreement fell apart, the price of green-bean coffee plunged from a 24-month average of $1.14 to $.82, a 42 percent drop. The retail price of roasted coffee, however, went from $2.93 down to $2.82, a drop of only 4 percent.[7] American consumers did not complain because they evidently believed that roasted coffee prices were based on green-bean costs.

Cost-based pricing is also unfair when it is inequitable. The price may not reflect what the good is really worth because the costs can include debatable charges. Take, for example, the allocation of overhead costs.[8]

The pharmaceutical industry claims that one of the reasons that medicine is so expensive is the cost of research and development (R&D). But which R&D costs should be allocated to any one medicine? Only the R&D that went into that particular pill? That is what buyers think would be fair.

But the pharmaceutical companies think it fair that each medication should include a proportion of all the R&D costs, much of which never results in a successful medicine. How else can companies recoup these costs? So the fairness of overhead allocations is a matter of debate.

The cost part of cost-plus prices also includes executive pay, which has recently increased to new heights. A prime example is the president of ExxonMobil, who is paid $144,573 a day.[9] Consumers think such compensation is unfairly high. According to a Bloomberg poll in 2006, 81 percent of Americans think that executives are paid too much.[10] A majority of company directors, the very ones who set executive compensation, also think executive pay is excessive.[11]

Now that the Securities and Exchange Commission has approved new disclosure rules, the total compensation of top executives has become public knowledge. According to a study by Mercer Human Resource Consulting for the *Wall Street Journal*, the median total direct compensation in 2006 was $6.5 million.[12] This indicates a huge gulf between the top executive and the average worker. Such a disparity naturally causes additional debate.

One side claims that the pay is equitable due to the extraordinary work required of executives; the other side insists it is inequitable since executives' pay is not connected to their performance. A gross example of such inequity is the Home Depot chief who left the ailing company with a "pay for failure package" worth more than $210 million.[13]

In addition to costs, the fairness of the "plus" part of cost-plus pricing is also of concern. Where does it go? Obviously, one part goes to profit. As we saw in Chapter 12, customers condone profits as long as the company is acting fairly. But when the company is suspected of unfair actions, then profits are scrutinized for fairness.

But what constitutes a "fair" profit?

According to the norm of equity, a fair profit is one that reflects the extra benefit provided by the company—the services, quality control, innovation, and so on. Does an 86 percent profit margin on Microsoft Windows reflect the extra benefit provided by Microsoft? Many consumers think it does not.[14] Or is the record-making $39.5 billion made by ExxonMobil in 2006 equitable?[15]

In its defense, ExxonMobil points out that their 8.2 percent profit is less than the 18.6 percent profit in pharmaceuticals and 18 percent profit in banking.[16] But 70 percent of Americans already think that pharmaceutical company profits are too high.[17] And "too high" profits—however that term is defined—imply a "too high" price for the consumer. And too high prices are deemed unfair.

Cost-plus pricing can also violate social norms when the costs are opaque: consumers cannot understand them.[18] In the case of airlines, some customers still seem to think they should be priced according to cost. They figure logically that it must cost more to fly a plane from New York to San Francisco than from New York to Indianapolis. Hence, it makes sense for the airfare to be higher for flying to San Francisco. When consumers find that airfare can actually be higher for flying to Indianapolis, they judge it unfair.

Customer-Based Pricing

The final "C" of the "four C's" of pricing is the most controversial. This is customer-based pricing (including variations called "value-based," "demand-based," and "variable" or "dynamic pricing"). Customer-based pricing reflects the consumer's perceived value of the product or the service. When perceived value increases, demand should increase. According to the economists' idea of supply and demand, prices should then increase, assuming supply remains the same.

Basing a price on customer demand, the economists tell us, "makes certain that money is not left on the table." The problem is that customer-based pricing can be seen as fair or not fair depending on which norm is evoked: equity or need. Demand can be based on either perceived value, which is equitable, or perceived need, which is unfair.

When a price is based on the value perceived by customers, that is fair. Value-based pricing meets the norm of equity. What customers get is equivalent to what they pay.

Value-based pricing can have a huge impact on profits. Changing prices from strictly cost-based to value-based resulted in the Parker Hannifin Corporation's increasing net income from $130 million in 2002 to $673 million in 2006.[19] When the change resulted in a price higher than customers' reference price, they initially balked. But when the value of the item was explained, they accepted the price as fair.

However, although customer-based pricing can be considered fair if customers think it is based on value, it can be considered unfair if they think it is based on need. Taking advantage of need is not fair.[20]

Consider what happened to Coca-Cola when they introduced Coke vending machines that would charge higher prices in the summer due to increased demand. Consumers did not think about the greater value of Coke in hot weather; they just thought the company was taking advantage of their greater need for Coke in the summer. The public backlash was so vehement that the company had to quash the entire project.[21]

To guard against a potential backlash, many businesses do not increase prices based on demand. Theaters have traditionally not charged more for popular plays. Restaurants have not increased prices on weekends. Sports teams have set a price at the beginning of the season and have not changed it, even if their team was winning and the demand for tickets skyrocketed. Steve Jobs insisted on pricing all iTunes at $.99 rather than charging more for performances that were more popular.

Airlines, however, are well known for increasing prices due to demand, and they have spawned an enthusiastic new following. It has become popular for pricing strategists to recommend customer-based pricing, or what in the case of the airlines is called yield pricing.

For example, movie theaters are now contemplating lower ticket prices on low-attendance days.[22] iTunes is being pushed by the music industry to shift to demand-based pricing. The argument is that it is "the basic rule of economics: charge a higher price for artists in greater demand, while charging less for artists in scant demand."[23] That may be the basic rule of economics, and it may conform to the norm of equity, but it violates the norm of need.

In fact, based on need, what consumers believe is fair is for prices to *decrease* when demand for a needed product increases. And at least grocery stores respond to that belief. According to an economics study, grocery stores actually *reduce* the price of tuna during Lent, cut the price of cheese and crackers at Thanksgiving, and offer beer at a lower price in the summer.[24] Consumers think that is fair.

Part of the problem is how "need" is defined. Do customers think they "need" tuna during Lent or "need" beer for Independence Day? I suspect they think they do. They are like my students who tell me they "need" a cell phone, whereas I think it is a luxury. And, based on need, consumers think a price should be lower.

Consumers are particularly hostile to customer-based pricing when need is a matter of life and death, for example, the urgent demand of hurricane victims for water or of patients for medication. In defense of the pharmaceutical companies, health care economist Alan Garber said, "It would be unfair to portray them as greedy or irresponsible if they charge what they can get."[25] But from the consumers' viewpoint, charging as much as customers will pay when they are desperate is taking advantage of demand based on need. That is unfair.

Supporting consumers' belief that prices should be lower due to demand is the idea of economies of scale. Consumers appear to think that greater demand will force greater supply, thereby lowering the cost per item. This is often the case in the electronics industry. The great interest in big-screen televisions has meant that their prices have been cut in half. The tremendous demand for the iPod is expected to bring its price down. That is thought to be fair.

Customer-based prices are also fair when the customers—not the sellers—set the price. The customer then has voice. Examples are negotiations, as discussed in Chapter 16, and auctions.

In auctions, consumers have full control over the price they pay. Each bidder has a different objective and may have only partial information, but together they settle on a price through their collective actions. In a recent study, 83 percent of the respondents attributed the outcomes of auctions to their own actions.[26]

An auction price is equitable in that it represents a consensus as to the "true" value of an item. Each person has a voice in determining that value, and that is fair.

As sociologist Charles Smith writes, "To many people, including most economists, the idea that auctions function to establish a 'fair' price is incontrovertible."[27] He tells the story of a museum director who was forced to auction some paintings even though he felt certain he could get a higher price in a private sale. But the donors of the art considered an auction price fairer.

With the advent of eBay, auctions have become increasingly popular, and even very high prices are accepted as fair. For example, Diana Duyser sold her 10-year-old pizza slice with a burn mark resembling the Virgin Mary on eBay for $28,000.[28] Although exorbitant, the price was fair because all bidders had equal opportunity to estimate the value of the unusual pizza slice.

Auctions are now being extended into new areas. Tickets to superstar tours are now being auctioned by Ticketmaster. The result is that tickets with a face value of $350 are being sold at $400 to $500. Although more than the face value, these prices are less than what the scalpers are asking. A Ticketmaster executive calls the online bidding "a market solution to an industry problem. It makes it a much more level playing field."[29] That is thought to be fair because it is the buyers, not the sellers, who are setting the price.

Auctions, however, are not necessarily fair. They are not, for example, a fair way to set the price of medicine. A company called Pharmabid established a web site in 1999 where physicians and hospitals could bid for drugs, blood products, and medical supplies. When I checked recently, the site was no longer up. Auctioning medicine is considered unfair because it takes advantage of a need.

Auctions also do not necessarily establish a fair and equitable price. A notorious example is Google that auctioned off shares in its initial public offering (IPO). The goal was to be fair and transparent, to establish a realistic price for the stock and raise the maximum amount of money. The result was not as planned. The company expected a price between $108 and $135. The actual closing price was $85, but immediately after the close of the auction the price of the stock rose 18 percent to $100.34.[30] The company did not get a fair price.

Auctions can result in not only unfairly low but also unfairly high prices. The *winner's curse* refers to the unfairness of the winning bid's being actually *more* than the value placed on the good by anyone else. Such a price is higher than the consensual evaluation of value. In recognition of this problem, some auctions sell the item to the highest bidder at the penultimate price, the price that at least one other bidder was willing to pay.

Another concern in auctions is that sellers do not always disclose full information. This is evident in horse trading. Traditionally, "it was considered perfectly fair for sellers to do all sorts of things to make their horses look better and sounder."[31] Such practices, however, were in the past curbed by the sellers' need to protect their reputation within the small group of horse traders. Today, however, there are many new buyers and sellers in the market. So the industry has had to introduce a code of ethics allowing sellers to return a horse bought at auction under unfair conditions.[32]

Clearly unfair—and illegal—was the price fixing by Christie's and Sotheby's auction houses. For years, they coordinated fees to sellers, including an agreement as to which customers would be charged low fees or no fees at all.[33] They thereby violated the social norm of equality, which says that all customers should be treated the same. As a result, the auction houses have had to pay $512 million in compensation to customers who had been treated unfairly.[34]

Other Pricing Strategies

In addition to the basic "four C's" of pricing, other pricing tactics are also fair or unfair depending on whether they meet the social norms of fairness. One such practice is *buffer pricing*, where the seller absorbs small price increases and decreases.[35] It is fair because the price meets the norm of consistency.

Another tactic is *buffet pricing* used in popular "all-you-can-eat" Chinese restaurants, where unlimited quantities are available at a predetermined price. Customers find this fair because they can assure themselves of an equitable exchange by taking more or less of what is offered. By the same token, set-price stores such as Dollar Stores are fair because customers can determine for themselves what is equitable: customers can control whether the value of what they get is equivalent to a dollar.

Bundling, where two products are sold together, is personally fair when it results in a lower price but socially unfair when it gives a company an unfair advantage. This is the case of "tying" products: of making the sale of one item "tied" to the sale of a second item. The classic example is when customers of Kodak could buy replacement parts for their Kodak equipment only when they also hired Kodak to make the repairs.[36] Such coercion is not only unfair but also illegal.

Unbundling, where products previously sold as a bundle are then sold separately, can also be either fair or unfair. It is fair because it is equitable. When the English airlines Flybe and Ryanair started charging for checked baggage, they explained that it was a fair deal because "passengers unburdened by bags will no longer have to pay toward carrying other people's suitcases."[37] So everyone paid for only the service they received and no one subsidized what others received.

But unbundling is not fair when it is an unpleasant surprise. For instance, in the past, any luggage was included in the airfare. But now British Airways is charging £120 [$240] extra for overweight bags. This is unfair because it is unexpected.[38]

Unbundling also makes it difficult for consumers to compare prices because they cannot judge apples to apples. Some stores charge an extra fee for restocking; some do not. Some web sites charge for shipping and handling; some do not. The price violates the norm of transparency. That is not fair.

Maintaining a Fair Price Reputation

To combat accusations of unfair prices, all a company needs to do is—obviously—to price fairly, which means not violating the social norms. (See "So How Is a Company Supposed to Price Fairly?" on page 178.) It is, however, sometimes difficult to follow these rules because of conflicting claims on fairness.

Stockholders demand a fair return. Employees demand a fair wage. Suppliers require a fair profit. So the price cannot be determined solely on the basis of what consumers think is fair. A company has to strike a balance of what is fair to everyone involved.

If a company does not get the fair price balance right, then customers boycott. Or employees strike. Or investors pull out. Or suppliers quit. Or all of the above.

But when a company does get the balance right, their reputation is burnished.

A case in point is Johnson & Johnson, which for seven straight years was ranked number one out of the 60 most visible companies in the Annual Reputation Quotient® RQ^{SM} survey conducted by Harris Interactive.[39] The reputation of Johnson & Johnson is partly based on their baby products and partly based on their handling of the Tylenol scare in 1982. At that time, some crazy person laced Tylenol capsules with cyanide. Seven people died. Johnson & Johnson recalled more than 31 million bottles, which cost the company over $100 million.[40]

It appears that consumers respond to clear evidence that a price is based not just on greed, that a company has a concern for the welfare of their customers. Since Johnson & Johnson was willing to forfeit profits to benefit the customer, consumers developed trust in the benevolence of the company. As a result, although the price fairness of other pharmaceutical companies is often questioned in the press, Johnson & Johnson is conspicuous for its absence.

This year, however, Johnson & Johnson was beaten in the RQ^{SM} survey by Microsoft.[41] In the past, the profit margins of Microsoft have been called unfair, bringing into question the fairness of their price. But the generosity of the Gates Foundation has demonstrated that the company is not motivated by greed. The company's reputation has consequently soared.

Researchers have established that a good reputation counters suspicions of price unfairness: when companies have a reputation of fairness, they are given the benefit of the doubt when they increase prices.[42] The opposite, however, also holds. Evidence from the RQ^{SM} Survey suggests that when customers think that a company prices unfairly, the company's reputation suffers. For example, three oil companies that have high prices and record profits are among the lowest 10 companies in reputation.

A reputation, however, is not built on just a low price. In the RQ^{SM} Survey, Starbucks, with its high prices, is ranked as number 28 in reputation but Wal-Mart, with its low prices, is ranked as number 40. Wal-Mart ranks low despite its massive public relations campaign. This has been a lesson to other companies. What companies are learning is that deeds—like those of Johnson & Johnson and Microsoft—count more than words.

In particular, pharmaceutical companies like Novartis are demonstrating with deeds that they are good corporate citizens. They have instituted programs to make medications available to people who need them but cannot afford them. They are providing free tuberculosis and leprosy treatment in the developing world.[43]

Evidence that the programs of the pharmaceutical companies are having a positive impact is shown by the significant increase in the reputation of Merck between 2005 and 2006: in the RQ^{SM} Survey, the company's ranking increased from number 45 to number 39. The increase reflects the $540 million that Merck contributed in 2004 to patient assistance, making it the second highest contributor to charity, next only to the Gates Foundation.[44]

In addition to good deeds, companies need to show clearly that they are adhering to the social norms of pricing. They need to make their pricing policies transparent. They need to explain when the price is unavoidable due to external circumstances. They need to train their customer service representatives to give the reasons behind the price, to demonstrate the value that customers are receiving for what they are giving up. And companies need to inform their own employees.

As an example, I have a friend in Borneo who runs a small inn. When he wants to increase prices, he has a meeting of his entire staff to discuss the proposed price increases. Everyone then understands the reasons and can present the new price to customers with confidence. The entire organization takes pride in its price.

In Sum . . .

The basic "four C's" of pricing strategy are custom-based, competitive-based, cost-based, and customer-based. Customers think both custom-based and competitive-based pricing are personally fair. They consider custom-based pricing as fair because it follows the descriptive norms that have been established as the tradition. And they accept competitive-based pricing as fair because it results in the lowest possible price. But they judge cost-based and customer-based pricing as being either socially fair or socially unfair depending on the circumstances.

If the seller follows the social norms, the price is fair. It is fair to charge the normal price and to make the normal profit. But it is unfair to be greedy. It is fair to make an equitable exchange. But it is unfair to take advantage of the customer.

If companies violate the social norms, consumers will think the price is wrong. They will not pay it—and may even boycott and rebel. That is the price companies pay for pricing unfairly.

Definitions

Competitive-based pricing: Basing price on competitors' prices (also called *market-based pricing*).

Cost-based pricing: Basing price on costs plus profit (also called *cost-plus pricing*).

Customer-based pricing: Basing price on what a customer is willing to pay (also called *demand-based, value-based, dynamic,* or *yield pricing*).

Custom-based pricing: Basing price on what is traditional in an industry.

Winner's curse: When the successful bidder in an auction has to pay more than any other person was willing to pay.

Buffer pricing: When the seller maintains the same price despite small cost variations.

Buffet pricing: When seller charges a flat price for unlimited use of a product.

Bundling: When more than one item is included in a price.

Unbundling: When items previously included in a price are sold separately.

So how is a company supposed to price fairly?

By not violating the social norms of fair pricing!

1. The price should be kept relatively stable over time.
2. The price should be set according to industry tradition.
3. The price should be based on uncontrollable, external forces.
4. The price should reflect the true worth of the good.
5. The price should be determined by unbiased methods.
6. The same price should be charged to everyone, but adjusted for the needy.
7. The method for setting prices should be transparent.
8. The customer should be given a voice in setting the price.
9. The price should be based on the cost of supplies and labor plus reasonable profit.
10. The price should match or beat competition.

Notes

Chapter 1

1. Elizabeth Douglass and Gary Cohn, "Zones of Contention in Gasoline Pricing," *Los Angeles Times*, June 19, 2005, www.latimes.com.
2. Liz Fedor, "Airlines Might Be Ready to Close Fare Gap," *Minneapolis Star Tribune*, January 4, 2005, www.startribune.com.
3. Franklin Paul, "Kodak Launches Printer to Compete with HP, Others," *Washington Post*, February 6, 2007, www.washingtonpost.com.
4. Anne Broache, "Supreme Court Rules in Printer Ink Dispute," March 1, 2006, news.com.com.
5. "Kodak's New Battle Plan: Cheap Printer Ink," February 6, 2007, www.techdirt.com.
6. Franklin Paul, "Kodak Launches Printer to Compete with HP, Others," February 6, 2007.
7. Ruaridh Nicoll, "Electricity Cut-Off Sparks South African Township Riot," *The Guardian*, August 8, 1997.
8. Anita Ramasastry, "Websites that Charge Different Customers Different Prices," *FindLaw's Legal Commentary*, 2005, www.writ.findlaw.com.
9. Lisa E. Bolton, Luk Warlop, and Joseph Alba, "Consumer Perceptions of Price (Un)Fairness," *Journal of Consumer Research* 29 (March 2003): 474–491.
10. Peter R. Darke and Darren W. Dahl, "Fairness and Discounts: The Subjective Value of a Bargain," *Journal of Consumer Psychology* 13, no. 3 (2003): 328–338, 334.
11. Sarah R. Brosnan and Frans B. M. de Waal, "Monkeys Reject Unequal Pay," *Nature* 425 (2003): 297–299.
12. "Animal Behavior, Fair and Square," *The Economist*, September 20, 2003: 77.
13. Antonio Damasio, *Descartes' Error: Emotion, Reason and the Human Brain* (London: Penguin Books, 1994).

Chapter 2

1. Diana Wood, *Medieval Economic Thought* (Cambridge: Cambridge University Press, 2002): 114.
2. Ibid., p. 12.
3. Ibid., p. 79.

4. Joel Kaye, *Economy and Nature in the Fourteenth Century: Money, Market Exchange, and the Emergence of Scientific Thought* (Cambridge: Cambridge University Press, 1998): 7.

5. Ibid., 3.

6. Wood, 2002, p. 11.

7. Richard E. Rubenstein, *Aristotle's Children* (Orlando, FL: Harcourt, 2004): 184.

8. Aristotle, *The Nicomachean Ethics*, ed. and trans. David Ross (Oxford: Oxford University Press, 1998): 1133a.

9. Ibid.

10. Ibid.

11. Wood, 2002, p. 137.

12. Walter Nicholson, *Microeconomic Theory: Basic Principles and Extensions*, 3rd ed. (New York: The Dryden Press, 1985): 13.

13. Thomas Aquinas, *Commentary on Nicomachean Ethics*, vol. 2, trans., C. I. Litzinger (Chicago: Henry Regnery, 1964).

14. John Baldwin, *The Medieval Theories of the Just Price: Romanists, Canonists and Theologians in the Twelfth and Thirteenth Centuries* (Philadelphia: Transactions of the American Philosophical Society, 1959), n.s. 49, pt. 4.

15. Thomas Aquinas, *Summa Theologica*, 2a2ae, Question 77, Article 3.

16. Marjorie Grice-Hutchinson, *The School of Salamanca: Readings in Spanish Monetary Theory* (Oxford: Clarendon Press, 1952): 27.

17. Alejandro A. Chafuen, *Faith and Liberty: The Economic Thought of the Late Scholastics* (Lanham, MD: Lexington Books, 2003): 114.

18. Wood, 2002, p. 137.

19. Raymond De Roover, "The Concept of the Just Price: Theory and Economic Policy," *Journal of Economic History* 18 (December 1958): 422–438, 424.

20. Wood, 2002, p. 143.

21. Ibid., p. 139.

22. Sally Blount, "Whoever Said that Markets Were Fair?" *Negotiation Journal* 16, no. 3 (2000): 237–252.

23. Daniel Kahneman, Jack L. Knetsch, and Richard H. Thaler, "Fairness and the Assumptions of Economics," *Journal of Business* 59, no. 4 (1986): S285–S300; Daniel Kahneman, Jack L. Knetsch, and Richard H. Thaler, "Fairness as a Constraint on Profit Seeking: Entitlements in the Market," *American Economic Review* 76 (September 1986): 728–741.

24. David Herlihy, "The Concept of the Just Price: Discussion," *Journal of Economic History* 18 (December 1958): 437–438.

Chapter 3

1. Christel Rutte and David Messick, "An Integrated Model of Perceived Unfairness in Organizations," *Social Justice Research* 8, no. 3 (1995): 239–261.

2. Leon Festinger, *A Theory of Cognitive Dissonance* (Stanford: Stanford University Press, 1957).

3. Ibid.

4. Sarah Maxwell, "Rule-Based Price Fairness and Its Effect on Willingness to Purchase," *Journal of Economic Psychology* 23, no. 2 (2002): 193–212.
5. George C. Homans, *Social Behavior: Its Elementary Forms* (New York: Harcourt Brace, 1961); J. Stacy Adams, "Toward an Understanding of Inequity," *Journal of Abnormal and Social Psychology* 67 (1963): 422–436; Peter Blau, *Exchange and Power in Social Life* (New York: Wiley, 1967).
6. John W. Thibaut and Harold H. Kelley, *The Social Psychology of Groups* (New York: Wiley, 1959); John W. Thibaut and Laurens Walker, *Procedural Justice: A Psychological Analysis* (Hillsdale, NJ: Erlbaum, 1975).
7. Alvin W. Gouldner, "The Norm of Reciprocity: A Preliminary Statement," *American Sociological Review* 25, no. 2 (1960): 161–178.
8. Richard Oliver and John E. Swan, "Consumer Perceptions of Interpersonal Equity and Satisfaction in Transactions: A Field Survey Approach," *Journal of Marketing* 53 (April 1989): 21–35; Richard Oliver and John E. Swan, "Equity and Disconfirmation Perceptions as Influences on Merchant and Product Satisfaction," *Journal of Consumer Research*, 16 (December 1989): 372–383.
9. J. Stacy Adams, "Toward an Understanding of Inequity," *Journal of Abnormal Social Psychology*, 67 (1963): 422–436.
10. Joel E. Urbany, Thomas J. Madden, and Peter R. Dickson, "All's Not Fair in Pricing: An Initial Look at the Dual Entitlement Principle," *Marketing Letters* 1, no. 1 (1989): 17–25.
11. Margaret Campbell, "Perceptions of Price Fairness: Antecedents and Consequences," *Journal of Marketing Research* 36 (May 1999): 187–199.

Chapter 4

1. Robert B. Cialdini and Raymond R. Reno, "A Focus Theory of Normative Conduct: A Theoretical Refinement and Reevaluation of the Role of Norms in Human Behavior," *Advances in Experimental Social Psychology* 24 (1990): 240–248.
2. Robert Axelrod, "An Evolutionary Approach to Norms," *American Political Science Review* 80 (1986): 1095–1111.
3. Émile Durkheim, *The Division of Labor in Society*, trans., George Simpson (Glencoe, IL: Free Press, 1933 [1893]).
4. Guillermina Jasso, "Rule Finding about Rule Making: Comparison Processes and the Making of Rules," in Michael Hechter and Karl-Dieter Opp (eds.), *Social Norms* (New York: Russell Sage Foundation, 2001): 348–393.
5. Ragnar Rommetveit, *Social Norms and Roles* (Minneapolis: University of Minnesota Press, 1954).
6. For similar ideas but from a different angle, see James Surowiecki, *The Wisdom of Crowds* (New York: Anchor Books, 2005).
7. E. Allan Lind and Tom R. Tyler, *The Social Psychology of Procedural Justice* (New York: Plenum, 1988); Tom R. Tyler and E. Allan, "A Relational Model of Authority in Groups," in M. Zanna (ed.), *Advances in Experimental Social Psychology*, vol. 25, (San Diego: Academic Press, 1992): 115–191.
8. Douglass C. North, *Institutions, Institutional Change and Economic Performance* (Cambridge: Cambridge University Press, 1990): 6.

9. See, e.g., Daniel Kahneman, Jack L. Knetsch, and Richard H. Thaler, "Fairness as a Constraint on Profit Seeking: Entitlements in the Market," *American Economic Review* 76 (September 1986): 728–741.
10. See, e.g., Hechter and Opp (eds.), 2001.
11. See, e.g., Christina Bicchieri, *The Grammar of Society: The Nature and Dynamics of Social Norms* (Cambridge: Cambridge University Press, 2006).
12. See, e.g., Robert C. Ellickson, *Order without Law: How Neighbors Settle Disputes* (Cambridge: Harvard University Press, 1991).
13. See, e.g., Jan B. Heide and George John, "Do Norms Matter in Marketing Relationships?" *Journal of Marketing* 56 (April 1992): 32–44.
14. See, e.g., Gary Goertz and Paul F. Diehl, "Toward a Theory of International Norms," *Journal of Conflict Resolution* 36 (December 1992): 634–664.
15. Oliver Williamson, *The Economic Institutions of Capitalism: Firms, Markets, Relational Contracting* (New York: Free Press, 1975).
16. Dale T. Miller, "The Norm of Self Interest," *American Psychologist* 54 (December 1999): 1053–1060.
17. Heide and John, 1992.
18. Goertz and Diehl, 1992.
19. David M. Messick and Keith Sentis, "Fairness, Preference and Fairness Biases," in David Messick and Karen Cook (eds.), *Equity Theory*, (New York: Praeger, 1983): 61–94.
20. Bicchieri, 2006.
21. Ellickson, 1991.
22. Joachim Kruger and Russell Clement, "The Truly False Consensus Effect: An Ineradicable and Egocentric Bias in Social Perception," *Journal of Personality and Social Psychology* 67, no. 4 (1994): 596–619.
23. Anthony Giddens, *The Constitution of Society* (Berkeley: University of California Press, 1984): 22.
24. Christine Horne, "Sociological Perspectives on the Emergence of Social Norms," in Michael Hechter and Karl-Dieter Opp (eds.), *Social Norms* (New York: Russell Sage Foundation, 2001): 3–34.
25. Ibid.
26. Barbara Stewart, "$9.50 for the Movies? Vallone Urges a Boycott," *New York Times*, March 2, 1999.
27. "Consumer Boycott of Glaxo Gains Steam with Protest by Seniors," February 21, 2003, www.SeniorJournal.com.
28. Abbie Hoffman, *Steal This Book* (Pirate Editions 1971), www.tenant.net/Community/steal/steal.html.

Chapter 5

1. Norman Finkel, *Not Fair! The Typology of Commonsense Unfairness* (Washington, DC: American Psychological Association, 2001): 56.
2. Craig L. Carr, *On Fairness* (Aldershot, UK: Ashgate Publishing Ltd., 2000).
3. Ibid., p. 8.
4. Ibid., p. 7.
5. Ibid., p. 9.

6. Daniel Kahneman, Jack L. Knetsch, and Richard H. Thaler, "Fairness as a Constraint on Profit Seeking: Entitlements in the Market," *American Economic Review* 76 (September 1986): 728–741.

7. Ibid., p. 729.

8. Bruno S. Frey and Werner W. Pommerehne, "On the Fairness of Pricing: An Empirical Survey among the General Population," *Journal of Economic Behavior and Organization* 20 (1993): 295–307.

9. Raymond Gorman and James B. Kehr, "Fairness as a Constraint on Profit Seeking: Comment," *American Economic Review* 82, no. 1 (1992): 355–358.

10. Sarah Maxwell, "What Makes a Price Increase Seem 'Fair'?" *Pricing Strategy and Practice: An International Journal* 3, no. 4 (1995): 21–27.

11. Antonio Damasio, *Descartes' Error: Emotion, Reason and the Human Brain* (London: Penguin Books, 1994): 193.

12. Ibid., p. 49.

13. Antonio Damasio, *Looking for Spinoza: Joy, Sorrow, and the Feeling Brain* (Orlando, FL: Harcourt, 2003): 153.

Chapter 6

1. William Samuelson and Richard Zeckhauser, "Status Quo Bias in Decision Making," *Journal of Risk and Uncertainty* 1 (March 1988): 7–59.

2. Ibid., p. 38.

3. Richard S. Lazarus, "From Psychological Stress to the Emotions: A History of Changing Outlooks," *Annual Review of Psychology* 44 (1993): 1–21.

4. Hooman Estelami, "The Price is Right . . . or is it? Demographic and Category Effects on Consumer Price Knowledge," *Journal of Product and Brand Management* 7, no. 3 (1998): 254–266.

5. Ibid.

6. See, e.g., E. Berscheid et al., "Outcome Dependency, Attention, Attribution, and Attraction," *Journal of Personality and Social Psychology* 34 (1976): 978–989.

7. David M. Messick and Keith Sentis, "Fairness, Preference and Fairness Biases," in David Messick and Karen Cook (eds.), *Equity Theory* (New York: Praeger, 1983).

8. Linda Babcock and George Loewenstein, "Explaining Bargaining Impasses: The Role of Self-Serving Biases," *Journal of Economic Perspectives* 11, no. 1 (1997): 109–126.

9. Richard Oliver and John Swan, "Consumer Perceptions of Interpersonal Equity and Satisfaction," *Journal of Marketing* 53, no. 2 (1989): 21–34.

10. Dennis Rockstroh, "Store Price Scanners: Shoppers Beware," *Mercury News*, September 14, 2005, www.typepad.com.

11. Sarah Maxwell and Nicholas Maxwell, "The Perception of a Fair Price: Self-Interest and Social Norms in Individualist vs. Collectivist Cultures," *International Conference of the Academy of Marketing Science* (Ann Arbor, MI: Books on Demand, 1995).

12. Jacob Jacoby and Jerry C. Olson, "Consumer Response to Price: An Attitudinal, Information Processing Perspective," in Yoram Wind and Marshall

Greenberg (eds.), *Moving Ahead with Attitude Research* (Chicago: American Marketing Society, 1977).

13. Manohar U. Kalwani et al., "A Price Expectations Model of Customer Brand Choice," *Journal of Marketing Research* 27 (August 1990): 251–261.

14. David Leonhardt, "The Shock of the New Entry Fee," *New York Times*, September 26, 2004.

15. Dalia Sussman, "Poll: Americans Angry About Gas Prices," *ABC News*, August 22, 2005, abcnews.go.com.

16. Dhruv Grewal and Larry Compeau, "Pricing and Public Policy: A Research Agenda and an Overview," *Journal of Public Policy & Marketing* 18, no. 1 (1999): 3–10.

17. Noah Rothbaum, "10 Things Your Rental Car Company Won't Tell You," June 13, 2006, aol.smartmoney.com.

18. David Streitfeld, "Amazon Mystery: Pricing of Books," *Los Angeles Times*, January 2, 2007, www.calendarlive.com.

19. Julio Rothemberg, "Fair Pricing," 2004, www.people.hbs.edu.

20. A. S. Blinder, et al., *Asking About Prices: A New Approach to Understanding Price Stickiness* (New York: Russell Sage Foundation, 1998): 309.

21. Samuelson and Zeckhauser, 1988.

22. Richard Thaler, "Mental Accounting and Consumer Choice," *Marketing Science* 3 (Summer 1985): 199–214.

23. Russell Winer, "A Reference Price Model of Brand Choice for Frequently Purchased Products," *Journal of Consumer Research* 13 (September 1986): 250–256.

24. James M. Lattin and Randolf E. Bucklin, "Reference Effects of Price and Promotion on Brand Choice Behavior," *Journal of Marketing Research* 26, no. 3 (1989): 229–310.

25. Gurumurthy Kalyanaram and John D. Little, "A Price Response Model Developed from Perceptual Theories" (working paper, Sloan School of Management, Massachusetts Institute of Technology, Cambridge, MA, 1987).

26. Peter R. Dickson and Alan G. Sawyer, "The Price Knowledge and Search of Supermarket Shoppers," *Journal of Marketing* 54, no. 3 (1990): 42–53.

27. Chris Janiszewski and Donald R. Lichtenstein, "A Range Theory Account of Price Perception," *Journal of Consumer Research* 25 (March 1999): 353–368.

28. Kent B. Monroe and Angela Y. Lee, "Remembering Versus Knowing: Issues in Buyers' Processing of Price Information," *Journal of the Academy of Marketing Science* 27, no. 2 (1999): 207–225.

29. Tracy A. Suter and Scot Burton, "Believability and Consumer Perceptions of Implausible Reference Prices in Retail Advertisements," *Psychology & Marketing* 13, no. 1 (1996): 37–54.

30. Federal Trade Commission, *FTC Guides against Deceptive Pricing*, www.ftc.gov/bcp/guides/decptprc.htm: Section 233.1.

31. "Florida Begins Probe of 'Reference' Prices Used for Macy's Sales," *Wall Street Journal* (Eastern Edition), January 7, 1997.

32. Patrick J. Kaufman, N. Craig Smith, and Gwendolyn K. Ortmeyer, "Deception in Retailer High-Low Pricing: A 'Rule of Reason' Approach," *Journal of Retailing* 70, no. 2 (1994): 115–138.

Chapter 7

1. Tracie Rozhon, "Mrs. Clinton 'Listens,' This Time to House Prices," *New York Times*, August 12, 1999.
2. Richard Harrington, "Ticket Auction Trend May Cost You," July 6, 2006, MontereyHerald.com.
3. Vera Baird, "Getting Carter—The Future of Legal Aid," *The Times*, July 4, 2006, www.timesonline.co.uk.
4. Morton Deutsch, *Distributive Justice: A Social-Psychological Perspective* (New Haven: Yale University Press, 1985).
5. Jason A. Coquitt and Jerome M. Cherthoff, "Explaining Injustice: The Interactive Effect of Explanation and Outcome on Fairness Perceptions and Task Motivation," *Journal of Management* 28, no. 5 (2002): 591–610.
6. Jen-Hung Huan and Chia-Yen Lin, "The Explanation Effects on Consumer Perceived Justice, Satisfaction and Loyalty Improvement: An Exploratory Study," *The Journal of American Academy of Business* 7, no. 2 (2005): 212–218.
7. John C. Shaw, Eric Wild and Jason A Conquitt, "To Justify or Excuse? A Meta-Analytic Review of the Effects of Explanation," *Journal of Applied Psychology* 88, no. 3 (2003): 444–458.
8. Ibid.
9. Janice Bohm and Bryan Hendricks, "Effects of Interpersonal Touch, Degree of Justification, and Sex of Participants in Compliance with Request," *The Journal of Social Psychology* 137, no. 4 (1997): 460–469.
10. Sarah Maxwell, "Rule-Based Price Fairness and Its Effect on Willingness to Purchase," *Journal of Economic Psychology* 23, no. 2 (2002): 193–212.
11. Michael B. Lupfer et al., "Folk Conceptions of Fairness and Unfairness," *European Journal of Social Psychology* 30 (2000): 405–428.
12. Dan Ariely, George Loewenstein and Drazen Prelec, "'Coherent Arbitrariness:' Stable Demand Curves without Stable Preferences," *The Quarterly Journal of Economics* 118, no. 1 (2003): 73–106; Dan Ariely, George Loewenstein, and Drazen Prelec, "Tom Sawyer and the Construction of Value," *Journal of Economic Behavior & Organization* 60, no. 1 (2006): 1–28.
13. "Comings & Goings," *New York Times*, April 9, 2006.
14. Richard L. Oliver and John E. Swan, "Equity and Disconfirmation Perceptions as Influences on Merchant and Product Satisfaction," *Journal of Consumer Research* 16 (December 1989): 372–383.
15. Margaret Neale, Vandra L. Huber, and Gregory B. Northcraft, "The Framing of Negotiations: Contextual Versus Task Frame," *Organizational Behavior and Human Decision Making* 39 (1987): 228–241.
16. Richard L. Oliver and John E. Swan, "Consumer Perceptions of Interpersonal Equity and Satisfaction in Transactions: A Field Survey Approach," *Journal of Marketing* 53 (April 1989): 21–35.

17. Edward E. Sampson, "On Justice as Equality," *Journal of Social Issues* 31, no. 3 (1975): 45–64.
18. John Rawls, *A Theory of Justice* (Cambridge: Harvard University Press, 1971).
19. Hal R. Varian, "Distributive Justice, Welfare Economics, and the Theory of Fairness," *Philosophy and Public Affairs* 4 (1975): 223–247.
20. Kelly L. Haws and William O. Bearden, "Dynamic Pricing and Consumer Fairness Perceptions," *Journal of Consumer Research* 33, no. 3 (2006): 304–311.
21. Peter R. Darke and Darren W. Dahl, "Fairness and Discounts: The Subjective Value of a Bargain," *Journal of Consumer Psychology* 13, no. 3 (2003): 328–338.
22. Tamar Lewin, "Students Find $100 Textbooks Cost $50 Purchased Overseas," *New York Times*, October 21, 2003.
23. Daniel Kahneman, Jack Knetsch, and Richard Thaler, "Fairness and the Assumptions of Economics," *Journal of Business* 59 (October 1986): S285–S300; Robert Forsythe et al., "Fairness in Simple Bargaining Experiments," *Games and Economic Behavior* 6 (1994): 347–369.
24. Gary E. Bolton and Rami Zwick, "Anonymity versus Punishment in Ultimatum Bargaining," *Games and Economic Behavior* 10 (1995): 95–121.
25. Sampson, 1975.
26. Karen F. Stein, "Explaining Ghetto Consumer Behavior: Hypotheses from Urban Sociology," *Journal of Consumer Affairs* 14, no. 1 (1980): 232–242.
27. Morton Deutsch, "Equity, Equality, and Need: What Determines Which Value Will Be Used as the Basis of Distributive Justice?" *Journal of Social Issues* 31, no. 3 (1975): 137–149.
28. Milt Freudenheim, "Low Payments by U.S. Raise Medical Bills Billions a Year," *New York Times*, June 1, 2006.
29. "Lautenschlager to File Complaints against Two Area Hospitals," *Milwaukee Business Journal*, November 7, 2005, Milwaukee.bizjournal.com.
30. Sue Kirchhoff, "Efforts Renewed to Control Excessive Cost of Payday Loans," *USA Today*, December 1, 2006.
31. Bernard Wasow, "A New Minimum Benefit for Social Security," The Social Security Network, April 12, 2004, www.socsec.org.
32. Melissa Campanelli, "What's in Store for EDLP?" *Sales and Marketing Management* 145, no. 9 (1993): 56–59.
33. Alex Berenson, "A Cancer Drug Shows Promise, at a Price That Many Can't Pay," *New York Times*, February 15, 2006, www.nytimes.com.
34. "Price Gouging on Cancer Drugs?" *New York Times*, February 17, 2006, www.nytimes.com.
35. Ruaridh Nicoll, "Electricity Cut-Off Sparks South African Township Riot," *The Guardian*, August 8, 1997.
36. Deutsch, 1975.

Chapter 8

1. Fritz Heider, *The Psychology of Interpersonal Relations* (New York: Wiley, 1958); Harold H. Kelley, "The Processes of Causal Attribution," *American Psychologist* 28 (February 1973): 107–123; Bernard Weiner, *An Attributional Theory of Motivation and Emotion* (New York: Springer-Verlag, 1986).

2. Bernard Weiner, "Attributional Thoughts about Consumer Behavior," *Journal of Consumer Research* 27, no. 3 (2000): 382–387.
3. Ibid.
4. Matthew Rabin, "Incorporating Fairness into Game Theory and Economics," *American Economic Review* 83, no. 5 (1993): 1281–1302.
5. Sally Blount, "When Social Outcomes Aren't Fair: The Effect of Causal Attributions on Preferences," *Organizational Behavior and Human Decision Processes* 63, no. 2 (August 1995): 131–144.
6. Margaret Campbell, "Why Did You Do That? The Important Role of Inferred Motive in Perceptions of Price Fairness," *Journal of Product and Brand Management* 8, no. 2 (1999): 145–153.
7. Sarah Maxwell, "The Effects of Differential Textbook Pricing: On-Line vs. In-Store," *Journal of Media Economics* 16, no. 2 (2003): 87–95.
8. Margaret Campbell, "Perceptions of Price Fairness: Antecedents and Consequences," *Journal of Marketing Research* 36 (May 1999): 187–199.
9. Rajiv Vaidyanathan and Praveen Aggarwal, "Who Is the Fairest of Them All? An Attributional Approach to Price Fairness Perceptions," *Journal of Business Research* 56, no. 6 (2003): 453–459.
10. Arthur M. Okun, *Prices and Quantities: A Macroeconomic Analysis* (Washington DC: The Brookings Institution, 1981).
11. Michael Tsiros, Vikas Mittal, and William T. Ross, Jr., "The Role of Attributions in Customer Satisfaction: A Reexamination," *Journal of Consumer Research* 31, no. 2 (2004): 478–483.
12. Valerie Folkes, Susan Koletsky, and John L. Graham, "A Field Study of Causal Inference and Consumer Reaction: The View from the Airport," *Journal of Consumer Research* 13 (March 1987): 534–539.
13. N. T. Feather and J. G. Simon, "Fear of Success and Causal Attribution for Outcome," *Journal of Personality* 41 (1973): 525–542.
14. Sarah Maxwell, "Biased Attributions of a Price Increase: Effects of Culture and Gender," *Journal of Consumer Marketing* 16, no. 1 (1999): 9–23.
15. Jaebeom Suh and Jeffrey Hess, "Individualism vs. Collectivism: Cultural Moderation of Consumer Attribution," *Proceedings, American Marketing Association* (Summer 1996): 188–192.
16. Harold H. Kelley, "The Process of Causal Attribution," *American Psychologist* 28 (February 1973): 107–123; Gifford W. Bradley, "Self-Serving Biases in the Attribution Process; A Reexamination of the Fact or Fiction Question," *Journal of Personality and Social Psychology* 36, no. 1 (1978): 56–71.
17. Weiner, 1986.

Chapter 9

1. Jerald Greenberg, "Stress Fairness to Fare No Stress: Managing Workplace Stress by Promoting Organizational Justice," *Organizational Dynamics* 33, no. 4 (2004): 352–364.
2. John Thibaut and Laurens Walker, *Procedural Justice: A Psychological Analysis* (Hillsdale, NY: Erlbaum, 1975).
3. E. Allan Lind and Tom R. Tyler, *The Social Psychology of Procedural Justice* (New York: Plenum, 1988).

4. Kwok Leung and Wai-Kwan Li, "Psychological Mechanisms of Process-Control Effects," *Journal of Applied Psychology* 75, no. 6 (1990): 613–620.
5. Kelly L. Haws and William O. Bearden, "Dynamic Pricing and Consumer Fairness Perceptions," *Journal of Consumer Research* 33, no. 3 (2006): 304–311.
6. "Lentil as Anything," www.lentilasanything.com.
7. Barbara Meyer, "Textbook Market Unfair: Few Alternatives Available," *Kansas State Collegian*, March 10, 2004, www.kstate.collegian.com.
8. N. K. Malhotra, "Information Load and Consumer Decision Making," *Journal of Consumer Research* 8 (March 1982): 419–430.
9. Sarah Maxwell, "Hyperchoice and High Prices: An Unfair Combination," *Journal of Product and Brand Management* 14, no. 7 (2005): 448–454.
10. Edward E. Zajac, *Fairness or Efficiency: An Introduction to Public Utility Pricing* (Cambridge, MA: Ballinger Publishing, 1978); Edward E. Zajac, *Political Economy of Fairness* (Cambridge, MA: MIT Press, 1995).
11. Douglas N. Jones and Patrick C. Mann, "The Fairness Criterion in Public Utility Regulations: Does Fairness Still Matter?" *Journal of Economic Issues* 35, no. 1 (2001): 153–172.
12. Joe Sharkey, "Business Travel: One Critic Shows the Mounting Animosity over Different Air Fares for Business and Leisure Fliers," *New York Times*, March 6, 2002.
13. Roy Furchgott, "You Say You Didn't Buy It. But Did You Read the Tiny Type?" *New York Times*, December 7, 1997.
14. Sarah Maxwell, "Rule-Based Price Fairness and its Effect on Willingness to Purchase," *Journal of Economic Psychology* 23, no. 2 (2002): 191–212.
15. Diana Wood, *Medieval Economic Thought* (Cambridge: Cambridge University Press, 2002).
16. Uwe E. Reinhardt, "The Pricing of U.S. Hospital Services: Chaos behind a Veil of Secrecy," *Health Affairs* 25, no. 1 (2006): 57–69.

Chapter 10

1. Robert Axelrod, "An Evolutionary Approach to Norms," *American Political Science Review* 80, no. 4 (1986): 1095–1111.
2. Richard DeRidder and Rama C. Tripathi, *Norm Violation and Intergroup Relations* (Oxford, UK: Clarendon Press, 1992): 22.
3. George C. Homans, *The Human Group* (New York: Harcourt Brace, 1950): 123.
4. Dale T. Miller and Neil Vidmar, "The Social Psychology of Punishment Reactions," in Melvin J. Lerner and Sally C. Lerner (eds.), *The Justice Motive in Social Behavior: Adapting to Times of Scarcity and Change* (New York: Plenum Press, 1981): 145–172.
5. Jeffrey P. Carpenter, Peter Hans Matthews and Okomboli Ong'ong'a, "Why Punish? Social Reciprocity and the Enforcement of Prosocial Norms," *Journal of Evolutionary Economics* 24 (2004): 407–429.
6. Matthew Rabin, "Incorporating Fairness into Game Theory and Economics," *The American Economic Review* (December 1993): 1281–1302.

7. Frans B. M. DeWaal, "The Chimpanzee's Sense of Social Regularity and Its Relation to the Human Sense of Justice," *American Behavioral Scientist* 34, no. 3 (January/February 1991): 335–348.

8. Michael E. Price, Leda Cosmides, and John Tooby, "Punitive Sentiment as an Anti-Free Rider Psychological Device," *Evolution and Human Behavior* 23, no. 3 (May 2002): 203–231.

9. Herbert Gents, "Strong Reciprocity and Human Sociality," *Journal of Theoretical Biology* 206, no. 2 (September 21, 2000): 169–179.

10. Alvin W. Gouldner, "The Norm of Reciprocity: A Preliminary Statement," *American Sociological Review* 25, no. 2 (1960): 161–178.

11. Gary Goertz and Paul F. Diehl, "Toward a Theory of International Norms," *Journal of Conflict Resolution* 36 (December 1992): 634–664.

12. Friedrich A. Hayek, *The Road to Serfdom* (Chicago: University of Chicago Press, 1994 [1944]).

13. Gregory Gundlach and Ravi S. Achrol, "Governance in Exchange: Contract Law and its Alternatives," *Journal of Public Policy and Marketing* 12 (October 1993): 141–155.

14. Ragnar Rommetveit, *Social Norms and Roles* (Minneapolis: University of Minnesota Press, 1954).

15. Robert Piron and Luis Fernandez, "Are Fairness Constraints on Profit-Seeking Important?" *Journal of Economic Psychology* 16 (1995): 73–96.

16. Roger Bougie, Rik Pieters, and Marcel Zeelenberg, "Angry Customers Don't Come Back, They Get Back: The Experience and Behavioral Implications of Anger and Dissatisfaction in Services," *Journal of the Academy of Marketing Science* 31, no. 4 (2003): 377–393.

17. Jim Rendon, "What Gas Stations Won't Tell You," July 11, 2006, aol.smartmoney.com.

18. Sara H. Goo, "Underdogs in Battle Against Gas Gougers," September 23, 2005, washingtonpost.com.

19. Daniel Kahneman, Jack L. Knetsch, and Richard H. Thaler, "Fairness as a Constraint on Profit Seeking: Entitlements in the Market," *American Economic Review* 76 (September 1986): 728–741.

20. Jean-Robert Tyran and Dirk Engelmann, "To Buy or Not to Buy? An Experimental Study of Consumer Boycotts in Retail Markets," *Economica* 72 (2005): 1–16.

21. Ipsos-Reid Survey, cited by Mark Dolliver, "Boomers as Boycotters," *Adweek*, (Eastern edition), December 4, 2000: 44.

22. Price, Cosmides, and Tooby, 2002.

23. Natalie Angier, "The Urge to Punish Cheats: It Isn't Merely Vengeance," *New York Times*, January 22, 2002.

24. Nada Nasr Bechwati and Maureen Morrin, "Outraged Consumers: Getting Even at the Expense of Getting a Good Deal," *Journal of Consumer Psychology* 13, no. 4 (2003): 440–453.

25. Carpenter, Matthews, and Ong'ong'a, 2004.

26. Ernst Fehr and Klaus M. Schmidt, "A Theory of Fairness, Competition, and Cooperation," *Quarterly Journal of Economics* (August 1999): 817–868.

27. Alan G. Sanfey et al., "The Neural Basis of Economic Decision-Making in the Ultimatum Game," *Science* 300 (2003): 1755–1758.

28. Daria Knoch, et al., "Diminishing Reciprocal Fairness by Disrupting the Right Prefrontal Cortex," *Sciencexpress*, October 5, 2006, www.sciencexpress.org.

29. D. DeQuervain et al., "The Neural Basis of Altruistic Punishment," *Science* 305 (2004): 1254–1258.

30. J. Keith Murnighan and Madan M. Pillutla, "Fairness versus Self-Interest: Asymmetric Moral Imperatives in Ultimatum Bargaining," in Roderick M. Kramer and David M. Messick (eds.), *Negotiation as a Social Process*, (Thousand Oaks, CA: Sage Publications, 1995), 240–267.

31. Ernst Fehr and Urs Fischbacher, "Third-Party Punishment and Social Norms," *Evolution and Human Behavior* 25 (2004): 63–87.

32. Fehr and Schmidt, 1999.

33. Alvin E. Roth et al., "Bargaining and Market Behavior in Jerusalem, Ljubljana, Pittsburg, and Tokyo: An Experimental Study," *American Economic Review* 81 (December 1991): 1068–1095.

34. Joseph Henrich et al., "Costly Punishment Across Human Societies," *Science* 312, no. 5781 (June 23, 2006): 1767–1770.

35. Miller and Vidmar, 1981.

36. Sarah Maxwell, "Sanctioning Unfair Pricing: Making the Punishment Fit the Crime," *Proceedings, Summer Conference* (Chicago: American Marketing Association, 2003).

37. Bruce Mohl, "Wal-Mart Settles Lawsuit on Item-Pricing for $7.35M," *The Boston Globe*, January 22, 2004, www.consumerwatchdog.org.

Chapter 11

1. Federal Highway Administration, "Highway Statistics," 2006, www.fhwa.dot.gov.

2. "For Oil Giants, Pricey Gas Means Big Profits," ABC News, January 25, 2006, abcnews.go.com

3. Tom Curry, "What Is Price 'Gouging'? And Can It Be Stopped?" MSNBC, April 26, 2006, www.msnbc.msn.com.

4. Pete Domenici, Representative from New Mexico, quoted in "Big Oil Defends Profits," CBS News, November 9, 2005, www.cbsnews.com.

5. White House, "President Discusses Energy at National Small Business Conference," press release, April 27, 2005, www.whitehouse.gov.

6. Curry, 2006.

7. Robert A. Dahl, "The Concept of Power," *Behavioral Science* 2 no. 3 (July 1957): 201–215.

8. Kurt Eichenwald, "Archer Daniels Said to Settle Sweetened Price-Fixing Case," *New York Times*, June 18, 2004.

9. Stefano DellaVigna and Ulrike Malmendier, "Contract Design and Self-Control: Theory and Evidence," *The Quarterly Journal of Economics* 119, no. 2 (May 2004): 353–384.

10. Gary L. Frazier and Sudhir H. Kale, "Manufacturer-Distributor Relationships: A Sellers' Versus Buyers' Market Perspective," *International Marketing Review* 6, no. 6 (1989): 7–26.

11. F. Robert Dwyer, Paul H. Schurr, and Sejo Oh, "Developing Buyer-Seller Relationships," *Journal of Marketing* 51 (April 1987): 11–27.

12. Francis Bacon, *Religious Meditations, Of Heresies* (Philadelphia: William Bradford, 1688), electronic resource, www.library.fordham.edu.

13. "Crowned at Last," *The Economist*, March 31, 2005, www.economist.com.

14. Behrang Rezabakhsh et al., "Consumer Power: A Comparison of the Old Economy and the Internet Economy," *Journal of Consumer Policy* 29 (2006): 3–36.

15. John R. French and Bertram Raven, "The Bases of Social Power," in Dorwin Cartwright (ed.), *Studies in Social Power* (Ann Arbor: University of Michigan Press, 1959): 150–167.

16. X. Pan, B. T. Ratchford, and V. Shankar, "The Evolution of Price Dispersion in Internet Retail Markets," *Advances in Applied Microeconomics* 12 (2003): 85–105.

17. "Crowned at Last" 2005.

18. Linda D. Molm, "Imbalanced Structures, Unfair Strategies: Power and Justice in Social Exchange," *American Sociological Review* 59, no. 1 (1994): 98–121.

19. F. Robert Dwyer, "Are Two Better than One? Bargaining Behavior and Outcomes in an Asymmetrical Power Relationship," *Journal of Consumer Research* 11 (September 1984): 680–693.

20. Daniel Kahneman, Jack L. Knetsch, and Richard H. Thaler, "Fairness as a Constraint on Profit Seeking: Entitlements in the Market," *American Economic Review* 76 (September 1986); 728–741.

21. Robert H. Frank, *Passions within Reason: The Strategic Role of the Emotions* (New York: W. W. Norton, 1988).

22. Jeffrey Bradach and Robert Eccles, "Price, Authority and Trust," *Annual Review of Sociology* 15 (1989): 97–106.

23. "E-Commerce," *The Economist: The World in 2007*: 94.

24. L. Walker, et al., "Reactions of Participants and Observers to Modes of Adjudication," *Journal of Applied Social Psychology* 4 (1974): 295–310.

Chapter 12

1. Kanchan Vasdev, "All 200 Milk Samples Fail Test," *Tribune News Service*, August 13, 2006, www.tribuneindia.com.

2. Akshay R. Rao and Mark E. Bergen, "Price Premium Variations as a Consequence of Buyers' Lack of Information," *Journal of Consumer Research* 19, no. 3 (1992): 412–424.

3. David M. Messick and Roderick M. Kramer, "Trust as a Form of Shallow Morality," in Karen Cook (ed.), *Trust in Society*, (New York: Russell Sage Foundation, 2001): 89–117.

4. Roy J. Lewicki, Daniel J. McAllister, and Robert J. Bier, "Trust and Distrust: New Relationships and Realities," *Academy of Management Review* 23, no. 3 (1998): 438–458.

5. Shelly Taylor, "A Categorization Approach to Stereotyping," in D. L. Hamilton (ed.), *Cognitive Processes in Stereotyping and Intergroup Behavior,* (Hillsdale, NJ: Erlbaum, 1981): 88–114.

6. Oliver Williamson, "Calculativeness, Trust and Economic Organization," *Journal of Law and Economics* 36 (1993): 453–486.

7. Mark Granovetter, "Economic Action and Social Structure: The Problem of Embeddedness," *American Journal of Sociology* 91, no. 3 (1985): 481–510.

8. Kenneth Arrow, *The Limits of Organization* (New York: Norton, 1974).

9. Leonard L. Berry, "Retailers with a Future," *Marketing Management* 5 (Spring 1996): 38–46.

10. Amanda Vickers and Jackie Smith, "Why Consumer Trust Is the Key to Repeat Business," *The Wise Marketer,* January 2005, www.thewisemarketer.com.

11. Glen L. Urban, "The Trust Imperative" (working paper no. 4302-03, Sloan School of Management, Massachusetts Institute of Technology, 2003), http://ssrn.com/abstract=400421 or DOI: 10.2139/ssrn.400421.

12. John Drummond, "The Value of Being a 'Trusted' Company," *Corporate Responsibility Management* 2, no. 4 (2006): 12–13.

13. Donald L. Potter, "Moving from a DRTV 'Need-It-Now' Sell to a 'Trust-Marketing' Relationship," *Response Magazine,* February 1, 2005, www.responsemagazine. com.

14. Lynn Jeffress and Jean-Paul Mayanobe, "A World Struggle Is Underway: An Interview with Jose Bove," *Z Magazine,* June 2001, www.thirdworldtraveler. com.

15. Messick and Kramer, 2001.

16. Derek Creevey, "Trust Shifting from Traditional Authorities to Peers, Edelman Trust Barometer Finds," January 24, 2005, www.edelman.com.

17. Jeffrey Bradach and Robert Eccles, "Price, Authority and Trust," *Annual Review of Sociology* 13 (1989): 97–118.

18. Larue T. Hosmer, "Trust: The Connecting Link between Organizational Theory and Philosophical Ethics," *Academy of Management Review* 20, no. 2 (1995): 379–403.

19. Roger C. Mayer, James H. Davis, and F. David Schoorman, "An Integration Model of Organizational Trust," *Academy of Management Review* 20, no. 3 (1995): 709–844.

20. Ernst Fehr, Urs Fischbacher, and Michael Kosfeld, "Neuroeconomic Foundations of Trust and Social Preferences: Initial Evidence," *American Economic Review* 95, no. 2 (2005): 346–351.

21. Francis Fukuyama, *Trust* (New York: Simon & Schuster, 1995): 26.

22. James Coleman, "Social Capital in the Creation of Human Capital," *American Journal of Sociology* 94 (1988): S95–S120; Robert D. Putnam, "The Prosperous Community: Social Capital and Public Life," *American Prospect* 13 (1993): 35–42.

23. Fukuyama, 1995.

24. Yankelovich, "A Crisis of Confidence: Rebuilding the Bonds of Trust," *State of Consumer Trust Report,* 2004, www.compad.com.au.

25. Russell Hardin, "Conceptions and Explanations of Trust," in Karen Cook (ed.), *Trust in Society* (New York: Russell Sage Foundation, 2001): 3–39.

26. Peter Blau, *Exchange and Power in Social Life* (New York: Wiley, 1967).

27. See, e.g., Frank K. Sonnenberg, "Trust Me, Trust Me Not," *Journal of Business Strategy* 15, no. 1 (January/February 1994): 14–16; John D. Butler Jr., "Toward Understanding and Measuring Conditions of Trust: Evolution of a Conditions of Trust Inventory," *Journal of Management* 17, no. 3 (1991): 643–663.

28. See, e.g., Marshall Sashkin and Richard L. Williams, "Does Fairness Make a Difference?" *Organizational Dynamics* 19, no. 2 (1990): 56–71.

29. L. G. Zucker, "Production of Trust: Institutional Sources of Economic Structure, 1840–1920," in B. M. Staw and L. L. Cummings (eds.), *Research in Organization Behavior*, vol. 8, (Greenwich, CT: JAI Press, 1986): 53–111.

30. Hosmer, 1995.

31. Una McMahon-Beattie, "Future of Revenue Management: Trust and Revenue Management," *Journal of Revenue and Pricing Management* 4, no. 4 (2005): 406–407.

32. Margaret Campbell, "Perceptions of Price Fairness: Antecedents and Consequences," *Journal of Marketing Research* 36 (May 1999): 187–199.

33. Morton Deutsch, "Trust and Suspicion," *The Journal of Conflict Resolution* 2, no. 4 (1958): 265–279.

34. Campbell, 1999.

35. John W. Huppertz, Sidney J. Arenson, and Richard H. Evans, "An Application of Equity Theory to Buyer-Seller Exchange Situations," *Journal of Marketing Research* 15 (May 1978): 250–260.

36. Rosemary Kalapurakal, Peter R. Dickson, and Joel E. Urbany, "A Conceptual Model of Price Fairness Judgments" (working paper, Ohio State University, 1992): 17.

37. Robert Bies and Thomas Tripp, "Beyond Distrust: 'Getting Even' and the Need for Revenge," in Roderick Kramer and Tom R. Tyler (eds.), *Trust in Organizations*, (Thousand Oaks, CA: Sage Publications, 1996): 252–283.

38. Fred M. Feinberg, Aradhna Krishna, and Z. John Zhang, "Do We Care What Others Get? A Behaviorist Approach to Targeted Promotions," *Journal of Marketing Research* 39, no. 3 (2002): 277–291.

39. Joel Brockner and Phyllis A. Siegel, "Understanding the Interaction between Procedural and Distributive Justice," in Roderick M. Kramer and Tom R. Tyler (eds.), *Trust in Organizations*, (Thousand Oaks, CA: Sage Publications, 1996): 390–410.

40. Yankelovich, 2004.

41. Thomas T. Nagle and Reed K. Holden, *The Strategy and Tactics of Pricing* (Englewood Cliffs, NJ: Prentice-Hall, 1995).

42. Kees van den Bos and Henk A. M. Wilke, "When Do We Need Procedural Fairness? The Role of Trust in Authority," *Journal of Personality and Social Psychology* 75, no. 6 (1998): 1449–1458.

43. Jean Ensminger, "Reputations, Trust, and the Principal Agent Problem," in Karen Cook (ed.), *Trust in Society*, (New York: Russell Sage Foundation, 2001): 185–201.

44. Yankelovich, 2004.

45. Brockner and Segal, 1996.

46. Sunanda N. Ganju, "Gender Revolution after White Revolution," *India Together*, September 20, 2005, www.indiatogether.org.

Chapter 13

1. Anna Shoup, "The Global Warming Debate: Emissions Trading Ins and Outs," June 5, 2006, www.pbs.org/newshour.
2. Collin Dunn, "The Social Costs of Greenhouse Gas Emissions," February 10, 2006, www.treehugger.com.
3. "A Soluble Problem," *The Economist*, March 24, 2000: 20.
4. John Peet, "Water, Water Everywhere: And Scarcely a Drop of Common Sense in Its Pricing," *The Economist: The World in 2004*: 18.
5. Ronald Bailey, "The Case for Selling Human Organs," *Reasonline*, April 18, 2001, reason.com.
6. John Stossel, interviewed on *Your World with Neil Cavuto*, Fox News, June 13, 2006, mediamatters.org.
7. Claire Andre and Manuel Velasquez, "Kidneys for Sale," *Issues in Ethics* 1, no. 2 (1988), www.scu.edu/ethics.
8. Claudia Kalb, "Ethics, Eggs and Embryos," *Newsweek*, June 20, 2005: 52.
9. Norbert Schechter, "Economic Damages under New York Wrongful Death Statute" June, 2006, www.nysscpa.org.
10. Jim Yardley, "3 Deaths in China Reveal Disparity in Price of Lives," *New York Times*, April 14, 2006.
11. Randy Kennedy, "The Day the Traffic Disappeared," *New York Times*, April 20, 2003.
12. "Charge Late Fees for Missed Appointments?" *The [Non]billable Hour*," June 27, 2006, thenonbillablehour.typepad.com.
13. "Road Pricing," August 28, 2006, en.wikipedia.org.
14. Adam Raphael, "Road Pricing: Queue or Pay?" *The Economist: The World in 2003*: 79.
15. Randy Cohen, "Line Up," *New York Times Magazine*, July 24, 2005.
16. Sheryl E. Kimes and Jochen Wirtz, "Has Revenue Management Become Acceptable?" *Journal of Service Research* 6, no. 2 (2003): 125–137.
17. Dhruv Grewal, David M. Hardesty, and Gopalkrishnan R. Iyer, "The Effects of Buyer Identification and Purchase Timing on Consumers' Perceptions of Trust, Price Fairness and Repurchase Intentions," *Journal of Interactive Marketing* 18, no. 4 (2004): 87–100, www.interscience.com.
18. "American Socialism: Battling with Demons," *The Economist*, September 24, 2005: 41.
19. "Copying Rights," *Newsweek*, March 26, 2007: 11.
20. David Rowell, "Airline Zen: Less Is More," November 2001 (updated February 2005), www.thetravelinsider.info.

Chapter 14

1. See, e.g., Ofer H.Azar, "Optimal Monitoring with External Incentives: The Case of Tipping," *Southern Economic Journal*, 71 no. 1 (2004): 170–181.
2. Orn B. Bodvarsson and William A Gibson, "Economics and Restaurant Gratuities: Determining Tip Rates," *American Journal of Economics and Sociology* 56, no. 2 (1997): 187–203.

3. Robert H. Frank, *Passions within Reason: The Strategic Role of the Emotions* (New York: Norton, 1988).
4. Jeff D. Opdyke, "Love & Money: 10%? 15%? 20%? We Are What We Tip," *Wall Street Journal*, July 10, 2005.
5. Ibid.
6. Sarah Maxwell, "Fair Price, Fair Practice: Dual Entitlements for the Consumer," *Proceedings, Fordham Pricing Conference* (New York: Fordham University, 2005).
7. Daniel Kahneman, Jack L. Knetsch, and Richard H. Thaler, "Fairness as a Constraint on Profit Seeking: Entitlements in the Market," *American Economic Review*, 76 (September 1986): 728–741.
8. Sarah Maxwell, "KKT Revisited" (working paper, Fordham Pricing Center, Fordham University, New York, 2006).
9. Michael Conlin, Michael Lynn, and Ted O'Donoghue, "The Norm of Restaurant Tipping," *Journal of Economic Behavior and Organization* 52, no. 3 (2003): 297–308; Michael Lynn and Michael McCall, "Gratitude and Gratuity: A Meta-Analysis of Research on the Service-Tipping Relationship," *Journal of Socio-Economics* 29, no. 2 (2000): 203–214.
10. Uri Ben-Zion and Edi Karni, "Tip Payments and the Quality of Service," in O. C. Ashenfelter and W. E. Oates (eds.), *Essays in Labor Market Analysis*, (New York: Wiley, 1977): 37–44.
11. Bodvarsson and Gibson, 1997.
12. Kerry Seagrave, *Tipping: An American Social History of Gratuities* (Jefferson, NC: McFarland, 1998).
13. William Scott, *The Itching Palm: A Study of the Habit of Tipping in America* (Philadelphia: Penn Publishing Company, 1916).
14. Danielle Archlbagi, "Tips and Democracy," *Dissent*, Spring 2004, www.dissent. magazine.org.
15. Ofer H. Azar, "The Social Norm of Tipping: Does It Improve Social Welfare?," *Journal of Economics* 85, no. 2 (2005): 141–149.
16. Jeanne Sahadi, "Tipping Revisited: Readers Respond," June 5, 2003, cnnmoney. printthis.clickability.com
17. Bodvarsson and Gibson, 1997, p. 187.
18. Natalie MacLean, "Gratuitous Praise," February 11, 2005, www.smh.com.au/ articles.
19. Michael Lynn, George M. Zinkhan, and Judy Harris, "Consumer Tipping: A Cross-Country Study," *Journal of Consumer Research* 20, no. 3 (1993): 478–488.
20. James Surowiecki, "Check, Please," *The New Yorker*, September 5, 2005: 58.
21. Michael Lynn, "Restaurant Tipping and Service Quality: A Tenuous Relationship," *Cornell Hotel and Restaurant Administration Quarterly* 42, no. 1 (2001): 14–20.
22. Chris, August 8, 2005, majikthise.typepad.com.
23. "History," *National Restaurant Association* (2005), www.restaurant.org/ aboutus/history.
24. Nancy Benac, "Tipping Debate," July 3, 2002, www.icrsurvey.com.
25. Ofer H. Azar, "What Sustains Social Norms and How They Evolve? The Case of Tipping," *Journal of Economic Behavior and Organization* 54, no. 1 (2004): 49–57.

26. Ibid.

27. Seagrave, 1998.

28. The Associated Press 2002 Poll, in "Tipping Notes," *Topeka Capital Journal*, August 25, 2002, www.cjonline.com.

29. Bodvarsson and Gibson, 1997.

30. R. Mildred, August 28, 2005, majikthise.typepad.com.

31. *Letitia Baldrige's New Complete Guide to Executive Manners* (New York: Rawson Associates, Macmillan Publishing Company, 1993).

32. Warren St. John, "Time to Render unto Doormen," *New York Times*, December 21, 2003.

33. Sean Foley, August 28, 2005, majikthise.typepad.com.

34. Stevenson Swanson, "Tips Giving Way to Service Charges?" *Charlotte Observer*, October 14, 2005, www.charlotte.com.

35. Matthias Klaes, "Some Remarks on the Place of Psychological and Social Elements in a Theory of Custom," *American Journal of Economics and Sociology* 61, no. 2 (2002): 523.

36. "Forget the Tip . . . Market Trends Drive a Wage," 2005, www.thinkandask.com.

Chapter 15

1. Anita Ramasastry, "Websites that Charge Different Customers Different Prices," June 20, 2005, writ.news.findlaw.com.

2. Martha Heller, "Is Dynamic Pricing Really So Bad?" October 25, 2000, comment.cio.com/soundoff.

3. D. Streitfeld, "On the Web, Price Tags Blur," *Washington Post*, September 27, 2000.

4. Howard Marmorstein, Jeanne Rossomme, and Dan Sarel, "Unleashing the Power of Yield Management in the Internet Era: Opportunities and Challenges," *California Management Review* 45, no. 3 (2003): 147–167.

5. Joseph Turow, "Open to Exploitation: American Shoppers Online and Offline," (Annenberg Public Policy Center, University of Pennsylvania, 2005), www.appcpenn.org.

6. Debbie Bocian, Keith Ernst, and Wei Li, "Unfair Lending: The Effect of Race and Ethnicity on the Price of Subprime Mortgages," Center for Responsible Lending, May 31, 2006, www.responsiblelending.org.

7. Jacque Storm, "Gender-Based Price Discrimination: Does It Require a New Solution or Enforcement of an Old Law?" South Dakota Legislative Research Council (Issue Memorandum 96–22, 2000).

8. Joanna Grossman, "The End of 'Ladies' Night' in New Jersey: A Controversial Ruling Deems the Practice Sex Discrimination against Men," 2004, lawjig@hofstra.edu.

9. Edward E. Zajac, *Fairness or Efficiency: An Introduction to Public Utility Pricing* (Cambridge, MA: Ballinger, 1978).

10. Judith Dancoff, "Done Deals," *MM Magazine* (January/February 2002): 13.

11. Richard Thaler, "Mental Accounting and Consumer Choice," *Marketing Science* 4 (Summer 1985): 199–214.

12. Michael J. McCarthy, "Taking the Value Out of Value-Sized: Shoppers Flock to Discounters, But It Isn't Always Cheaper; The Cool Whip Conundrum," *Wall Street Journal*, August 14, 2002.

13. David E. Sprott, Kenneth C. Manning, and Anthony D. Miyazaki, "Grocery Price Setting and Quantity Surcharges," *Journal of Marketing* 67, no. 3 (2003): 34–45.

14. Ellen Garbarino and Sarah Maxwell, "Social Norms and Judged Fairness as Mediators of Trust-Breaking Due to Dynamic Posted Prices," *Proceedings, Fordham Pricing Conference* (New York, Fordham University, 2004).

15. "Broken Promises: When Your Program Changes the Rules," 2005, www.insideflyer.com.

16. Fred M. Feinberg, Aradhna Krishna, and Z. John Zhang, "Do We Care What Others Get? A Behaviorist Approach to Targeted Promotions," *Journal of Marketing Research* 39, no. 3 (2002): 277–291.

17. Decision No. 587-C-A-2002, "In the Matter of a Complaint Filed by Tom Sherlock against Air Canada," October 30, 2002, www.cta-otc.gc.ca.

18. Paul Krugman, "What Price Fairness?" *New York Times*, October 4, 2000.

19. Sarah Maxwell, "Rule-Based Price Fairness and Its Effect on Willingness to Purchase," *Journal of Economic Psychology* 23, no. 2 (2002): 191–212.

20. "What You Pay at Target, Wal-Mart May Depend on Where You Live: Different Neighborhoods Have Different Prices," November 30, 2005, www.thedenverchanel.com.

21. Ibid.

22. Lan Xia, Kent B. Monroe, and Jennifer L. Cox, "The Price Is Unfair! A Conceptual Framework of Price Fairness Perceptions," *Journal of Marketing* 68 (October 2004): 1–15.

23. Lan Xia, Monika Kukar-Kinney, and Kent B. Monroe, "The Effects of Promotion Restrictions on Perceptions of Promotion and Price Fairness," *Proceedings, Fordham Pricing Conference* (New York, Fordham University, 2005).

24. Ramasastry, 2005.

25. Feinberg, Krishna, and Zhang, 2002.

26. "Getting Personal: Will Engaging in Dynamic Pricing Help or Hurt Your Business?" *Entrepreneur*, October 2005, www.allbusiness.com.

27. "How Technology Tailors Price Tags," *Wall Street Journal* (Eastern Edition), June 21, 2001.

Chapter 16

1. Diana Wood, *Medieval Economic Thought* (Cambridge: Cambridge University Press, 2002).

2. Howard Raiffa, *The Art and Science of Negotiation: How to Resolve Conflicts and Get the Best Out of Bargaining* (Cambridge, MA: Belknap Press, 1982).

3. M. H. Bazerman and J. Carroll, "Negotiator Cognition," in B. Staw and L. L. Cummings (eds.), *Research in Organizational Behavior*, Vol 9, (Greenwich, CT: JAI Press, 1987): 247–288.

4. Otomar J. Bartos, "Simple Model of Negotiation: A Sociological Point of View," *Journal of Conflict Resolution* 21, no. 4 (December 1977): 565–579.

5. George Loewenstein et al., "Biased Judgments of Fairness in Bargaining," *The American Economic Review* 85, no. 5 (1993): 1337-1343.
6. Linda Loewenstein and George Loewenstein, "Explaining Bargaining Impasses: The Role of Self-Serving Biases," *Journal of Economic Perspectives* 11, no. 1 (1997): 109–126.
7. Linda Babcock et al., "Biased Judgments of Fairness in Bargaining," *American Economic Review* 85, no. 5 (1995): 1337–1343.
8. Ian Ayres, "Further Evidence of Discrimination in New Car Negotiations and Estimates of Its Cause," islandia.law.yale.edu/ayers/carint.htm.
9. Sarah Maxwell, "The Social Norms of Discrete Consumer Exchange: Classification and Quantification," *American Journal of Economics and Sociology* 58, no. 4 (October 1999): 999–1018.
10. George F. Loewenstein, Leigh Thompson, and Max H. Bazerman, "Social Utility and Decision Making in Interpersonal Contexts," *Journal of Personality and Social Psychology* 57, no. 3 (1989): 426–441.
11. Robyn Dawes and Richard Thaler, "Anomalies of Cooperation," *Journal of Economic Perspective* 2, no. 3 (1988): 187–197.
12. A. C. Filley, *Interpersonal Conflict Resolution* (Glenview, IL: Scott, Foresman, 1975); Dean G. Pruitt, *Negotiation Behavior* (New York: Academic Press, 1981); Evert van de Vliert, *Theoretical Frontiers of Complex Interpersonal Conflict Behavior* (Hove, UK: Erlbaum, Taylor, and Francis, 1996).
13. See, e.g., O. Ben-Yoav and D. G. Pruitt, "Resistance to Yielding and the Expectation of Cooperative Future Interaction in Negotiation," *Journal of Experimental Social Psychology* 20 (1984): 323–353.
14. Tom Tyler and Steven L. Blader, "Justice and Negotiation," in Michele J. Gelfand and Jeanne M. Brett (eds.), *The Handbook of Negotiation and Culture* (Stanford, CA: Stanford University Press, 2004): 295–312.
15. Aimee Drolet, Richard Larrick, and Michael W. Morris, "Thinking of Others: How Perspective Taking Changes Negotiators' Aspirations and Fairness Perceptions as a Function of Negotiator Relationship," *Basic and Applied Social Psychology* 20, no. 1 (1998): 23–31.
16. Sarah Maxwell, Pete Nye, and Nicholas Maxwell, "Less Pain, Same Gain: The Effects of Priming Fairness in Price Negotiations," *Journal of Psychology and Marketing* 16, no. 7 (1999): 545–562.
17. Ibid.
18. Sarah Maxwell, Pete Nye, and Nicholas Maxwell, "The Wrath of the Fairness-Primed Negotiator When the Reciprocity Norm Is Violated," *Journal of Business Research* 56, no. 2 (2003): 399–409.
19. Dean G. Pruitt, *Negotiation Behavior* (New York: Academic Press, 1981).
20. James K. Esser and S. S. Komorita, "Reciprocity and Concession Making in Bargaining," *Journal of Personality and Social Psychology* 31, no. 5 (1975): 864–872.
21. Linda D. Molm, Nobuyuki Takahashi, and Gretchen Peterson, "In the Eye of the Beholder: Procedural Justice in Social Exchange," *American Sociological Review* 68, no. 1 (2003): 128–152.
22. Randy Cohen, "Mea Culpa," *New York Times Magazine*, April 4, 2001: 6.
23. Pruitt, 1981.

24. Jeffry Rubin and Bert Brown, *The Social Psychology of Bargaining and Negotiation* (New York: Academic Press, 1975).
25. Ibid.
26. Charles B. McClintock and William B. Liebrand, "The Role of Interdependence Structure, Individual Value Orientation and Other's Strategy in Social Decision Making: A Transformational Analysis," *Journal of Personality and Social Psychology* 55, no. 3 (1988): 396–409.
27. See, e.g., Gary L. Frazier and Raymond C. Rody, "The Use of Influence Strategies in Interfirm Relationships in Industrial Product Channels," *Journal of Marketing* 55, no. 1 (1991): 52–69.
28. Maxwell, Nye, and Maxwell, 2003.
29. James J. White, "Machiavelli and the Bar: Ethical Limitations on Lying in Negotiation," *American Bar Foundation Research Journal* (1980): 926–938.
30. Eleanor H. Norton, "Bargaining and the Ethics of Process," *What's Fair: Ethics for Negotiators* (San Francisco: Jossey-Bass, 2004): 292.
31. Thomas Aquinas, *Summa Theologica*, 2a2ae, Question 77, Article 3 (New York: Benzinger Bros., 1947–48).
32. Pruitt, 1981.
33. William Ross and Jessica LaCroix, "Multiple Meanings of Trust in Negotiation Theory and Research: A Literature Review and Integrative Model," *International Journal of Conflict Management* 7, no. 4 (1996): 314–360.
34. Karen S. Cook et al., "The Distribution of Power in Exchange Networks: Theory and Experimental Results," *American Journal of Sociology* 89 (1983): 275–305.
35. Linda D. Molm, Theron M. Quist, and Phillip A. Wiseley, "Reciprocal Justice and Strategies of Exchange," *Social Forces* 72 (1993): 19–44.
36. Kenneth R. Evans and Richard F. Beltramini, "A Theoretical Model of Consumer Negotiated Pricing: An Orientation Perspective," *Journal of Marketing* 51 (April 1987): 58–73.
37. J. Eliashberg et al., "Assessing the Predictive Accuracy of Two Utility-Based Theories in Marketing Channel Negotiation Context," *Journal of Marketing Research* 23 (1986): 101–110.
38. Margaret Neale and Max Bazerman, *Cognition and Rationality in Negotiation* (New York: Free Press, 1991): 156.
39. Matt Michel, June, 2001, www.plumbers.org/pdl/opt.html quoted by Frank Blau, "What Is a 'Fair' Price?" August 27, 2001, www.pmmag.com.

Chapter 17

1. Robert Barra, Long Island State Assemblyman, AP release (2006) www.weax.com.
2. Harris Interactive Online Survey, conducted for Tax Foundation, March 8–16, 2006, www.taxfoundation.org.
3. Charles Bennett, "Preliminary Results of the National Research Program's Reporting Compliance Study of Tax Year 2001 Individual Returns," Internal Revenue Service (2005).
4. James Alm and Benno Torgler, "Cultural Differences and Tax Morale in the United States and in Europe," *Journal of Economic Psychology* 27, no. 2 (2006): 224–246.

5. Benjamin Barber, interviewed by Gwen Ifill, *The Newshour with Jim Lehrer*, April 16, 2001, www.pbs.org/newshour/.
6. "Tax Quotes," Internal Revenue Service, www.irs.gov.
7. "Taxpayer Attitude Survey," IRS Oversight Board (2005), www.irsoversight board.treas.gov.
8. "A Barometer of Modern Morals," Pew Research Center, March 28, 2006, pewresearch.org.
9. NBC News Poll, Blum & Weprin Associates, April 3–5, 2005, www.pollingreport. com.
10. James Alm, Gary H. McClelland, and William D. Schulze, "Changing the Social Norm of Tax Compliance by Voting" (working paper No. 98-17, *Center for Economic Analysis*, University of Colorado, Boulder, 1998); Benno Torgler, "Tax Morale, Rule-Governed Behaviour and Trust," *Constitutional Political Economy* 14, no. 2 (2003): 119–140.
11. James Alm, Jorge Martinez-Vazquez, and Benno Torgler, "Russian Attitudes Toward Paying Taxes—Before, During and After the Transition," (working paper no. 2005-27, Center for Research in Economics, Management and the Arts, 2005): 18.
12. Stephen Coleman, "The Minnesota Income Tax Compliance Experiment: State Tax Results," Minnesota Department of Revenue (1996), www. socialnorm.org/CaseStudies/taxcompliance.php.
13. Harris Interactive Online Survey, conducted for Tax Foundation, March 8–16, 2006, www.taxfoundation.org.
14. "Fact Sheets: History of the U.S. Tax System," United States Department of the Treasury, www.ustreas.gov/education/fact-sheets/taxes/ustax.
15. Fox News/Opinion Dynamics Poll, March 29–30, 2005, www.pollingreport.com.
16. Dru Sefton, "Enthusiasts Don't Mind Having to Pay Taxes," *New Orleans Times Picayune*, March 24, 2002, www.responsiblewealth.org.
17. Tax Foundation, "Poll Shows Majority of U. S. Adults Support Major Tax Reform, Willing to Give up Some Deductions to Make Tax System Simpler," April 5, 2006, www.taxfoundation.org.
18. Gallup Poll, April 4–7, 2005, www.pollingreport.com.
19. "Description and Analysis of Proposals to Replace the Federal Income Tax," Joint Committee on Taxation, JCS-18-95, June 5, 1995, 58–59.
20. "April's Hard Truths," *The Economist*, April 15, 2006: 34.
21. "Americans Feel They Pay Fair Share of Taxes, Says Poll," May 2, 2005, NewsTarget.com.
22. "Flat Tax," RateEmpire.com.
23. "Estonian Economist and Former Chairman of the Country's Parliamentary Budget Committee in September 2005," www.zeit.de/2005/36/Osteuropa.
24. Professor Annette Nellen, San José State University, www.cob.sjsu.edu/facstaff/.
25. Harris Interactive Online Survey, 2006.
26. "April's Hard Truths," 2006.
27. Rob Morgan, "High Cigarette Tax Would Pay in Several Ways," *The State*, April 16, 2006, www.thestate.com.
28. Jonathan Tamari, "Cigarette Taxes May Go up Again," *Asbury Park Press*, March 17, 2006, www.app.com.

29. Christian Wardlaw and Ingrid Loeffler Palmer, "Calculating Luxury Taxes on Automobiles," 2001, Edmunds.com.

30. Bob Jamieson, "Why Is Gasoline So Expensive?" *World News Tonight*, April 15, 2006, www.abcnews.go.com.

31. Andrew Bary, "Toll-Road Sales: Paying Up," *Barron's*, May 8, 2006: 17–20.

32. Harris Interactive Online Survey, 2006.

33. Chris Edwards, "Democrats' Challenge on Tax Complexity," *Washington Times*, July 23, 2004, www.washingtontimes.com.

34. Robert J. Samuelson, "The Guardians of Complexity," *Newsweek*, April 17, 2006: 47.

35. Executive Summary of President' Advisory Panel of Federal Tax Reform (2005): xiii.

36. Ibid.

37. James Alm and Benno Torgler, "Cultural Differences and Tax Morale in the United States and in Europe," *Journal of Economic Psychology* 27 (2006): 224–246.

38. NBC News Poll, 2005.

39. Benno Torgler, "Tax Morale in Latin America," *Public Choice* 122, no.1 (2005): 133–157.

40. Paul Webley et al., *Tax Evasion: An Experimental Approach* (Cambridge: Cambridge University Press, 1991).

41. J. T. Scholz and M. Lubell, "Cooperation, Reciprocity and the Collective Action Heuristic," *American Journal of Political Science* 45 (2001): 160–178.

42. Edward L. Deci, *Intrinsic Motivation* (New York: Plenum Press, 1975).

43. Torgler, 2005.

44. Benno Torgler, "Cross-Cultural Comparison of Tax Morale and Tax Compliance: Evidence from Costa Rica and Switzerland," *International Journal of Comparative Sociology* 45, no. 17 (2004): 17–43.

45. Lars P. Feld and Benno Torgler, "Tax Morale after the Reunification of Germany: Results from a Quasi-Natural Experiment," (working paper 210, University of California, Berkeley, 2007).

46. Ibid.

47. James Alm, Jorge Martinez-Vazquez, and Benno Torgler, "Russian Attitudes Toward Paying Taxes – Before, During and After the Transition," (working paper no. 2005-27, Center for Research in Economics, Management and the Arts, 2005).

48. Torgler, 2005.

49. Bo Rothstein, *Social Traps and the Problem of Trust* (Cambridge: Cambridge University Press, 2005).

50. Sefton, 2002.

51. M. Ray Perryman, "Paying Taxes Is as American as Disliking Taxes," *San Antonio Business Journal*, May 3, 2002, sanantonio.bizjournals.com.

Chapter 18

1. J. Q. Wilson, *The Moral Sense* (New York: Free Press, 1993).

2. Sarah Maxwell, "Social Norms of Consumer Pricing, Indian Style," *Proceedings: International Society for Marketing and Development* (Legon, Ghana, 2000); Veronica Feder Mayer and Marcos Goncalves Avila, "A Qualitative

Investigation about Community Standards of Fairness in the Brazilian Market: Inferences, Emotions and Culture," *Proceedings: Fordham Pricing Conference* (New York: Fordham University, 2004); Sarah Maxwell et al., "Reactions to a Service Price Increase: What Makes It Seem Fair," *Proceedings: Academy of Marketing Science Cross Cultural Conference* (Seoul, South Korea, 2006).

3. Harry C. Triandis, *Individualism & Collectivism* (Boulder, CO: Westview Press, 1995): 43.

4. Geert Hofstede, *Cultures and Organizations: Software of the Mind* (New York: McGraw-Hill, 1997).

5. Ibid.

6. Mesquita Batja and Nico H. Frijda, "Cultural Variations in Emotions: A Review," *Psychological Bulletin* 112, no. 2 (1992): 179–204.

7. K. Leung and M. H. Bond, "The Impact of Cultural Collectivism on Reward Allocation," *Journal of Personality and Social Psychology* 47 (1984): 793–804.

8. K. Leung and E. A. Lind, "Procedural Justice and Culture: Effects of Culture, Gender, and Investigator Status on Procedural Preferences," *Journal of Personality and Social Psychology* 50 (1986): 1134–1140.

9. Ken-ichi Obuchi, Tomohiro Kumagai, and Emi Atsumi, "Motives of and Responses to Anger in Conflict Situations: A Cross-Cultural Analysis," *Tohoku Psychologica Folia* 61, (2002): 11–21.

10. Raymond R. Liu and Peter McClure, "Recognizing Cross-Cultural Differences in Consumer Complaint Behavior and Intentions: An Empirical Examination," *Journal of Consumer Marketing* 18, no. 1 (2001): 54–71.

11. Harry S. Watkins and Raymond Liu, "Collectivism, Individualism and In-Group Membership: Implications for Consumer Complaining Behaviors in Multicultural Contexts," *Journal of International Consumer Marketing* 8, no. 3/4 (1996): 69–96.

12. Marsha Richins and Bronislaw J. Verhage, "Cross-Cultural Differences in Consumer Attitudes and their Implications for Complaint Management," *International Journal of Research in Marketing* 2 (1985): 197–206.

13. Francis Fukuyama, *Trust* (New York: Simon and Schuster, 1995).

14. Ibid.

15. Nancy R. Buchan, Rachel T. A. Croson and Eric J. Johnson, "When Do Fair Beliefs Influence Bargaining Behavior? Experimental Bargaining in Japan and the United States," *Journal of Consumer Research* 31, no. 1 (2004): 181–190.

16. Michael Lynn, George M. Zinkhan, and Judy Harris, "Consumer Tipping: A Cross-Country Study," *Journal of Consumer Research* 20, no. 3 (1993): 478–488.

17. Hofstede, 1997.

18. Bella Feygin, *The Theory and Practice of Price Formation in the USSR* (Falls Church, VA: Delphic Associates, Inc., 1983).

Chapter 19

1. Margaret Campbell, "Perceptions of Price Fairness: Antecedents and Consequences," *Journal of Marketing Research* 36 (May 1999): 187–199.

2. Outi Uusitalo and Maija Rökman, "Change in Pricing Strategy: The Case of Finnish Grocery Retailing," *Proceedings: Fordham Pricing Conference* (New York: Fordham University, 2004).

3. Jonathan Epstein, "Rising Credit Card Fees Are Costing Consumers Billions," *Buffalo News*, July 17, 2005, www.buffalonews.com.

4. Lisa E. Bolton, and Joseph W. Alba, "Price Fairness: Good and Service Differences and the Role of Vendor Costs," *Journal of Consumer Research* 33 (September 2006): 258–265.

5. Enzo Pesciarelli, "Aspects of the Influence of Francis Hutcheson on Adam Smith," *History of Political Economy* 31, no. 3 (1999): 525–545.

6. "How Textbooks Are Priced," Barnes and Noble Bookstores, Inc. (1995).

7. "Coffee: World Coffee Situation," *Foreign Agricultural Service*, United States Department of Agriculture, 1987–1991; Sarah Maxwell "Before and After the International Coffee Agreement," (working paper, Florida International University, 1991).

8. William Baumol, *Superfairness* (Cambridge MA: MIT Press, 1986).

9. Jad Mouawad, "For Leading Exxon to Its Riches, $144,573 a Day," *New York Times*, April 15, 2006.

10. "Shakers: CEO's Pay Too Much for Affluent Investors," *International Herald Tribune*, March 22, 2006, www.iht.com.

11. "In the Money: A Special Report on Executive Pay," *The Economist*, January 20, 2007: 3–4.

12. "The Boss's Pay: The WSJ/Mercer 2006 CEO Compensation Survey," *Wall Street Journal*, April 9, 2007.

13. "Ousted Home Depot Chief's Golden Handshake Irks Investors," January 4, 2007, www.accountingweb.com.

14. "Microsoft's 87% Windows Profit Margin Draws Criticism from Consumer Groups," *Ananova*, January 14, 2005, www.ananova.com.

15. "Exxon's Profit Will Be Hard to Top," *Wall Street Journal*, February 2, 2007.

16. Simon Romero and Edmund Andrews, "At Exxon Mobil, a Record Profit but No Fanfare," *New York Times*, January 31, 2006: A1.

17. "New National UConn Poll Shows Public Strongly Believes Prescription Drug Prices Unfair; Support Price Controls," University of Connecticut, July 27, 2005, www.uconn.edu/newsmedia.

18. Lisa Bolton, Luk Warlop, and Joseph Alba, "Consumer Perceptions of Price (Un)Fairness," *Journal of Consumer Research* 29 (2003): 474–491.

19. Timothy Aeppel, "Seeking Perfect Prices, CEO Tears up the Rules," *Wall Street Journal*, March 27, 2007.

20. Bruno S. Frey and Werner W. Pommerehne, "On the Fairness of Pricing: An Empirical Survey among the General Population," *Journal of Economic Behavior and Organization* 20 (1993): 295–307.

21. David Leonhardt, "Why Variable Pricing Fails at the Vending Machine," *New York Times*, June 27, 2005, www.nytimes.com.

22. David Leonhardt, "Changes Ahead for a Theater Near You," *New York Times*, February 15, 2006.

23. Thomas Mennecke, "iTunes Sticks with 99 Cent Structure," May 2, 2006, www.slyck.com.

24. Judith A. Chevalier, Anil K. Kashyap, and Peter E. Rossi, "Why Don't Prices Rise during Periods of Peak Demand? Evidence from Scanner Data," *American Economic Review* 93, no. 1 (2003): 15–37.

25. Anita Kunz, "Drug Prices: What's Fair?" *Business Week*, December 10, 2001, 61–70.

26. Kelly L. Haws and William O. Bearden, "Dynamic Pricing and Consumer Fairness Perceptions," *Journal of Consumer Research* 33 (December, 2006): 304–311.

27. Charles Smith, *Auctions: The Social Construction of Value* (Berkeley, CA: University of California Press, 1989): 80.

28. Elizabeth Esfahani, "The Mother of Stunt Marketers," *Business 2.0*, July 2005: 60.

29. Jefferson Graham, "Ticketmaster Uses Auctions to Fight Online Scalpers," *USA Today*, May 22, 2006, www.usatoday.com.

30. Thomas Hildreth, "Google's Dutch Auction IPO: Is There a Take Away Lesson for the Rest of Us?" www.mclane.com.

31. Smith, 1989.

32. Sarah Lyall, "No Gift Horses Here, So Look in Their Mouths," *New York Times*, August 14, 2005.

33. Douglas Frantz, Carol Vogel, and Ralph Blumenthal, "Files of Ex-Christie's Chief Fuel Inquiry into Art Auction," *New York Times*, October 8, 2000.

34. Lee Rosenbaum, "A Touch of Class-Action," *Wall Street Journal*, February 15, 2001.

35. Peter R. Dickson and Rosemary Kalapurakal, "The Use and Perceived Fairness of Price-Setting Rules in the Bulk Electricity Market," *Journal of Economic Psychology* 15 (1994): 427–448.

36. Arik Johnson, "Tying Arrangements: Illegal Tying Is One of the Most Common Antitrust Claims," Aurora WDC, March 9, 2007, www.aurorawdc.com.

37. "Light Up: Why Airlines Have Started Charging for Check-in Bags," *The Economist*, February 11, 2006: 60.

38. Dan Milmo, "BA Says It Will Charge £120 for Excess Baggage," *Guardian*, February 9, 2007, www.guardian.com.uk.

39. Ronald Alsop, "How Boss's Deeds Buff a Firm's Reputation," *Wall Street Journal*, January 31, 2007.

40. Tamara Kaplan, "The Tylenol Crisis," www.personal.psu.edu.

41. Alsop, 2007.

42. Campbell, 1999.

43. Novartis International, *Corporate Citizenship Review*, January 2007.

44. "Donating Our Dollars and Hours: Charitable Giving in the United States," July 3/10, 2006: 65.

Glossary

Advantageous inequity: Getting more than we give in an exchange; getting more than the other party to the exchange gets or more than other people get.

Anger: A highly charged negative emotional state that consists of feelings of fury, rage, resentment, and hostility to others.

Aristotle: Fourth century B.C. Greek philosopher rediscovered in the High Middle Ages and revered for his work in logic and ethics.

Attributional bias: Tendency to blame events on either another person, or oneself, or fate.

Attribution theory: How everyday people explain the cause of everyday events.

Augustine: Fourth century A.D. theologian, author of many books on theology and held as an authority of the church by the Scholastics.

Bait and switch: The illegal practice of advertising a low price to bring customers into the store but then saying that the item is sold out and showing them a higher priced alternative.

Behavioral regularity: A habitual action repeated over time, but not backed by a social norm.

Buffer pricing: When the seller maintains the same price despite small cost variations.

Buffet pricing: When seller charges a flat price for unlimited use of a product.

Bundling: When more than one item is included in a price.

Buyers' market: A situation where buyers have greater power than the seller due to supply having outstripped demand.

Candy-bar pricing: Increasing profits by decreasing the size of the product rather than increasing the price.

Class society: A society that supports obvious levels of social rankings.

Coercive norms: Rules imposed by a more powerful person to further his or her own self-interest.

Collectivist culture: Culture in which people take their identity from the group in which they belong.

Competitive-based pricing: Basing price on competitors' prices (also called *market-based pricing*).

Competitive negotiation strategy: The use of aggressive negotiating techniques: making small concessions and bluffing with threats to leave.

Congestion pricing: Charging for traffic into the center part of a city; adjusting charge by time of day to reduce peak hour traffic.

Consumption tax: Same as a "fair" tax: a tax on amount spent rather than the amount earned.

Context-based trust: Short-term optimistic expectation that another person will be trustworthy.

Control: Belief that an event can be influenced by person responsible.

Cooperative negotiation strategy: The use of conciliatory negotiating techniques: making large concessions and not bluffing with threats to leave.

Cooperative norms: Rules that develop within an ongoing relationship to the benefit of both parties involved.

Cost-based pricing: Basing price on costs plus profit (also called *cost-plus pricing*).

Crowding out: The replacement of internal, intrinsic motivation with external motivation.

Cultural trust: The expectation that people in one's group will act in accordance with the social norms.

Culture: The values, beliefs, and attitudes of a society; what has been called "the software of the mind."

Custom-based pricing: Basing price on what is traditional in an industry.

Customer-based pricing: Basing price on what a customer is willing to pay (also called *demand-based, value-based, dynamic* or *yield pricing*).

Decentralized norms: Ubiquitous rules that evolve over time to facilitate exchange, whether economic or social.

Demand: Consumers' desire for a product or service combined with their ability to pay for it.

Descriptive norms: Consensual rules of expected actions and outcomes based on custom and tradition.

Dictator: The person in dictator games who is given the money and decides the allotment.

Dictator games: A research method in which one person is given a sum of money that is to be shared with another person; if the other person refuses his or her allotted share, neither receives anything.

Discriminatory pricing: Charging different prices to different people for the same product or service (also called *differential pricing*).

Distress: A negative emotional state that consists of feelings of disappointment, annoyance or mild irritation.

Distributive fairness: When an outcome adheres to the social norms of how goods (or prices) should be allocated.

Dorsal striatum: Section of the brain that processes rewards, makes you feel good.

Dual concern model: A negotiation model in which both parties have a concern for not only their own self-interest but also the interest of the other.

Dynamic pricing: Discriminatory pricing that can change quickly: usually applied to discriminatory prices on the Internet.

Egalitarian society: A society that supports all people being on the same level.

Emotional tag: The association of feelings like "good" or "bad" to beliefs like social norms.

Emotion: A strong feeling that arises subjectively rather than cognitively, from the gut rather than from the brain.

Engrosser: One who buys up all goods before they get to market in order to gain monopoly power.

Envy-free allocations: A distribution of benefits so no one is jealous of the bundle of benefits received by another.

Expert power: The ability to manipulate prices due to superior knowledge.

Exponentially decaying weighted average: A mathematical method of adjusting a rolling average so that more recent events are given greater weight.

Fairness heuristic theory: The idea that giving another person authority increases one's sensitivity to issues of fairness and concerns about the other's trustworthiness.

Fair tax: A tax based on a percentage of all sales.

Five-finger discount: Stealing, particularly shoplifting.

Flat culture: Where differences in power and status are less accepted; where the norm is that all people should be treated equally.

Flat tax: A tax where everyone pays the same percentage of income.

Focus group: A market research technique in which six to ten consumers are gathered together to share their ideas with a moderator.

Forestaller: One who discourages or prevents normal sales by buying merchandise before it gets to market or by keeping others from bringing their goods to market.

Freeloader: Someone who takes advantage of the benefits earned by others.

Freeware: Software provided at no cost over the net.

Haggling: Negotiating a price: bargaining, dickering.

Heuristic: A "rule-of-thumb" method of solving problems; for example, always ordering the second cheapest bottle of wine on the menu.

Hierarchical culture: Where differences in power and status are accepted; where the norm is that individuals with more power should be granted special privileges.

Individualist culture: Where people take their identity from their own individual accomplishments.

Individual trust: A predisposition to have optimistic expectations about events or behavior.

In-group: The group of similar individuals—extended family and close friends—in a collectivist society.

Legitimate power: The ability to influence another person's actions such as setting a price.

Luxury tax: Tax on big-ticket nonessentials.

Market solutions: Allowing supply and demand to determine prices without government interference.

Meta-analysis: Analysis encompassing many other studies.

Metanorm: Norm encompassing many other norms, for example, the norm of fairness.

Model: A simplified representation of how ideas are related, often shown graphically.

Monopoly: Exclusive control over the sale of a product or service.

Moral rectitude: A firm belief that one's actions are right and legitimate, in accordance with the social norms.

Motivation: Urge to act.

Norm of equality: The rule that all people should be charged the same amount; all people should have equal opportunity to get the lowest possible price.

Norm of equity: The rule that what you pay should match the value of what you receive.

Norm of impartiality: The rule that the pricing process should not be influenced by personal favoritism.

Norm of need: The rule that special considerations should be given to those who are less fortunate.

Norm of rationality: The rule that economic decisions should be based on reasoning rather than emotions, with self interest often considered the primary reason.

Norm of reciprocity: The rule that a kindness should be repaid with a kindness, a harm with a harm.

Norm of self-interest: The erroneously assumed rule that people act only in their own self interest.

Norm of transparency: The rule that the pricing process should be clear and understandable.

Norm of voice and choice: The rule that consumers should have some control over pricing process.

Norms of outcome: Consensually agreed upon rules of who should be charged what in different circumstances.

Norms of process: Consensually agreed upon rules of how prices should be determined.

Opportunism: Taking advantage of a situation for one's own self-interest.

Outcomes: The end result of a distribution strategy: the price actually charged to the customer.

Permanence: Belief that an action will be repeated in the future.

Personal fairness: Preference for what is considered acceptable outcomes and procedures based on the legitimate expectations of descriptive norms.

Pollution rights: An assigned allotment of pollution that a country can produce and potentially trade with other countries.

Power: The ability to make other people do what you want them to do even when they do not want to do so.

Power distance: The extent to which a culture accepts preferential treatment of some groups based on their power: hierarchical.

Prescriptive norms: Consensual rules of appropriate actions and outcomes based on community values: "should" statements.

Price bundle: When more than one item or service are included in the price; for example, including the tires in the price of a car.

Price elasticity: The extent to which the quantity sold responds to the price charged, the assumption being that as the price increases, sales will decrease.

Price negotiations: Bargaining over only the price, not the product or service.

Price optimization software: Computer software that determines discriminatory prices based on local customer demand: usually applied to discriminatory prices in retailing.

Price segmentation: Grouping together consumers based on their price sensitivity.

Price sensitivity: A consumer's willingness to purchase when the price increases or decreases.

Priming: Planting an idea so that it becomes important when decisions are made.

Procedural fairness: When a process adheres to the social norms of how people should act in different situations.

Progressive tax: A tax that has more impact as income increases: for example, the current income tax system where the percentage of tax increases when the income a person earns increases.

Quantity discount: A lower price based on buying a larger quantity.

Reciprocal negotiation strategy: Copying whatever opponents do in bargaining: making large concessions when they do and being stingy when they are, counterbluffing when they bluff.

Reference price: The standard against which a price is judged cheap or expensive, fair or unfair: based on prior experience and information in the environment.

Regressive tax: A tax that has less impact as income increases; for example, a sales tax that is the same percentage for everyone, no matter how much income a person earns.

Responder: The person in dictator games who decides on acceptance or rejection of the dictator's allotment.

Responsibility: Person, inanimate object, or force that is named and blamed for an adverse action.

Rolling average: An average based on a set number of past events over time; for example, averaging the past three months at the end of each month.

Sanction: Punishment that ensures compliance with the social norms.

Sanction power: The ability to control another person's actions through rewards and punishments.

Scholastics: Group of philosophical theologians whose school of thought, strongly influenced by Aristotle, dominated the High Middle Ages.

Script: A set of rules prescribing a sequence of appropriate actions; for instance, how a negotiation is to be conducted.

Self-serving bias: The inclination to think that what benefits oneself is more fair.

Sellers' market: A situation where sellers have greater power than buyers due to demand being greater than supply.

Service charge: Percentage automatically added to restaurant bills for service provided.

Sin tax: Tax on items that are generally considered harmful to society or individuals.

Social capital: A network of cooperative relationships based on commonly accepted social norms that facilitate productive activity.

Social fairness: Judgment that outcomes and procedures are "just" based on the standards of prescriptive norms.

Social homeostasis: A state of social equilibrium; the status quo.

Social norms: Tacitly understood and consensually agreed upon rules of a society.

St. Albert the Great: Brilliant thirteenth-century A.D. Scholastic who was the teacher of Thomas Aquinas; with Aquinas, he translated and interpreted Aristotle.

St. Thomas Aquinas: Best known thirteenth-century A.D. Scholastic who is recognized for synthesizing the work of Aristotle with the precepts of the church.

Tax morale: Having an intrinsic motivation to pay taxes.

Transaction costs: The costs associated with making an economic exchange.

Trust: The belief that another person will act in your best interest even when she or he has the power to take advantage of you.

Unbundling: When items previously included in a price are sold separately.

Universal norm: A social rule believed to be held in all cultures.

Use tax: Taxing the use of a product instead of the sale of it.

Value: Subjectively perceived material worth of item or service, which is measured quantitatively by the price.

Win-lose negotiation: Bargaining in which one person's gain is another person's loss as in price negotiations.

Win-win negotiation: Bargaining over price, product, and services so that both negotiators come out ahead.

Yield pricing: Discriminatory pricing that changes based on predicted demand; usually applied to discriminatory prices for airfares.

Zero-sum game: Where one person's gain is another person's loss; for instance, negotiating the price of a used car.

Zone of agreement: The range of prices between the highest price the buyer will pay and the lowest price the seller will accept; settlement is expected to take place within this zone.

References

Adams, J. Stacy. 1963. Toward an understanding of inequity. *Journal of Abnormal and Social Psychology* 67: 422–436.

Alm, James, Gary H. McClelland, and William D. Schulze. 1998. Changing the social norm of tax compliance by voting. Working Paper No. 98–17. Center for Economic Analysis. Boulder: University of Colorado.

——, Jorge Martinez-Vazquez, and Benno Torgler. 2005. Russian attitudes toward paying taxes—before, during and after the transition. Working paper no. 2005–27. Center for Research in Economics, Management and the Arts.

——, and Benno Torgler. 2006. Cultural differences and tax morale in the United States and in Europe. *Journal of Economic Psychology* 27 (2): 224–246.

Ariely, Dan, George Loewenstein, and Drazen Prelec. 2003. "Coherent arbitrariness": Stable demand curves without stable preferences. *The Quarterly Journal of Economics* 118 (1): 73–106.

——. 2006. Tom Sawyer and the construction of value. *Journal of Economic Behavior & Organization* 60 (1): 1–28.

Arrow, Kenneth. 1974. *The limits of organization.* New York: Norton.

Axelrod, Robert. 1986. An evolutionary approach to norms. *American Political Science Review* 80: 1095–1111.

Azar, Ofer H. 2004. Optimal monitoring with external incentives: The case of tipping. *Southern Economic Journal* 71 (1): 170–181.

——. 2004. What sustains social norms and how they evolve? The case of tipping. *Journal of Economic Behavior and Organization* 54 (1): 49–57.

——. 2005. The social norm of tipping: Does it improve social welfare? *Journal of Economics* 85 (2): 141–149.

Babcock Linda, George Loewenstein, Samuel Issacharoff, and Colin Camerer. 1995. Biased judgments of fairness in bargaining. *The American Economic Review* 85 (May): 1337–1343.

———, and George Loewenstein. 1997. Explaining bargaining impasses: The role of self-serving biases. *Journal of Economic Perspectives* 11 (1): 109–126.

Baldridge, Letitia. 1993. *Letitia Baldridge's new complete guide to executive manners.* New York: Rawson Associates, Macmillan Publishing Company.

Baldwin, John. 1959. *The medieval theories of the just price: Romanists, canonists and theologians in the twelfth and thirteenth centuries.* Transactions of the American Philosophical Society. n.s. 49. pt. 4. Philadelphia.

Bartos, Otomar J. 1977. Simple model of negotiation: A sociological point of view. *Journal of Conflict Resolution* 21 (4): 565–579.

Batja, Mesquita and Nico H. Frijda. 1992. Cultural variations in emotions: A review. *Psychological Bulletin* 112 (2): 179–204.

Baumol, William. 1986. *Superfairness.* Cambridge: MIT Press.

Bazerman, M. H., and J. Carroll. 1987. Negotiator cognition. *Research in Organizational Behavior,* Vol 9. Ed. B. Staw and L. L. Cummings. Greenwich, CT: JAI Press: 247–288.

Bechwati, Nada Nasr, and Maureen Morrin. 2003. Outraged consumers: Getting even at the expense of getting a good deal. *Journal of Consumer Psychology* 13 (4): 440–453.

Ben-Yoav, O., and D. G. Pruitt. 1984. Resistance to yielding and the expectation of cooperative future interaction in negotiation. *Journal of Experimental Social Psychology* 20: 323–353.

Ben-Zion, Uri, and Edi Karni. 1977. Tip payments and the quality of service. In O. C. Ashenfelter and W. E. Oates (eds.), *Essays in Labor Market Analysis.* New York: Wiley.

Berry, Leonard L. 1996. Retailers with a future. *Marketing Management* 5 (Spring): 38–46.

Berscheid, E., W. Graziano, T. Monson, and M. Dermer. 1976. Outcome dependency, attention, attribution, and attraction. *Journal of Personality and Social Psychology* 34: 978–989.

Bicchieri, Christina. 2006. *The grammar of society: The nature and dynamics of social norms.* Cambridge, UK: Cambridge University Press.

Bies, Robert, and Thomas Tripp. 1996. Beyond distrust: "Getting even" and the need for revenge. In Roderick Kramer and Tom R. Tyler (eds.), *Trust in Organizations.* Thousand Oaks, CA: Sage Publications: 252–283.

Blau, Peter. 1967. *Exchange and power in social life.* New York: John Wiley.

Blinder, A. S., E. R. D. Canetti, D. E. Lebow, and J. B. Rudd. 1998. *Asking about prices: A new approach to understanding price stickiness.* New York: Russell Sage Foundation.

Blount, Sally. 1995. When social outcomes aren't fair: The effect of causal attributions on preferences. *Organizational Behavior and Human Decision Processes* 63 (2): 131–144.

———. 2000. Whoever said that markets were fair? *Negotiation Journal* 16 (3): 237–252.

Bodvarsson, Orn B., and William A Gibson. 1997. Economics and restaurant gratuities: Determining tip rates. *The American Journal of Economics and Sociology* 56 (February): 187–203.

Bohm, Janice, and Bryan Hendricks. 1997. Effects of interpersonal touch, degree of justification, and sex of participants in compliance with request. *The Journal of Social Psychology* 137 (4): 460–469.

Bolton, Gary E., and Rami Zwick. 1995. Anonymity versus punishment in ultimatum bargaining. *Games and Economic Behavior* 10: 95–121.

Bolton, Lisa E., Luk Warlop, and Joseph Alba. 2003. Consumers perceptions of price (un)fairness. *Journal of Consumer Research* 29 (March): 474–491.

———, and Joseph W. Alba. 2006. Price fairness: Good and service differences and the role of vendor costs. *Journal of Consumer Research* 33 (September): 258–265.

Bougie, Roger, Rik Pieters, and Marcel Zeelenberg. 2003. Angry customers don't come back, they get back: The experience and behavioral implications of anger and dissatisfaction in services. *Journal of the Academy of Marketing Science* 31 (4): 377–393.

Bradach, Jeffrey, and Robert Eccles. 1989. Price, authority and trust. *Annual Review of Sociology* 15: 97–106.

Bradley, Gifford W. 1978. Self-serving biases in the attribution process: A reexamination of the fact or fiction question. *Journal of Personality and Social Psychology* 36 (January): 56–71.

Brockner, Joel, and Phyllis A. Siegel. 1996. Understanding the interaction between procedural and distributive justice. In Roderick M. Kramer and Tom R. Tyler (eds.), *Trust in Organizations.* Thousand Oaks, CA: Sage Publications.

Brosnan, Sarah R., and Frans B. M. de Waal. 2003. Monkeys reject unequal pay. *Nature* 425: 297–299.

Buchan, Nancy R., Rachel T. A. Croson, and Eric J. Johnson. 2004. When do fair beliefs influence bargaining behavior? Experimental bargaining in Japan and the United States. *Journal of Consumer Research* 31 (1): 181–190.

Butler, John D., Jr. 1991. Toward understanding and measuring conditions of trust: Evolution of a conditions of trust inventory. *Journal of Management* 17 (3): 643–663.

Campanelli, Melissa. 1993. What's in store for EDLP? *Sales and Marketing Management* 145 (9): 56–59.

Campbell, Margaret. 1999. Perceptions of price fairness: Antecedents and consequences. *Journal of Marketing Research* 36 (2): 187–199.

———. 1999. Why did you do that? The important role of inferred motive in perceptions of price fairness. *Journal of Product and Brand Management* 8 (2): 145–153.

Carpenter, Jeffrey P., Peter Hans Matthews, and Okomboli Ong'ong'a. 2004. Why punish? Social reciprocity and the enforcement of prosocial norms. *Journal of Evolutionary Economics* 24: 407–429.

Carr, Craig L. 2000. *On fairness*. Aldershot, UK: Ashgate Publishing Ltd.

Chafuen, Alejandro A. 2003. *Faith and liberty: The economic thought of the late Scholastics*. Lanham, MD: Lexington Books.

Chevalier, Judith A., Anil K. Kashyap, and Peter E. Rossi. 2003. Why don't prices rise during periods of peak demand? Evidence from scanner data. *American Economic Review* 93 (1): 15–37.

Cialdini, Robert B., and Raymond R. Reno. 1990. A focus theory of normative conduct: A theoretical refinement and reevaluation of the role of norms in human behavior. *Advances in Experimental Social Psychology* 24: 240–248.

Coleman, James. 1988. Social capital in the creation of human capital. *American Journal of Sociology* 94: S95–S120.

Conlin, Michael, Michael Lynn, and Ted O'Donoghue. 2003. The norm of restaurant tipping. *Journal of Economic Behavior and Organization* 52 (3): 297–308.

Cook, Karen S., Richard M. Emerson, Mary R Gillmore, and Toshio Yamagishi. 1983. The distribution of power in exchange networks: Theory and experimental results. *American Journal of Sociology* 89: 275–305.

Coquitt, Jason A., and Jerome M. Cherthoff. 2002. Explaining injustice: The interactive effect of explanation and outcome on fairness perceptions and task motivation. *Journal of Management* 28 (5): 591–610.

Dahl, Robert A. 1957. The concept of power. *Behavioral Science* 2 (3): 201–215.

Damasio, Antonio. 1994. *Descartes' error: Emotion, reason and the human brain.* London: Penguin Books.

———. 2003. *Looking for Spinoza: Joy, sorrow, and the feeling brain.* Orlando, FL: Harcourt, Inc.

Darke, Peter R., and Darren W. Dahl. 2003. Fairness and discounts: The subjective value of a bargain. *Journal of Consumer Psychology* 13 (3): 328–338.

Dawes, Robyn, and Richard Thaler. 1988. Anomalies of cooperation. *The Journal of Economic Perspective* 2 (3): 187–197.

Deci, Edward L. 1975. *Intrinsic motivation.* New York: Plenum Press.

DellaVigna, Stefano, and Ulrike Malmendier. 2004. Contract design and self-control: Theory and evidence. *The Quarterly Journal of Economics* 119 (2): 353–384.

DeQuervain D., U. Fischbacher, V. Treyer, M. Schellhamer, U. Schnyder, A. Buk, and E. Fehr. 2004. The neural basis of altruistic punishment. *Science* 305: 1254–1258.

DeRidder, Richard, and Rama C. Tripathi. 1992. *Norm violation and intergroup relations.* Oxford, UK: Clarendon Press.

De Roover, Raymond. 1958. The concept of the just price: Theory and economic policy. *Journal of Economic History* 18 (December): 422–438.

Deutsch, Morton. 1958. Trust and suspicion. *The Journal of Conflict Resolution* 2 (4): 265–279.

———. 1975. Equity, equality, and need: What determines which value will be used as the basis of distributive justice? *Journal of Social Issues* 31 (3): 137–149.

———. 1985. *Distributive justice: A social-psychological perspective.* New Haven, CT: Yale University Press.

DeWaal, Frans B. M. 1991. The chimpanzee's sense of social regularity and its relation to the human sense of justice. *The American Behavioral Scientist* 34 (3): 335–348.

Dickson, Peter R., and Alan G. Sawyer. 1990. "The price knowledge and search of supermarket shoppers." *Journal of Marketing* 54 (3): 42–53.

———, and Rosemary Kalapurakal. 1994. The use and perceived fairness of price-setting rules in the bulk electricity market. *Journal of Economic Psychology* 15: 427–448.

Drolet, Aimee, Richard Larrick, and Michael W. Morris. 1998. Thinking of others: How perspective taking changes negotiators' aspirations and fairness perceptions as a function of negotiator relationship. *Basic and Applied Social Psychology* 20 (1): 23–31.

Drummond, John. 2006. The value of being a "trusted" company. *Corporate Responsibility Management* 2 (4): 12–13.

Durkheim, Émile. [1893] 1933. *The division of labor in society.* Trans. George Simpson. Glencoe, IL: Free Press.

Dwyer, F. Robert. 1984. Are two better than one? Bargaining behavior and outcomes in an asymmetrical power relationship. *Journal of Consumer Research* 11 (September): 680–693.

———, Paul H. Schurr, and Sejo Oh. 1987. Developing buyer-seller relationships. *Journal of Marketing* 51 (April): 11–27.

Eliashberg, J., S. A. LaTour, A. Rangaswamy, and L. W. Stern. 1986. Assessing the predictive accuracy of two utility-based theories in marketing channel negotiation context. *Journal of Marketing Research* 23: 101–110.

Ellickson, Robert C. 1991. *Order without law: How neighbors settle disputes.* Cambridge: Harvard University Press.

Ensminger, Jean. 2001. Reputations, trust, and the principal agent problem. In Karen Cook (ed.), *Trust in Society.* New York: Russell Sage.

Esser, James K., and S. S. Komorita. 1975. Reciprocity and concession making in bargaining. *Journal of Personality and Social Psychology* 31 (5): 864–872.

Estelami, Hooman. 1998. The price is right . . . or is it? Demographic and category effects on consumer price knowledge. *Journal of Product and Brand Management* 7 (3): 254–266.

Evans, Kenneth R., and Richard F. Beltramini. 1987. A theoretical model of consumer negotiated pricing: An orientation perspective. *Journal of Marketing* 51 (April): 58–73.

Feather, N. T., and J. G. Simon. 1973. Fear of success and causal attribution for outcome. *Journal of Personality* 41: 525–542.

Fehr, Ernst, and Urs Fischbacher. 2004. Third-party punishment and social norms. *Evolution and Human Behavior* 25: 63–87.

———, Urs Fischbacher, and Michael Kosfeld. 2005. Neuroeconomic foundations of trust and social preferences: Initial evidence. *American Economic Review* 95 (February): 346–351.

———, and Klaus M. Schmidt. 1999. A theory of fairness, competition, and cooperation. *The Quarterly Journal of Economics* (August): 817–868.

Feinberg, Fred M., Aradhna Krishna and Z. John Zhang. 2002. Do we care what others get? A behaviorist approach to targeted promotions. *Journal of Marketing Research* 39 (3): 277–291.

Feld, Lars P., and Benno Torgler. 2007. Tax morale after the reunification of Germany: Results from a quasi-natural experiment. Working paper 210. Berkeley: University of California.

Festinger, Leon. 1957. *A theory of cognitive dissonance.* Stanford: Stanford University Press.

Feygin, Bella. 1983. *The theory and practice of price formation in the USSR.* Falls Church, VA: Delphic Associates, Inc.

Filley, A. C. 1975. *Interpersonal conflict resolution.* Glenview, IL: Scott, Foresman.

Finkel, Norman. 2001. *Not fair! The typology of commonsense unfairness.* Washington, DC: American Psychological Association.

Folkes, Valerie, Susan Koletsky, and John L. Graham. 1987. A field study of causal inference and consumer reaction: The view from the airport. *Journal of Consumer Research* 13 (March): 534–539.

Forsythe, Robert, Joel Horowitz, N. Savin, and Martin Sefton. 1994. Fairness in simple bargaining experiments. *Games and Economic Behavior* 6: 347–369.

Frank, Robert H. 1988. *Passions within reason: The strategic role of the emotions.* New York: Norton.

Frazier, Gary L. and Sudhir H. Kale. 1989. Manufacturer-distributor relationships: A sellers' versus buyers' market perspective. *International Marketing Review* 6 (6): 7–26.

———, and Raymond C. Rody. 1991. The use of influence strategies in interfirm relationships in industrial product channels. *Journal of Marketing* 55 (1): 52–69.

French, John R., and Bertram Raven. 1959. The bases of social power. In Dorwin Cartwright (ed.), *Studies in social power.* Ann Arbor: University of Michigan Press.

Frey, Bruno S., and Werner W. Pommerehne. 1993. On the fairness of pricing: An empirical survey among the general population. *Journal of Economic Behavior and Organization* 20: 295–307.

Fukuyama, Francis. 1995. *Trust.* New York: Simon & Schuster.

Garbarino, Ellen, and Sarah Maxwell. 2004. Social norms and judged fairness as mediators of trust-breaking due to dynamic posted prices. *Proceedings, Fordham Pricing Conference.* New York: Fordham University.

Gents, Herbert. 2000. Strong reciprocity and human sociality. *Journal of Theoretical Biology* 206 (2): 169–179.

Giddens, Anthony. 1984. *The constitution of society.* Berkeley: University of California Press.

Goertz, Gary, and Paul F. Diehl. 1992. Toward a theory of international norms. *Journal of Conflict Resolution* 36 (December): 634–664.

Gorman, Raymond, and James B. Kehr. 1992. Fairness as a constraint on profit seeking: Comment. The *American Economic Review* 82 (1): 355–358.

Gouldner, Alvin W. 1960. The norm of reciprocity: A preliminary statement. *American Sociological Review* 25 (2): 161–178.

Granovetter, Mark. 1985. Economic action and social structure: The problem of embeddedness. *American Journal of Sociology* 91 (3): 481–510.

Greenberg, Jerald. 2004. Stress fairness to fare no stress: Managing workplace stress by promoting organizational justice. *Organizational Dynamics* 33 (4): 352–364.

Grewal, Dhruv, and Larry Compeau. 1999. Pricing and public policy: A research agenda and an overview. *Journal of Public Policy & Marketing* 18 (1): 3–10.

———, David M. Hardesty, and Gopalkrishnan R. Iyer. 2004. The effects of buyer identification and purchase timing on consumers' perceptions of trust, price fairness and repurchase intentions. *Journal of Interactive Marketing* 18 (4): 87–100.

Grice-Hutchinson, Marjorie. 1952. *The school of Salamanca: Readings in Spanish monetary theory.* Oxford: Clarendon Press.

Gundlach, Gregory and Ravi S. Achrol. 1993. Governance in Exchange: Contract Law and its Alternatives. *Journal of Public Policy and Marketing* 12 (October): 141–155.

Hardin, Russell. 2001. Conceptions and explanations of trust. In Karen Cook (ed.), *Trust in Society.* New York: Russell Sage: 3–39.

Haws, Kelly L., and William O. Bearden. 2006. Dynamic pricing and consumer fairness perceptions. *Journal of Consumer Research* 33 (3): 304–311.

Hayek, Friedrich A. 1994 [1944]. *The road to serfdom.* Chicago: University of Chicago Press.

Hechter, Michael, and Karl-Dieter Opp (eds.). 2001. *Social norms.* New York: Russell Sage Foundation.

Heide, Jan B., and George John. 1992. Do norms matter in marketing relationships? *Journal of Marketing* 56 (April): 32–44.

Heider, Fritz. 1958. *The psychology of interpersonal relations.* New York: Wiley.

Henrich, Joseph, Richard McElreath, Abigail Barr, Jean Ensminger, Clark Barrett, Alexander Bolyanatz, Juan Camilo Cardenas, Michael Gurven, Edwins Gwako, Natalie Henrich, Carolyn Lesorogol, Frank Marlowe, David Tracer, and John Ziker. 2006. Costly punishment across human societies. *Science* 312 (5781): 1767–1770.

Herlihy, David. 1958. The concept of the just price: Discussion. *Journal of Economic History* 18 (December): 437.

Hoffman, Abbie. 1971. *Steal this book.* New York: Pirate Editions.

Hofstede, Geert. 1997. *Cultures and organizations: Software of the mind.* New York: McGraw-Hill.

Homans, George C. 1950. *The human group.* New York: Harcourt Brace.

———. 1961. *Social behavior: Its elementary forms.* New York: Harcourt Brace.

Horne, Christine. 2001. Sociological perspectives on the emergence of social norms. In Michael Hechter and Karl-Dieter Opp (eds.), *Social norms.* New York: Russell Sage Foundation: 3–34.

Hosmer, Larue T. 1995. Trust: The connecting link between organizational theory and philosophical ethics. *Academy of Management Review* 20 (2): 379–403.

Huan, Jen-Hung, and Chia-Yen Lin. 2005. The explanation effects on consumer perceived justice, satisfaction and loyalty improvement: An exploratory study. *Journal of American Academy of Business* 7 (2): 212–218.

Huppertz, John W., Sidney J. Arenson, and Richard H. Evans. 1978. An application of equity theory to buyer-seller exchange situations. *Journal of Marketing Research* 15 (May): 250–260.

Jacoby, Jacob, and Jerry C. Olson. 1977. Consumer response to price: An attitudinal, information processing perspective. In Yoram Wind and Marshall Greenberg (eds.), *Moving ahead with attitude research.* Chicago: American Marketing Society.

Janiszewski, Chris, and Donald R. Lichtenstein. 1999. A range theory account of price perception. *Journal of Consumer Research* 25 (March): 353–368.

Jasso, Guillermina. 2001. Rule finding about rule making: Comparison processes and the making of rules. In Michael Hechter and Karl-Dieter Opp (eds.), *Social norm.* New York: Russell Sage Foundation: 348–393.

Jones, Douglas N., and Patrick C. Mann. 2001. The fairness criterion in public utility regulations: Does fairness still matter? *Journal of Economic Issues* 35 (1): 153–172.

Kahneman, Daniel, Jack L. Knetsch, and Richard H. Thaler. 1986. Fairness and the assumptions of economics. *Journal of Business* 59 (April): S285–S300.

————. 1986. Fairness as a constraint on profit seeking: Entitlements in the market. *American Economic Review* 76 (September): 728–741.

Kalapurakal, Rosemary, Peter R. Dickson, and Joel E. Urbany. 1992. A conceptual model of price fairness judgments. *Working paper.* Columbus: Ohio State University.

Kalwani, Manohar U., Chi Kin Yim, Heikki J. Rinne, and Yoshi Sugita. 1990. A price expectations model of customer brand choice. *Journal of Marketing Research* 27 (August): 251–261.

Kalyanaram, Gurumurthy, and John D. Little. 1987. A price response model developed from perceptual theories. Working paper. Cambridge: Sloan School of Management, MIT.

Kaufman, Patrick J., N. Craig Smith, and Gwendolyn K. Ortmeyer. 1994. Deception in retailer high-low pricing: A "rule of reason" approach. *Journal of Retailing* 70 (2): 115–138.

Kaye, Joel. 1998. *Economy and nature in the fourteenth century: Money, market exchange, and the emergence of scientific thought.* Cambridge: Cambridge University Press.

Kelley, Harold H. 1973. The processes of causal attribution. *American Psychologist* 28 (February): 107–123.

Kimes, Sheryl E. and Jochen Wurtz. 2003. Has revenue management become acceptable? *Journal of Service Research* 6(2): 125–137.

Klaes, Matthias. 2002. Some remarks on the place of psychological and social elements in a theory of custom. *American Journal of Economics and Sociology* 61 (2): 523.

Kruger, Joachim, and Russell Clement. 1994. The truly false consensus effect: An ineradicable and egocentric bias in social perception. *Journal of Personality and Social Psychology* 67 (2): 596–619.

Lattin, James M., and Randolf E. Bucklin. 1989. Reference effects of price and promotion on brand choice behavior. *Journal of Marketing Research* 26 (3): 229–310.

Lazarus, Richard S. 1993. From psychological stress to the emotions: A history of changing outlooks. *Annual Review of Psychology* 44: 1–21.

Leung, K., and M. H. Bond. 1984. The impact of cultural collectivism on reward allocation. *Journal of Personality and Social Psychology* 47: 793–804.

———, and E. A. Lind. 1986. Procedural justice and culture: Effects of culture, gender, and investigator status on procedural preferences. *Journal of Personality and Social Psychology* 50: 1134–1140.

———, and Wai-Kwan Li. 1990. Psychological mechanisms of process-control effects. *Journal of Applied Psychology* 75 (June): 613–620.

Lewicki, Roy J., Daniel J. McAllister and Robert J. Bier. 1998. Trust and distrust: New relationships and realities. *Academy of Management Review* 23 (3): 438–458.

Lind, E. Allan, and Tom R. Tyler. 1988. *The social psychology of procedural justice.* New York: Plenum.

Liu, Raymond R., and Peter McClure. 2001. Recognizing cross-cultural differences in consumer complaint behavior and intentions: An empirical examination. *Journal of Consumer Marketing* 18 (1): 54–71.

Loewenstein, George F., Leigh Thompson, and Max H. Bazerman. 1989. Social utility and decision making in interpersonal contexts. *Journal of Personality and Social Psychology* 57 (3): 426–441.

———, Samuel Issacharoff, Colin Camerer, and Linda Babcock. 1993. Biased judgments of fairness in bargaining. *American Economic Review* 85 (5): 1337–1343.

Lowenstein, Linda and George Lowenstein. 1997. Explaining bargaining impasses: the role of self-serving biases. *Journal of Economic Perspectives* 11(1): 109–126.

Lupfer, Michael B., Kelly P. Weeks, Kelly A. Doan, and David A. Houston. 2000. Folk conceptions of fairness and unfairness. *European Journal of Social Psychology* 30: 405–428.

Lynn, Michael. 2001. Restaurant tipping and service quality: A tenuous relationship. *Cornell Hotel and Restaurant Administration Quarterly* 42 (1): 14–20.

———, and Michael McCall. 2000. Gratitude and gratuity: A meta-analysis of research on the service-tipping relationship. *Journal of Socio-Economics* 29 (February): 203–214.

———, George M. Zinkhan and Judy Harris. 1993. Consumer tipping: A cross-country study. *Journal of Consumer Research* 20 (3): 478–488.

Malhotra, N. K. 1982. Information load and consumer decision making. *Journal of Consumer Research* 8 (March): 419–430.

Marmorstein, Howard, Jeanne Rossomme, and Dan Sarel. 2003. Unleashing the power of yield management in the internet era: Opportunities and challenges. *California Management Review* 45 (3): 147–167.

Maxwell, Sarah. 1991. Before and after the international coffee agreement. Working paper. Miami: Florida International University.

———, 1995. "What makes a price increase seem 'fair'?" Pricing Strategy and Practice: An International Journal 3 (4): 21–27.

———. 1999. Biased attributions of a price increase: Effects of culture and gender. *Journal of Consumer Marketing* 16 (1): 9–23.

———. 1999. The social norms of discrete consumer exchange: Classification and quantification. *American Journal of Economics and Sociology* 58 (4): 999–1018.

———. 2000. Social norms of consumer pricing, Indian style. International Society for Marketing and Development. Legon, Ghana: University of Ghana.

———. 2002. Rule-based price fairness and its effect on willingness to purchase. *Journal of Economic Psychology* 23 (2): 191–212.

———. 2003. The effects of differential textbook pricing: On-line vs. in-store. *Journal of Media Economics* 16 (February): 87–95.

———. 2003. Sanctioning unfair pricing: Making the punishment fit the crime. *Proceedings, Summer Conference.* Chicago: American Marketing Association.

———. 2005. Hyperchoice and high prices: An unfair combination. *Journal of Product and Brand Management* 14 (7): 448–454.

———. 2005. Fair price, fair practice: Dual entitlements for the consumer. *Proceedings, Fordham Pricing Conference.* New York: Fordham University.

———. 2006. KKT Revisited. Working paper, Fordham Pricing Center. Fordham University, New York.

———, and Nicholas Maxwell. 1995. The perception of a fair price: Self-interest and social norms in individualist vs. collectivist cultures. *International Conference of the Academy of Marketing Science.* Ann Arbor, MI: Books on Demand.

———, Pete Nye, and Nicholas Maxwell. 1999. Less pain, same gain: The effects of priming fairness in price negotiations. *Journal of Psychology and Marketing* 16 (7): 545–562.

———, Pete Nye, and Nicholas Maxwell. 2003. The wrath of the fairness-primed negotiator when the reciprocity norm is violated. *Journal of Business Research* 56 (2): 399–409.

————, Veronica Feder Mayer, Hans H. Stamer, Hermann Diller, and Marcos Gonçalves Avila. 2006. Reactions to a service price increase: What makes it seem fair. *Proceedings, Academy of Marketing Science Cross Cultural Conference.* Seoul, South Korea.

Mayer, Roger C., James H. Davis, and F.David Schoorman. 1995. An integration model of organizational trust. *Academy of Management Review* 20 (3): 709–844.

Mayer, Veronica, and Marcos Gonçalves Avila. 2004. A qualitative investigation about community standards of fairness in the Brazilian market: Inferences, emotions, and culture. *Proceedings, Fordham Pricing Conference.* New York: Fordham University.

McClintock, Charles B., and William B. Liebrand. 1988. The role of interdependence structure, individual value orientation and other's strategy in social decision making: A transformational analysis. *Journal of Personality and Social Psychology* 55 (3): 396–409.

McMahon-Beattie, Una. 2005. Future of revenue management: Trust and revenue management. *Journal of Revenue and Pricing Management* 4 (4): 406–407.

Messick, David M., and Keith Sentis. 1983. Fairness, preference and fairness biases. In David Messick and Karen Cook (ed.), *Equity theory.* New York: Praeger Publishers: 61–94.

————, and Roderick M. Kramer. 2001. Trust as a form of shallow morality. In Karen Cook (ed.), *Trust in Society.* New York: Russell Sage: 89–117.

Miller, Dale T. 1999. The norm of self interest. *American Psychologist* 54 (December): 1053–1060.

————, and Neil Vidmar. 1981. The social psychology of punishment reactions. In Melvin J. Lerner and Sally C. Lerner (eds.), *The justice motive in social behavior: Adapting to times of scarcity and change.* New York: Plenum Press: 145–172.

Molm, Linda D. 1994. Imbalanced structures, unfair strategies: Power and justice in social exchange. *American Sociological Review* 59 (1): 98–121.

————, Theron M. Quist, and Phillip A. Wiseley. 1993. Reciprocal justice and strategies of exchange. *Social Forces* 72: 19–44.

————, Nobuyuki Takahashi, and Gretchen Peterson. 2003. In the eye of the beholder: Procedural justice in social exchange. *American Sociological Review* 68 (1): 128–152.

Monroe, Kent B., and Angela Y. Lee. 1999. Remembering versus knowing: Issues in buyers' processing of price information. *Journal of the Academy of Marketing Science* 27 (2): 207–225.

Murnighan, J. Keith, and Madan M. Pillutla. 1995. Fairness versus self-interest: Asymmetric moral imperatives in ultimatum bargaining. In Roderick M. Kramer and David M. Messick (eds.), *Negotiation as a social process.* Thousand Oaks, CA: Sage Publications: 240–267.

Nagle, Thomas T., and Reed K. Holden. 1995. *The strategy and tactics of pricing.* Englewood Cliffs, NJ: Prentice-Hall.

Neale, Margaret, Vandra L. Huber, and Gregory B. Northcraft. 1987. The framing of negotiations: Contextual versus task frame. *Organizational Behavior and Human Decision Making* 39: 228–241.

———, and Max Bazerman. *Cognition and rationality in negotiation.* New York: Free Press.

Nicholson, Walter. 1985. *Microeconomic theory: Basic principles and extensions,* 3rd ed. New York: Dryden Press.

North, Douglass C. 1990. *Institutions, institutional change and economic performance.* Cambridge: Cambridge University Press.

Norton, Eleanor H. 2004. Bargaining and the ethics of process. *What's fair: Ethics for negotiators.* San Francisco: Jossey-Bass.

Obuchi, Ken-ichi, Tomohiro Kumagai, and Emi Atsumi. 2002. Motives of and responses to anger in conflict situations: A cross-cultural analysis. *Tohoku Psychologica Folia* 61: 11–21.

Oliver, Richard, and John E. Swan. 1989. Consumer perceptions of interpersonal equity and satisfaction in transactions: A field survey approach. *Journal of Marketing* 53 (April): 21–35.

———. 1989. Equity and disconfirmation perceptions as influences on merchant and product satisfaction. *Journal of Consumer Research* 16 (December): 372–383.

Okun, Arthur M. 1981. *Prices and quantities: A macroeconomic analysis.* Washington DC: Brookings Institution.

Pan, X., B. T. Ratchford, and V. Shankar. 2003. The evolution of price dispersion in internet retail markets. *Advances in Applied Microeconomics* 12: 85–105.

Pesciarelli, Enzo. 1999. Aspects of the influence of Francis Hutcheson on Adam Smith. *History of political economy* 31 (3): 525–545.

Piron, Robert, and Luis Fernandez. 1995. Are fairness constraints on profit-seeking important? *Journal of Economic Psychology* 16: 73–96.

Price, Michael E., Leda Cosmides, and John Toby. 2002. Punitive sentiment as an anti-free rider psychological device. *Evolution and Human Behavior* 23 (3): 203–231.

Pruitt, Dean G. 1981. *Negotiation behavior.* New York: Academic Press.

Putnam, Robert D. 1993. The prosperous community: Social capital and public life. *American Prospect* 13: 35–42.

Rabin, Matthew. 1993. Incorporating fairness into game theory and economics. *The American Economic Review* 83 (5): 1281–1302.

Raiffa, Howard. 1982. The art and science of negotiation: How to resolve conflicts and get the best out of bargaining. Cambridge, MA: Belknap Press.

Rao, Akshay R., and Mark E. Bergen. 1992. Price premium variations as a consequence of buyers' lack of information. *Journal of Consumer Research* 19 (3): 412–424.

Rawls, John. 1971. *A theory of justice.* Cambridge: Harvard University Press.

Reinhardt, Uwe E. 2006. The pricing of U.S. hospital services: Chaos behind a veil of secrecy. *Health Affairs* 25 (1): 57–69.

Rezabakhsh, Behrang, Daniel Bornemann, Ursula Hansen, and Ulf Schrader. 2006. Consumer power: A comparison of the old economy and the internet economy. *Journal of Consumer Policy* 29: 3–36.

Richins, Marsha and Bronislaw J. Verhage. 1985. Cross-cultural differences in consumer attitudes and their implications for complaint management. *International Journal of Research in Marketing* 2: 197–206.

Rommetveit, Ragnar. 1954. *Social norms and roles.* Minneapolis: University of Minnesota Press.

Ross, William, and Jessica LaCroix. 1996. Multiple meanings of trust in negotiation theory and research: A literature review and integrative model. *International Journal of Conflict Management* 7 (4): 314–360.

Roth, Alvin E., Vesna Prasnikar, Shmuel Zamir, and Masahiro Okuno-Fujiwara. 1991. Bargaining and market behavior in Jerusalem, Ljubljana, Pittsburg, and Tokyo: An experimental study. *American Economic Review* 81: 1068–1095.

Rothstein, Bo. 2005. *Social traps and the problem of trust.* Cambridge: Cambridge University Press.

Rubenstein, Richard E. 2004. *Aristotle's children.* Orlando, FL: Harcourt, Inc.

Rubin, Jeffry, and Bert Brown. 1975. *The social psychology of bargaining and negotiation.* New York: Academic Press.

Rutte, Christel, and David Messick. 1995. An integrated model of perceived unfairness in organizations. *Social Justice Research* 8 (3): 239–261.

Sampson, Edward E. 1975. On justice as equality. *Journal of Social Issues* 31 (3): 45–64.

Samuelson, William, and Richard Zeckhauser. 1988. Status quo bias in decision making. *Journal of Risk and Uncertainty* 1 (March): 7–59.

Sanfey, Alan G., James K. Rilling, Jessica A. Aronson, Leigh E. Nystrom, and Jonathan D. Cohen. 2003. The neural basis of economic decision-making in the ultimatum game. *Science* 300: 1755–1758.

Sashkin, Marshall and Richard L. Williams. 1990. Does fairness make a difference? *Organizational Dynamics* 19 (2): 56–71.

Scholz, J. T., and M. Lubell. 2001. Cooperation, reciprocity and the collective action heuristic. *American Journal of Political Science* 45: 160–178.

Scott, William. 1916. *The itching palm: A study of the habit of tipping in America.* Philadelphia, PA: Penn Publishing Company.

Seagrave, Kerry. 1998. *Tipping: An American social history of gratuities.* Jefferson, NC: McFarland.

Shaw, John C., Eric Wild and Jason A Conquitt. 2003. To justify or excuse? A meta-analytic review of the effects of explanation. *Journal of Applied Psychology* 88 (3): 444–458.

Smith, Charles. 1989. *Auctions: The social construction of value.* Berkeley, CA: University of California Press.

Sonnenberg, Frank K. 1994. Trust me, trust me not. *Journal of Business Strategy* 15 (1): 14–16.

Sprott, David E., Kenneth C. Manning, and Anthony D. Miyazaki. 2003. Grocery price setting and quantity surcharges. *Journal of Marketing* 67 (3): 34–45.

Stein, Karen F. 1980. Explaining ghetto consumer behavior: Hypotheses from urban sociology. *Journal of Consumer Affairs* 14 (January): 232–242.

Suh, Jaebeom, and Jeffrey Hess. 1996. Individualism vs. collectivism: Cultural moderation of consumer attribution. *Proceedings, American Marketing Association* (Summer): 188–192.

Surowiecki, James. 2005. *The wisdom of crowds.* New York: Anchor Books.

Suter, Tracy A., and Scot Burton. 1996. Believability and consumer perceptions of implausible reference prices in retail advertisements. *Psychology & Marketing* 13 (1): 37–54.

Taylor, Shelly. 1981. A categorization approach to stereotyping. In D. L. Hamilton (ed.), *Cognitive processes in stereotyping and intergroup behavior.* Hillsdale, NJ: Erlbaum: 88–114.

Thaler, Richard. 1985. Mental accounting and consumer choice. *Marketing Science* 3 (Summer): 199–214.

Thibaut, John W., and Harold H. Kelley. 1959. *The social psychology of groups.* New York: Wiley.

———, and Laurens Walker. 1975. *Procedural justice: A psychological analysis.* Hillsdale, NY: Erlbaum.

Torgler, Benno. 2003. Tax morale, rule-governed behaviour and trust. *Constitutional Political Economy* 14 (2): 119–140.

———. 2004. Cross-cultural comparison of tax morale and tax compliance: Evidence from Costa Rica and Switzerland. *International Journal of Comparative Sociology* 45 (17): 17–43.

———. 2005. Tax morale in Latin America. *Public Choice* 122(1): 133–157.

Triandis, Harry C. 1995. *Individualism & collectivism.* Boulder, CO: Westview Press.

Tsiros, Michael, Vikas Mittal, and William T. Ross Jr., 2004. The role of attributions in customer satisfaction: A reexamination. *Journal of Consumer Research* 31 (2): 478–483.

Tyler, Tom R., and E. Allan. 1992. A relational model of authority in groups. In M. Zanna (ed.), *Advances in experimental social psychology*, vol. 25. San Diego: Academic Press: 115–191.

———, and Steven L. Blader. 2004. Justice and negotiation. In Michele J. Gelfand and Jeanne M. Brett (eds.), *The handbook of negotiation and culture.* Stanford: Stanford University Press: 295–312.

Tyran, Jean-Robert, and Dirk Engelmann. 2005. To buy or not to buy? An experimental study of consumer boycotts in retail markets. *Economica* 72: 1–16.

Urbany, Joel E., Thomas J. Madden, and Peter R. Dickson. 1989. All's not fair in pricing: An initial look at the Dual Entitlement Principle. *Marketing Letters* 1 (1): 17–25.

Uusitalo, Outi, and Maija Rökman. 2004. Change in pricing strategy: The case of Finnish grocery retailing. *Proceedings, Fordham Pricing Conference.* New York: Fordham University.

Vaidyanathan, Rajiv, and Praveen Aggarwal. 2003. Who is the fairest of them all? An attributional approach to price fairness perceptions. *Journal of Business Research* 56 (6): 453–459.

van den Bos, Kees, and Henk A. M. Wilke. 1998. When do we need procedural fairness? The role of trust in authority. *Journal of Personality and Social Psychology* 75 (6): 1449–1458.

van de Vliert, Evert. 1996. *Theoretical frontiers of complex interpersonal conflict behavior.* Hove, UK: Erlbaum, Taylor, and Francis.

Varian, Hal R. 1975. Distributive justice, welfare economics, and the theory of fairness. *Philosophy and Public Affairs* 4: 223–247.

Walker, L., S. Latour, E. A. Lind, and J. Thibaut. 1974. Reactions of participants and observers to modes of adjudication. *Journal of Applied Social Psychology* 4: 295–310.

Watkins, Harry S., and Raymond Liu. 1996. Collectivism, individualism and in-group membership: Implications for consumer complaining behaviors in multicultural contexts. *Journal of International Consumer Marketing* 8 (3/4): 69–96.

Webley, Paul, Henry Robben, Henk Elffers, and Dick Hessing. 1991. *Tax evasion: An experimental approach.* Cambridge: Cambridge University Press.

Weiner, Bernard. 1986. *An attributional theory of motivation and emotion.* New York: Springer-Verlag.

———. 2000. Attributional thoughts about consumer behavior. *Journal of Consumer Research* 27 (3): 382–387.

White, James J. 1980. Machiavelli and the bar: Ethical limitations on lying in negotiation. *American Bar Foundation Research Journal* 926–938.

Williamson, Oliver. 1975. *The economic institutions of capitalism: Firms, markets, relational contracting.* New York: Free Press.

———. 1993. Calculativeness, trust and economic organization. *Journal of Law and Economics* 36: 453–486.

Wilson, J. Q. 1993. *The moral sense.* New York: Free Press.

Winer, Russell. 1986. A reference price model of brand choice for frequently purchased products. *Journal of Consumer Research* 13 (September): 250–256.

Wood, Diana. 2002. *Medieval economic thought.* Cambridge: Cambridge University Press.

Xia, Lan, Kent B. Monroe, and Jennifer L. Cox. 2004. The price is unfair! A conceptual framework of price fairness perceptions. *Journal of Marketing* 68 (October): 1–15.

————, Monika Kukar-Kinney, and Kent B. Monroe. 2005. The effects of promotion restrictions on perceptions of promotion and price fairness. *Proceedings, Fordham Pricing Conference.* New York: Fordham University.

Zajac, Edward E. 1978 *Fairness or efficiency: An introduction to public utility pricing.* Cambridge, MA: Ballinger Publishing.

————. 1995. *Political economy of fairness.* Cambridge, MA: MIT Press.

Zucker L. G. 1986. Production of trust: Institutional sources of economic structure, 1840–1920. In B. M. Staw and L. L. Cummings (eds.), *Research in Organization Behavior,* vol. 8. Greenwich, CT: JAI Press: 53–111.

Index